ENGAGING
—*the*—
CIVIL WAR

Chris Mackowski and Brian Matthew Jordan, Series Editors

A Public-History Initiative of Emerging Civil War
and Southern Illinois University Press

THE BONDS OF WAR

A STORY OF IMMIGRANTS AND ESPRIT DE CORPS IN COMPANY C, 96TH ILLINOIS VOLUNTEER INFANTRY

Diana L. Dretske

Southern Illinois University Press
Carbondale

Southern Illinois University Press
www.siupress.com

24 23 22 21   4 3 2 1

Cover illustration and frontispiece: *seated, left to right*: William B. Lewin, Loughlin
  Madden Jr., Edward Murray; *standing, left to right*: James B. Murrie and
  John Y. Taylor. The inspiration for this book, the photograph was taken at
  Camp Fuller, Rockford, Illinois, about September 21, 1862. *Bess Bower Dunn
  Museum of Lake County, Lake County Forest Preserves.*

Library of Congress Cataloging-in-Publication Data
Names: Dretske, Diana, author.
Title: The bonds of war : a story of immigrants and esprit de corps in
  Company C, 96th Illinois Volunteer Infantry / Diana L. Dretske.
Other titles: Story of immigrants and esprit de corps in Company C, 96th
  Illinois Volunteer Infantry
Description: Carbondale : Southern Illinois University Press, [2021] | Series:
  Engaging the Civil War | Includes bibliographical references and index.
Identifiers: LCCN 2020026358 (print) | LCCN 2020026359 (ebook)
  | ISBN 9780809338207 (paperback) | ISBN 9780809338214 (ebook)
Subjects: LCSH: United States. Army. Illinois Infantry Regiment, 96th
  (1862–1865). Company C | Illinois—History—Civil War, 1861–1865—
  Regimental histories. | United States—History—Civil War, 1861–1865—
  Regimental histories. | United States—History—Civil War, 1861–1865—
  Participation, Scottish American. | Scottish American soldiers—
  Illinois—Lake County—Biography. | United States—History—
  Civil War, 1861–1865—Participation, Irish American. | Irish
  American soldiers—Illinois—Lake County—Biography. | United
  States—History—Civil War, 1861–1865—Participation, British.
  | British Americans—Illinois—Lake County—Biography. | Newport
  (Ill. : Township)—Biography.
Classification: LCC E505.5 96th .D74 2021 (print) | LCC E505.5 96th (ebook)
  | DDC 973.7/4730922—dc23
LC record available at https://lccn.loc.gov/2020026358
LC ebook record available at https://lccn.loc.gov/2020026359

Printed on recycled paper ♻

For my husband,
Al Westerman

Contents

Illustrations

Acknowledgments

This book evolved out of a need to put names on faces in a group portrait where only Edward Murray's identity was known. The resultant research turned into blog posts highlighting forgotten soldiers of the 96th Illinois and sparked a sense that there was so much more I wanted to know. That pursuit took me beyond my institution's collections and turned into a personal endeavor. On weekends, and during any free time I could get, I sought out archives, historical societies, and little-known sources that might hold keys to these men's lives.

A project such as this happens with the support of many individuals, as well as the dedication of public and private agencies that preserve and provide access to irreplaceable historical materials. I wish to thank my colleague and friend, Katherine Hamilton-Smith, former director of the Lake County Discovery Museum, for being the first to support this project and inspiring others to understand the value of archives and historical research. My utmost thanks to my friend and former colleague Christine Pyle for reading and commenting on the manuscript and for unwavering support. Thanks to my colleague Ty Rohrer, manager of cultural arts for the Waukegan Park District, for reading early versions of chapters and encouraging this work. A special thank you to Beverly Millard and Ann Darrow of the Waukegan Historical Society, whose enthusiasm for local history is a gift to us all.

Sincere thanks to Glenna Schroeder-Lein, manuscripts librarian (retired) at the Abraham Lincoln Presidential Library, for providing insight into the Taylor Family (James M.) Papers. This strengthened my understanding of the Taylor brothers' lives in Scotland and Illinois. My gratitude to Dr. Steven D. Fratt, professor of history (retired) at Trinity International University, for reading my manuscript and making an immeasurable difference in my understanding of the complex world of Civil War armies and battlefields.

I am especially indebted to Sylvia Frank Rodrigue, executive editor at SIU Press, for seeing the potential in my early manuscript and believing in its value. Your guidance and good nature throughout this process was vital and very much appreciated. My sincere thanks to all the great staff at SIU Press, who helped in editing, designing, marketing, and keeping tabs on this project to make it the best it could be: Linda Jorgensen Buhman, Jen Egan, Amy

Etcheson, Tracy Gholson, Chelsey Harris, Wayne Larsen, Ryan Masteller, Angela Moore-Swafford, Kristine Priddy, Jerry Richardson, and Judy Verdich.

I wish to express my gratitude to the Engaging the Civil War series editors, Chris Mackowski and Brian Matthew Jordan, whose insightful comments through multiple revisions encouraged me to dig a little deeper and broaden the scope of my work. Thanks also to the anonymous readers who provided recommendations that were important to the work's evolution.

I had the privilege of meeting and corresponding with individuals related to my subjects: Millie Ramsay, descendant of Edward Murray; Margie Queen, descendent of William B. Lewin; Jack Murrie, relation of James B. Murrie; Jim Lodesky, descendant of Mary Taylor Bater; and Thomas E. Doyle, colleague of James M. Taylor's grandson. These connections revealed details and personal stories that brought me closer to my subjects. Special thanks and recognition to Margie Queen for generous access to Lewin family history, letters, and photographs.

My heartfelt thanks to my husband, Al Westerman; mom, Dody Dretske; brother and sister, Dan Dretske and Cindy Kolanko; and friends Leslie Rous, Lin Butler, Corinne Court, Katy Burgess, and Alexandria Solt. Thank you for your patience, love, and support, and for enduring years of hearing about a book that never seemed to get any closer to being done. At last, we made it!

ENGAGING
—*the*—
CIVIL WAR

For additional content that will let you engage this material further, scan the QR code on this page. It will take you to exclusive online material, additional photos and images, links to online resources, and related blog posts at www. emergingcivilwar.com.

A QR scanner is readily available for download through the app store on your digital device.

The Bonds of War

Introduction

"Few, I believe, realize today what it is to leave home and all that is dear and realize that you may never see them again."[1] These words, written by Scottish immigrant Edward Murray, were a reflection on leaving his wife and children after he enlisted in Company C of the 96th Illinois Volunteer Infantry in September 1862.

In the second year of the American Civil War, Murray made the decision to fight for the preservation of the Union and enlisted with four other immigrant men from Lake County, Illinois, the state's northeasternmost county. These comrades in arms commemorated their enlistment in a photographic portrait wearing newly issued Union-blue uniforms and creating the image that inspired this book. The 96th Illinois mustered in September 5, 1862, at Rockford, Illinois, and served in the war's Western Theater with the Army of Kentucky (October 1862–June 1863) and Army of the Cumberland (June 1863–June 1865). The 96th was engaged in the Tullahoma, Chattanooga, Atlanta, and Franklin-Nashville Campaigns, and at the Battles of Chickamauga, Lookout Mountain, Resaca, Kennesaw, Franklin, and Nashville, mustering out June 10, 1865.[2]

One hundred years after the portrait was taken, Murray's grandson donated the cased photo tintype to the county history museum, but by then only his grandfather was identified, and the connection between the men had been lost.[3] Through my research, Murray's companions were identified: Loughlin Madden Jr., James B. Murrie, William B. Lewin, and John Y. Taylor. With their names came their connection as neighbors and immigrants, and a door into their world began to open.

As immigrants their voluntary service in the Civil War cast them in a special light and was particularly intriguing to me. The familiar narrative of the American-born soldier was upended, and a new image of Union soldiers and what motivated them to enlist begged to be answered. As evidenced by the portrait, immigrants wholeheartedly responded to the call to arms, leaving a remarkable legacy of hundreds of thousands who fought. Without the great number of immigrants and sons of immigrants—estimated at 43 percent of the U.S. armed forces—the North could not have won the Civil War. Although most Northerners, whether native or foreign born, enlisted for the same reason—to preserve the Union—the stories of immigrant soldiers are largely unexamined. With such an impact on the fighting forces of the North, a re-envisioning of the identity of the "common soldier" presented an opportunity to gain a fresh perspective.[4]

Historian Ryan W. Keating explained that only by intimately exploring immigrant experiences and the differences between them "can we truly understand the motivations that drove these men to fight and die for the Union." In pursuit of this understanding, the story that follows weaves together the lives of Murray and his four comrades into a collective biography, utilizing a microhistorical approach to give voice to those who would otherwise remain forgotten. It is a challenge to research obscure subjects whose lives are sparsely documented, but their story can be regained by pursuing fragments of information from unpublished and little-known local sources and stitching them together with a wide assortment of official records. Part of the microhistorical methodology included reconstructing the men's social networks to reveal connections and influences, as well as scaling the historical analysis to gain perspective on national events and each man's personal identity as immigrant, soldier, and American. Through this lens, the lives of five immigrant men and their families from a small geographical area become the means to examining individual motives for enlisting to fight for the Union, and to studying the context of the culture as a whole. As historian István M. Szijártó explained, microhistorians view people of the past "as active individuals, conscious actors," and not merely "puppets on the hands of great underlying forces of history."[5]

Each of my five subjects left behind countries where privilege and monarchy ruled, arriving between 1841 and 1854 in the early settlement of Newport Township, Lake County, Illinois: Edward Murray, James B. Murrie, and John Y. Taylor from Scotland; William B. Lewin from England; and Loughlin Madden Jr. from Ireland. Their hopes for the future lay across the Atlantic in a young republic full of change and possibility. The nation they found gave them the freedom and opportunities they sought, but it was being torn asunder by sectional politics. They lived in a region of the state where antislavery sentiment was at its strongest. By the mid to late 1840s, the antislavery movement had become a significant part of the area's culture, and the county had shifted politically from Democratic to Whig and Liberty.[6]

It was during the second summer of the war that the Union's cause became more desperate with the failure of Maj. Gen. George B. McClellan's Peninsula Campaign to capture the Confederate capital of Richmond, Virginia. President Lincoln's call for six hundred thousand troops forced communities to meet quotas for enlistees. Men were eager to show their courage by volunteering rather than being drafted. Edward, Loughlin, James, William, and John united in a singular belief in the Union and a hope that military service would solidify their place as Americans. The 96th Illinois's historian, Charles A. Partridge, wrote that a "high grade of patriotism was required to nerve men to enlist" at so gloomy a period. At the start of the war, the Confederates had enjoyed a strategic and psychological advantage with early victories in the East, but in the spring of 1862, the focus shifted to the Western Theater with victories by Maj. Gen. Ulysses S. Grant at Fort Donelson and Shiloh, Tennessee. Illinois's volunteers were needed in the Western Theater where they could strike at the core of the Confederacy.[7]

With multiple regiments forming in the region, Murray and his companions chose to enlist in the 96th Illinois. The regiment was a joint venture of Lake County and Jo Daviess County (located in the state's northwest corner), since neither county had enough men to form its own regiment. With Lake County supplying four companies (B, C, D, G), and Jo Daviess County six companies (A, E, F, H, I, K), an arrangement was made through the political friendship of U.S. representative Elihu B. Washburne of Galena, and state senator Henry W. Blodgett of Waukegan. Out of the 1,046 men at the regiment's mustering, 29 percent were foreign born. This non-ethnic unit had pockets of strong enlistment of men from Germany, Ireland, Scotland and England. Murray and his comrades wanted to be considered Americans and to earn respect through their service to the Union. The necessity and even their preference to choose a non-ethnic unit (as opposed to one with a distinctive ethnic identity) reveals a confidence in fighting alongside their native-born neighbors, assimilating with them as they navigated the strange environment of army life, and embracing the esprit de corps of the regiment.[8]

By the time of Edward Murray's enlistment, he had achieved a place of respect as a family man, a farmer, and an elected township treasurer. He had been living in the United States for nearly three decades and conceivably felt more American than Scottish. His much younger comrade John Taylor had immigrated just eight years earlier and perceived his position quite differently. Months into his service, Taylor contemplated whether he and his comrades would "be respected and acknowledged as good American Citizens." Like many immigrant soldiers, Taylor sought gratitude for his service, and the greatest prize of all was to be accepted as an American. A little over a year after his muster, Murray lay wounded and paralyzed on the battlefield at Chickamauga, Georgia, on September 20, 1863. Murray's experience in the second bloodiest battle of the war was one that thousands of soldiers endured, whether immigrant or American born. As part of Maj. Gen. Gordon Granger's Reserve Corps, the 96th Illinois sent 419 commissioned officers and enlisted men into battle and suffered a total loss of 225 men.[9]

Although this book is not intended to be a comprehensive or traditional regimental history, the Civil War was the seminal event in these men's lives, and so it is essential to focus on their military service. It is my wish to breathe life into the five companions, allowing them to take center stage—and speak for themselves—as they were thrust into a world of sectional politics and war. The major actions in which the 96th Illinois participated are explored through the perspective of Edward, Loughlin, James, William, and John, who are the driving force of this narrative. For their experiences in the war to truly matter, we must know their personal stories and the complexity of their lives and beliefs. Through this collective biography, it is possible to recover the individuality that a traditional war narrative can suppress, and in the process highlight the service of a regiment in the Western Theater.[10]

While the 96th Illinois saw less fighting than many other units, it stands out, as Edward Murray wrote, as an "abolition regiment." Murray was particularly proud of how the regiment protected all who came into their lines that sought freedom. Though he did not enlist to abolish slavery, he was sympathetic to the plight of enslaved people, having taken to heart Baptist sermons on slavery's immorality. Those antislavery convictions were reinforced after witnessing the grim reality of the vile institution in the South. With the passage of the Emancipation Proclamation, there were men in the ranks who protested how the proclamation shifted the war's purpose from fighting to save the Union to fighting to free slaves. But the proclamation as a practical measure to restore the Union by denying the South its major source of labor was overwhelmingly supported by Union soldiers as a means to victory.[11]

The 96th was part of a movement of Illinois regiments who wrote resolutions supporting President Lincoln and denouncing the Northern peace movement. In January 1863, Peace Democrats had taken their elected seats in the Illinois legislature and demanded the retraction of the proclamation and the establishment of a peace commission to end the war. Historian Mark E. Neely Jr. noted that the peace movement in the north caused "a near-revolt of the Illinois line" that lasted from January 20 to April 22, 1863. As historian Jennifer L. Weber explained, many Union soldiers felt resentment for the "lack of support for their efforts" and believed that antiwar comments "undermined their ability to carry out the war successfully."[12]

Through Edward, Loughlin, James, William, and John, we can better understand the motivations of ordinary citizens—immigrants—who came to this country and embraced its ideals of freedom and liberty, and how national events ultimately thrust them into action. Their desire to preserve the Union led them to enlist, and their experiences as soldiers brought them face-to-face with the realities of slavery. They questioned their personal worth in a unit that spent much of its time digging fortifications and guarding wagon trains, and when sent into battle their courage and cohesion was tested. For those who survived, the postwar years came with life-altering wounds and survivor's guilt. Each man dealt with this differently, but all were motivated to support their families, contribute to their community, maintain their regimental affiliation, and commemorate their dead comrades.

The photograph taken at Camp Fuller in Rockford, Illinois, documented their bonds not only as soldiers and neighbors ready to fight for the nation's preservation but also as men who were unprepared for the hardships they would face. Without the portrait, their lives may never have been linked, this window into re-envisioning the common U.S. Civil War soldier been left unexplored, and the significance of the immigrant soldier's contribution to the Union's ultimate victory been reduced to names on the regiment's muster rolls.

These men lived but a stone's throw from my home. They traveled the same roads and admired the same burr oak trees, only 160 years before me. The realization of a shared connection of place gave me a daily reminder that their story and that of the immigrant Union soldier needed to be told.

1. ❄ Far from My Native Land

E dward Murray stepped inside the photographer's tent with his four companions—James B. Murrie, Loughlin Madden Jr., William B. Lewin, and John Y. Taylor. It was late September 1862, and the men were in military training at Camp Fuller, Rockford, Illinois. Each had emigrated from the British Isles with hopes fixed for the future on the United States. With that future imperiled, their enthusiasm to save the Union surged, and the five neighbors from rural Newport Township, Lake County, Illinois enlisted together in Company C, 96th Illinois Volunteer Infantry.

The comrades took their places for a crowded group portrait. Their transformation had never been more powerfully apparent than when they donned the Prussian blue coats and sky blue pants of the Union Army. They were now American soldiers.[1]

The men quickly jostled into place and stilled as they listened to the persistent drumbeat outside. The dichotomy of this private moment and the vigorous activity beyond the tent acted as a bridge between their lives as civilians and their duty as soldiers, solidifying the need to pull together more tightly and creating an esprit as a small bonded group. They would need each other's support in this strange environment devoid of the comforts of home. The group portrait commemorated their pride, commitment, and personal bonds as they assimilated into the larger regimental unit. The striking image captured the instant before they stepped onto the stage of war, where they would join in the struggle to preserve the Union.[2]

Edward Murray

Edward Murray's Irish-born parents knew the hardships of emigration and the struggle to improve their lot in life. William Murray and Agnes "Nancy" Riley were natives of County Derry (Londonderry), Ireland, a locale known for its linen and yarn. While in their youth, their respective families migrated to Scotland, where experience in textile working was valued. The couple met and married, and their fifth child, Edward, was born on December 19, 1828.[3]

William Murray worked as a spinner in a cotton factory in Glasgow. At forty-eight years old, he gave up his position to seek employment in textile factories in America, where he could begin a life far removed from the poor housing conditions of an overcrowded city. It was 1834, and William and Nancy felt that America held better prospects for their growing family.[4]

After a forty-five-day Atlantic crossing, the Murrays landed at New York City and continued on to New Berlin, New York. There, William Murray and his eldest children worked twelve-hour days making cloth on water-powered looms at Joseph Moss's cotton factory. But a depression in textile manufacturing prompted the Murrays to move several times in search of steady employment. Edward began working alongside his father and sisters. Child labor was common, and business owners paid children less. Though it helped his family, beginning work at such a young age meant that Edward's education was limited.[5]

By 1840, the continued instability of cloth-making work pressed William Murray to consider other options and a life beyond factories. The opening of lands in the west was well known through newspaper accounts and the constant outflow of people and wagons. The opportunity to own land—and the freedom it brought—was too much to resist. In 1841, the Murrays set out on the Erie Canal, taking it from Utica to Buffalo, New York.[6] Since its opening in 1825, the canal had sparked an explosion of trade and a dramatic rush of settlers in the first great western migration.

The canal brought hundreds of people from New York, Massachusetts, and surrounding states into Michigan and Illinois, creating pressure to open northeastern Illinois to non-native settlement by removing Native Americans. The Treaty of Chicago was signed between the U.S. government and the United Nations of Chippewa, Ottawa, and Potawatomi Indians on September 26, 1833. Five million acres, including the land now known as Lake County, Illinois, were sold. These were the last tracts of Native-occupied land in Illinois.[7]

At Buffalo the Murrays bought passage to Southport, Wisconsin (Kenosha), on the 185-foot steamer *Great Western*, one of the largest and finest steamers of the day. Its master, Capt. Augustus Walker, was a respected navigator on the lakes and known for his efforts in furthering steamboat interests, including lobbying for port improvements at Chicago. The *Great Western* traveled Lake Erie, Lake Huron, and finally down the length of Lake Michigan to land at Southport. With a population of 337 in 1840, the town bustled with a multitude of businesses to accommodate arriving passengers. The influx of settlers prompted an editorial in the *Southport Telegraph*: "Emigrants to this territory by way of the lakes has been at least three hundred percent greater this season. . . . A large portion of those who came to this country for the purpose of settling bear the evident characteristics of intelligence and enterprise."[8] The editor viewed the arriving immigrants as a boon to the town's growth and possibly his newspaper sales.

In August 1841, after making inquiries, William Murray found suitable land about six miles west of the shores of Lake Michigan in Newport Township, Lake County, Illinois. The area along the Wisconsin-Illinois state line was particularly beautiful with a gently rolling landscape, oak and hickory woodlands, and the abundant resource of the Des Plaines River. There were few settlers in the neighborhood and no money and no work, but the relative isolation reminded William and Nancy of their youth in the Irish countryside. They were now subsistence farmers, learning by trial and error as they plowed the black earth of Illinois and selling their harvest for cash or exchanging it for goods.[9]

This was a very different world from the one they had left. Glasgow, Scotland was crowded with upward of 275,000 inhabitants, whereas the whole of Lake County had a population of 2,905. Struggle and uncertainty were part and parcel for these first settlers. One of the Murrays' Irish neighbors, John Delany, wrote, "Although the settlers here were of different nationalities . . . [a]nything they could do for one another they did."[10]

Shortly after their arrival in 1841, the Murrays' eldest daughter, Catharine, wed Scotsman Daniel McCaskell. Within five years, two more daughters wed: Jane to Scotsman John Murrie, and Elizabeth to Irish Catholic Patrick English. These years of planting, harvesting, and settling into life in rural northeastern Illinois were tragically interrupted when Catharine Murray Mc-Caskell fell ill with tuberculosis. The dreaded disease, known as consumption for the way its victims wasted away, becoming pale and thin before dying, was an epidemic in mid-1800s America. People believed consumption was caused by "bad air" and the lack of seasoning to one's environment, such as the colder northern climate where the Murrays now lived. Catharine succumbed to the disease on March 25, 1851, leaving behind seven children.[11]

In 1852, Edward Murray took a step toward independence, buying eighty-two acres from his father for one hundred dollars. Edward continued living in the family's homestead with his parents and younger brother, but the land purchase anticipated his marriage to his neighbor Nancy Dixon, whom he had known for nearly a decade. Nancy was the eldest child of English immigrant John Dixon and New York native Rebecca Allen. Like William Murray, John Dixon had worked in a cotton mill in New York before coming west to acquire land, a common pattern in the early years of settlement. Edward and Nancy were married at the Dixon home on the bride's birthday, February 2, 1853. The couple's beginning was modest but promising. In December, they celebrated the birth of their first child and Edward's election as town collector.[12]

By his late twenties, Murray was a well-established farmer and had become civic minded. He furthered his standing in the community in 1860 when he was elected as Newport Township treasurer, discharging those duties, according to his biographical sketch, "with promptness and fidelity." Murray's relatively quick ascendancy in local politics was reflective of the acceptance of immigrants in this community and of Murray's ambition. Nationally, ethnic groups gained the attention of major political parties who saw them as a voting bloc.[13] In this sparsely settled area, it was imperative that neighbors worked together, creating a mutual reliance among the newcomers, whether immigrant or native born.

The Murrays lived in a region of the state where antislavery sentiment was at its strongest. By the 1840s, the antislavery movement had become part of the area's culture, much of it brought by settlers from New England and New York. One of the strongest voices against slavery was Rev. William B. Dodge, a known abolitionist and transplant from Salem, Massachusetts, who held the pulpit at the Millburn Congregational Church and was a familiar speaker at gatherings throughout the county. One such gathering was a Fourth of July picnic held in 1844 in Newport Township. The American celebration provided an opportunity for settlers to meet, appealing to immigrants as a chance to embrace their new country. Families brought food to share, including fish chowder, a variety of breads, pumpkin pie, and sorrel herb pie. A highlight of the day was the reading of the Declaration of Independence. The Revolutionary War and the signing of the Declaration had occurred within living memory of many Americans and meant a great deal to citizens of the young nation. Reverend Dodge gave the blessing and prayed for the freedom of the slaves. However, the public outcry against slavery heard at this celebration was not reflected in the temperament of Lake County voters. In the 1844 presidential election, the county voted Democrat, with 640 of the total 1,157 votes going for James K. Polk.[14]

Dodge's antislavery stance resonated with Amos Bennett, the county's first African American settler, who also attended the Independence Day gathering.

In 1835, Bennett, who was born a free man, brought his family west from Delhi, New York. By 1840, there were 3,598 free blacks in Illinois, but the Bennetts were the only African Americans residing in Lake County. Bennett and his family lived remarkably unaffected by the state's notorious Black Laws, first enacted in 1819 to restrict fundamental liberties to free African Americans. Bennett purchased land, sent his children to the local school, and ran (unsuccessfully) for public office. In part, Bennett's acceptance came from his knowledge of herbal remedies, which garnered him the title of "Dr. Bennett." With little access to physicians on the frontier, a self-reliant man with the skill to provide care was beneficial to all.[15]

In 1845, Libertyville in central Lake County held an antislavery convention at which Congregational clergyman and itinerant abolitionist Ichabod Codding spoke. Historian Henry Louis Gates Jr. noted that Codding spent a good portion of his time in Illinois "organizing Anti-Nebraska Democrats, Whigs, and political abolitionists into what would become the Republican Party." Also speaking at the convention was Sojourner Truth, who had escaped enslavement and become an impassioned and powerful political speaker for abolitionism and women's rights.[16]

In 1846, Dr. Richard Murphy, an Irish Lake County resident and former Illinois state legislator, spoke in Waukegan for the abolition of slavery. The same year, a local affiliate of the Illinois Liberty Party, the Lake County Liberty Association, was founded by Reverend Dodge and Seth Paine. The Liberty Party advocated for the full citizenship of African Americans and opposed discrimination.[17]

The Liberty Party's first true success in Lake County was the selection of antislavery advocate Hurlbut Swan as a delegate to the Illinois constitutional convention of 1847. The main function of the convention was to address the modernization of Illinois government and its banking system that had collapsed in the financial catastrophe of the Panic of 1837. Swan was most interested in speaking against Article 14 of the proposed new Illinois constitution, which aimed to limit citizenship to whites and prohibit people of color from immigrating to Illinois or being freed in the state by slaveholders. The state's long history of slavery dated back to French settlement in the 1680s, and as historian Jerome B. Meites explained, over two-thirds of the convention delegates were "born in states where chattel slavery was lawful." Swan could not overcome these odds, and his efforts to amend the article failed.[18]

Meites noted that when the new constitution was ratified by a vote on March 8, 1848, "Black exclusion passed in eighty-seven of the state's 101 counties. It lost in twelve northeastern counties, most definitively in Boone, where the vote was 94 percent against," and in Lake, with "85 percent against." The legislature enacted the Black Law in 1853, giving Illinois the shameful distinction of being the first Northern state to constitutionally ban African American immigration. In 1865, most of the Black Laws were repealed by the state legislature.[19]

Churches often led the shift in the position on slavery. In the 1830s, members of the three major denominations in Illinois—Baptist, Methodist, and Presbyterian—approved of freeing the slaves and sending them "back" to Africa, in what was called "African colonization." This was preferred over emancipating the slaves and having them remain in the United States, where it was presumed they would settle in the North and compete with whites for jobs. The colonization movement addressed Northerners' opposition to slavery, the belief that it was morally wrong, and that slavery was contrary to the principles of the Declaration of Independence that "all men are created equal." It also reflected, according to historian Sally Heinzel, the prejudice and self-interest of many whites, who were "unable to envision free blacks as productive, equal members of society."[20]

Edward Murray's views on slavery were influenced by his attendance at Baptist meetings. He became a Baptist in early adulthood, diverging from his father's Episcopal and his mother's Catholic affiliations. Historian Glen Jeansonne noted that the issue of slavery divided the Baptist Church, and in 1845 Southern and Northern Baptists "severed organizational relations" over the "morality of slavery." At Baptist meetings, Edward heard sermons that slavery was forbidden in the Bible and therefore a sin.[21]

Opposition to slavery grew more vocal in response to the Fugitive Slave Act of 1850. Through newspapers and word of mouth, the Murrays were aware of the growing discourse on sectional politics. A Whig convention in Waukegan in October 1850 passed a resolution opposing the "extension of human slavery over one foot more of territory belonging to the Union." Their opposition focused mainly on the economics of slavery. The growing anger over sectional politics began to register in the 1852 presidential election. Democrat Franklin Pierce won Lake County with 871 votes, but when the votes for Whig candidate Winfield Scott (760) and Free Soil candidate John P. Hale (555) were combined, it became clear that Lake County was shifting away from the Democratic Party. Newport Township voted in the majority for the antislavery Free Soil candidate.[22]

Lake County's greatest incidence of sectional outrage occurred on September 8, 1854, in response to the passage of the Kansas-Nebraska Act. Many

Northerners interpreted the act as an attack on the power of free states and an expansion of slavery. They held a particular antagonism for Illinois senator Stephen A. Douglas, whom they felt had betrayed his constituents and the country. The gathering of nearly six hundred Whigs, Democrats, and Free Soilers took place on the public square in Waukegan. As described in a letter to the editor of the *Chicago Tribune,* the evening culminated with "an effigy bearing the mournful initials S.A.D. . . . . publicly executed and burned." A resolution was written denouncing Douglas and read in part: "That the day is past when those *really small* can be bloated into Giants solely by the aid of political machinery and bad Whisky." On November 2, Douglas visited Waukegan, which county historian Charles A. Partridge explained had a "marked effect in closing up the lines again and producing harmony." Nearly two thousand gathered to hear him speak.[23]

While many Illinois Republicans supported the state's restrictive Black Laws, Murray was influenced by the strong antislavery culture in northern Illinois.[24]

Loughlin Madden Jr.

In October 1851, Loughlin Madden Jr. waited in the port of Liverpool, England, for a ship aptly named *America.* He was traveling with his widowed father, Loughlin Sr., and six siblings. The Maddens had traveled from Ireland by steamship to Liverpool, which had become Europe's largest emigration port due to its established transatlantic routes and the ability of emigrants to reach it by steamship and train. In 1851, nearly 160,000 passengers set sail from Liverpool for North America.[25]

The Maddens declared themselves as "farmers" on the ship's register, which meant they were tenant or subsistence farmers. They had the means to emigrate either by selling crops and livestock or by compensation from their landlord. They were poor, like the vast majority of Irish suffering from political and religious suppression and the extreme hardships brought on by potato famines without relief or aid from the British government. Every potato harvest from the summer of 1845 through the early 1850s had failed totally or partially, which was devastating in a country where the majority of inhabitants relied on the potato as their main source of food.[26]

The Maddens were just eight of the over one million Irish who emigrated in the 1840s and 1850s. Historian Kerby A. Miller explained that "thousands of panic-stricken people embraced emigration as their only escape from destitution and death." Unlike other immigrants, who sought liberty and freedom in the United States, the Famine Irish left their homeland because they feared death. Their emigration was "characterized by 'a note of doom, an air of finality.'"[27]

On board the *America*, Loughlin Madden Sr. and his children—Anne, John, Christopher, James, Loughlin Jr., Bridget, and Patrick—were in the company of their countrymen and women. The *America*'s passengers, a total of 348, were all from Ireland. After a voyage of about thirty-five days, the R.M. steamship *America* arrived in New York on November 7, 1851. As a farmer, Loughlin Sr. was keen to go west where good farmland was available. The fastest route was by Erie Canal packet boat and then steamship on the Great Lakes. They disembarked at Kenosha (formerly Southport) where they lived for the next several years.[28]

By June 1860, the family was living in Turk's Corners (Rosecrans), Newport Township, Lake County, Illinois, where they rented a farm. A strong impetus for settling in this community was its sizeable number of Irish families. By the 1840s, the locale was known as Irish Hills for its concentration of Irish and the gently rolling landscape. The availability of farmland and a community of fellow Irish were important for the Maddens' moral, spiritual, and physical sustenance, particularly in light of the national rise in nativism. The large influx of Irish and German Catholic immigrants to the United States in the 1840s and 1850s brought a backlash of anti-foreign and anti-Catholic sentiment epitomized by the American Party, also known as the Know Nothing Party.[29]

Nativist strongholds tended to be large cities in the eastern United States where masses of poor, suffering immigrants arrived daily and overwhelmed the relief organizations. There were also pockets of nativists in Chicago, St. Louis, and Milwaukee. As historian Michael J. McManus explained, American workers feared that the great number of immigrants would "depress wages, lower their standard of living, and limit upward mobility and opportunity." The nativists purported that immigrants "threatened the purity of American political institutions" since they lacked "familiarity with the nation's electoral traditions and practices," making them gullible to corrupt politicians.[30]

At the heart of anti-Catholic bigotry was the fear of "Romanism." McManus noted that native-born Protestants "warned of the dangers the alien menace posed to the Republic." The *Christian Advocate* asserted that the Know Nothings were trying to protect the country from "Romanism," which it considered "hostile to the principles of civil and religious liberty." It was believed that Catholics' devotion to the pope made them unable to "embrace the institutions of their adopted homeland." Historian Susannah Ural Bruce explained that it confounded some native-born Americans that the Irish (and Germans) "clung to their religious roots rather than adopting the predominant Protestant habits of the United States."[31]

For the Maddens, their sanctuary—St. Andrew's Catholic Church—was a log structure of modest proportions. Through this congregation, they became acquainted with Edward Murray's Catholic mother and Murray's Irish-born farm laborer Henry Furlong. Furlong married the eldest daughter, Anne Madden, creating a connection between the Maddens and their neighbors. While Catholic churches provided a sense of security and community, sectional politics were particularly concerning to the Famine emigrants. These Irish had been desperate to leave Ireland for the sake of survival, unlike the pre-Famine Irish, who had sought independence and economic opportunities. The prospect of emancipating millions of slaves threatened their precarious position on the bottom rung of society. Kerby A. Miller noted that most Irish aligned with the Democratic Party in part due to the "antagonism to the strong evangelical Protestant and anti-Irish Catholic strains" of the Whigs, Know Nothings, and Republicans. The rise of the Republican Party and Abraham Lincoln were unwelcome to this economically fragile group. Susannah Ural Bruce observed that the Irish position was further complicated by the fact that they viewed themselves "as much Irish as American," and the need for survival taught them "to protect their own interests." Support for a cause depended on how it impacted their family and their "dreams for Ireland and America, or both."[32]

James B. Murrie

For many immigrant families, the path to a new life was paved by loved ones who traveled to America before them. For the young James Murrie, the trailblazer was his uncle John Murrie, who sailed across winter seas from Scotland to New York, landing on January 19, 1842. When he arrived in northeastern Illinois, he had one hundred American dollars in his pocket, which he used to buy unclaimed government land west of the Des Plaines River in Newport Township. This location proved fortunate, because his neighbors were the Murrays. Daughter Jane Murray caught John's eye, and the couple married on October 3, 1845.[33]

In Scotland, older brother David Murrie Jr. followed John's success with interest. In the 1840s and early 1850s, Scotland faced economic depression and a potato famine in the Highlands and islands. In 1851, David was living in the parish of Beath, Fife, with his wife Janet Barrie and their sons James and Alexander, working as an "agricultural laborer." By then, David and Janet had suffered the loss of four children. With the knowledge of John's success in America and the prospect of a bright future farming alongside his brother and raising sons in the young republic, David was encouraged to uproot his family.[34]

James recalled that in 1852, when he was just a lad, they "bade good-by to their old home." When they reached America, the Murries continued by way of the Erie Canal and Great Lakes to Kenosha, Wisconsin. Within a few years, David was able to buy the property across the Des Plaines River from his younger brother. David and Janet Murrie soon welcomed daughters Jane, known as "Jennie," and Ellen. The Murries taught their children traditional Scottish folk songs and sent them to be educated at the Red Schoolhouse, named for its distinct color. A large stump near the corner of the school was used by young and old as a speaker's stand, and the newly settled Murries embraced this liberating and democratic form of public speaking.[35]

The Murries had belonged to the Presbyterian Church in Scotland, but in America they joined the Disciples of Christ (Christian Church). The Disciples of Christ members in central and northern Illinois were antislavery, but in the southern portion of the state a pro-slavery sentiment dominated. Exposed to this influence and living in a county with vocal abolitionists and antislavery societies, James Murrie adopted these sentiments. In 1856, at fourteen years old, James was old enough to take an interest in politics, but not to vote. His father and uncle supported John C. Frémont, the first presidential candidate of the antislavery Republican Party. By his eighteenth birthday on May 20, 1860, James had witnessed the rise of Abraham Lincoln and heard the rumbling threats of Southern secession.[36]

William Brighton Lewin

Henry and Jane Lewin and their nine children traveled from the countryside of Oxfordshire, England, to the bustling metropolis of London. Henry was a farmer, and although prosperous enough to employ several laborers, he made the decision to seek opportunities for himself and his family in the New World. It was 1853, and ten-year-old William "Billy" Lewin was about to set sail with his family for America on the bark *Kremlin*. The ship arrived in Boston on June 10, where the Lewins remained for several weeks before continuing to northeastern Illinois. Within a few years, Henry Lewin had purchased 120 acres straddling the Des Plaines River, and the family soon became acquainted with the Murrays, Murries, and Maddens.[37]

More than twenty years before the Lewins' arrival, Native Americans had been removed from the region by a series of treaties—the last being the Treaty of Chicago. Native people returned to the area to hunt wild game and honor their ancestors, and on one occasion a group of Native American men hunted and killed a deer near the Lewin homestead. They asked Henry Lewin for salt, which he provided, and the next morning he found "one fourth of a deer left to repay him for the salt."[38]

The Lewins were Methodists, and on those occasions when the circuit preacher came to their homestead, the eldest son ferried him across the river, as the nearest bridges were one mile in either direction. The family passed down the story that Henry Jr. "rebelled" against ferrying preachers and "wanted [his] brothers to take turns." On one crossing, "the river was high . . . and [he] caused the boat to tip." Thereafter, younger brothers John and William ferried the preacher.[39]

The Methodists, led by Rev. Salmon Stebbins, were well established in northern Lake County by the late 1830s. In 1844, the North and South denominations of the Methodist Church in America split over slavery, and the Lewins heard sermons against the institution. This message of moral concern was engrained in Billy Lewin. His sympathy for others also led him to take an interest in medicine. Though he did not receive a medical degree, the expertise in medicine that he gained was beneficial in a rural area where access to doctors was limited.[40] As a self-motivated and caring young man, Lewin had opinions on an acceptable resolution to slavery and saw promise in the rise of the Republican Party.

John Youngson Taylor

In a small rented house in the farming village of New Byth, Aberdeenshire, Scotland, John Taylor stood with his brothers and sisters at the wake of their beloved mother. It was the day before the Scottish New Year's Eve celebration of Hogmanay in 1845, a time when the family should have been celebrating with oatcakes and traditional songs. Instead, they mourned their forty-six year old mother, Isabella Lawrence Taylor, who left behind six children and an aging husband. John was just three years old. Isabella's death marked the end of a series of losses for the Taylors. Several months earlier, John's ten-year-old brother Samuel had died. The previous year, his half-sister Isabella had gone to America following their cousins, the John Thain family.[41]

Family patriarch Samuel Taylor supported his children as a house thatcher, bookbinder, and bookseller, and assisted the town in establishing a circulating library. Due to Samuel's fragile health and insufficient income, it was necessary for his children to work. The younger boys earned a small wage as sheepherders. Eight years after his wife's death, as Samuel was nearing his 72nd birthday, he continued to hear of tens of thousands of Scots departing for North America, Australia, and South Africa due to extreme poverty. The path to the New World was set, and Samuel encouraged his children to seek opportunities elsewhere.[42]

In April 1854, a twenty-one-year-old Mary and her brothers James (aged fourteen) and John (twelve) traveled to the bustling port of Aberdeen to begin their journey to join their sister Isabella, who had married James Low, and cousins in Illinois. It was cheaper to book passage to Canadian ports rather than to the United States, and with ships sailing frequently from Aberdeen to Quebec, the Taylors took this less expensive route to the New World. In Quebec, they transferred to a sidewheel steamer that traveled down the St. Lawrence River and around the Great Lakes. As their vessel approached Waukegan's harbor on Lake Michigan, the sight of the burgeoning port was the Taylors' first real glimpse of an American town.[43]

By June, the siblings were reunited with their sister, whom they had not seen for ten years. The Taylor siblings settled into the Low home and their new life in the abolitionist community of Millburn. The small town was settled by families from England, Scotland, and New England, and its Congregational church, led by Rev. William B. Dodge, was known for bold proclamations. On February 7, 1853, the congregation had voted on a resolution denouncing slavery: "a great system of oppression which deprives millions of our fellow beings of the civil, social, and moral rights and privileges which God granted a like to all the human family." The congregation stated that they would "withhold all acts of human fellowship from those who live in the practice of this sin [until] the oppressed go free."[44]

In Scotland, the Taylors' parents were members of the Baptist Church. James recalled that they "carefully looked after [our] religious training." Just weeks from first stepping on American soil, a twelve-year-old John Taylor found himself in the midst of this small but dynamic community. While the Millburn church was particularly forthright in its antislavery stance, the siblings heard similar sermons at other local Protestant churches, and from itinerant lecturers. On July 7, 1854, the Taylors had the opportunity to attend a lecture by Dr. R. L. Cooper, an African American abolitionist, who came to Millburn to speak on "Slavery and the Nebraska Measure." These public forums and the inspiring sermons of Reverend Dodge gave the Taylors a quick education on the deepening sectional politics.[45]

In 1856, John moved with his sister Isabella Low's family several miles down the road to O'Plain (Gurnee). The town's location at the intersection of two well-traveled roads was beneficial to James Low's livestock trade. On his way to school, John walked past a temperance tavern run by Wealthy Rudd. "Mother Rudd," as she was affectionately known, was rumored to have hidden African American freedom seekers on her property.[46]

News of the capture and death sentence of John Brown after his failed raid at Harpers Ferry, Virginia, on October 16–18, 1859, sent a shockwave through the North's antislavery communities. In an effort to take his antislavery war to the South, Brown and his supporters seized an armory in hopes of supplying weapons to enslaved men and freedom fighters. Brown was captured and charged with murder, slave insurrection, and treason against the state of Virginia. He was tried and given a death sentence. The emotional impact of Brown's raid widened the schism between North and South. Outrage over his impending execution brought the Millburn community together at the Congregational church on December 2, 1859. The congregation prayed and then adopted a resolution, which in part read, "We will do good to those that have escaped from bondage as we have the opportunity by supplying their present wants and aiding their flight."[47]

James and John Taylor accompanied their sisters to Congregational and Christian meetings, depending on whom they were living with or visiting at the time. It was not unusual for Protestants in rural areas to attend more than one church to hear different sermons or lecturers. The brothers attended Baptist meetings where they met the John Murrie and Edward Murray families. Through Christian Church meetings, they became acquainted with David Murrie and his son James. John Taylor also made connections with the Newport Township Stateline Road community by working as a farm laborer for John Murrie, David Murrie, and Edward Murray. Rural communities were intricately networked, and John had a reputation as an affable, hard-working, churchgoing lad.

For the Fourth of July, 1860, the Taylor brothers enjoyed the festivities in Waukegan. The *Chicago Press and Tribune* reported that the day's events included "trotting matches of the Northwestern Horse Growers' Association" at McKay's racetrack near the courthouse. Harness racing was wildly popular in northeastern Illinois and considered a farmer's sport. There were several political speakers, including Waukegan's republican mayor, Elisha P. Ferry. The speeches were of "Union-rending and heart-rending tendency." There was ample reason for the Taylors to ruminate on the prospect of war given the tone of the speeches, but if James's diary entry is any indication, it was of no consequence: "Went to Waukegan the Fourth. Went with John all day. Spent just 50 cents."[48]

The Taylor brothers set their sights on becoming teachers and enrolled in the abolitionist-leaning Waukegan Academy. After completing the rigorous curriculum, the Taylors held teaching positions in the winter months and continued to work as farm laborers during the growing season. For many young men, teaching was a stepping-stone to more substantial positions in the community. John and James were gaining independence and spreading their wings in the young republic.[49]

Between 1841 and 1854, Edward Murray, Loughlin Madden Jr., James B. Murrie, William B. Lewin, and John Y. Taylor immigrated to and settled in northeastern Illinois. These men and their families were part of a wave of migrants who looked to America for shelter and safe haven, economic opportunity, and most of all liberty, equality, and self-rule. It took a special mettle of person to venture onto the frontier where one had to build a life from scratch: breaking prairie, cutting oak trees for log homes and fences, planting seed and watching the skies for rain, and then hoping the market value of the harvest would make the backbreaking work worthwhile. These pioneering families faced illnesses attributed to "bad air" and adaptation to a new climate, debt from payments on land and farm equipment, and the emotional strain of being thousands of miles from loved ones left in the British Isles. Settlers persevered in these conditions in part through the goodwill of their neighbors.[50]

Since crops were harvested at the same time, farmers were often unable to assist one another, making it necessary to hire on helpers. Ed Murray worked his own farm, and James Murrie and Billy Lewin worked their family farms. John Taylor earned a living as a winter-term teacher and as a hired man for John Murrie and his brother-in-law Ed Murray. These men further cemented their connections at church meetings. Ed Murray, James Murrie, Billy Lewin, and John Taylor were Protestant and had occasion to meet at Baptist, Christian, Congregational, and Methodist services. It was also through the Protestant churches that they heard sermons on the evils of slavery.[51]

Through Catholic services, Loughlin Madden Jr. became acquainted with members of the Murray family. Through the farm community, he met neighbors such as the Lewins. A shared commonality of roots in the British Isles also brought these men together. For Ed Murray, James Murrie, and John Taylor, their Scottish ethnicity gave them a shared culture of holiday traditions and folk songs. All five men had lived under British rule, and they sought the freedom and refuge that America held. Their shared roots and experience as immigrants struggling to make a place for themselves in the New World helped them to form friendships.[52]

The ties these men made as kin and neighbors strengthened when their adopted country needed them most. Their greatest challenge lay on the horizon.

2. ❀ May God Save the Union

On the evening of April 2, 1860, a man of "humble appearance" spoke in front of a capacity crowd in Waukegan. The guest speaker was Abraham Lincoln, who in recent months had become a household name inspiring men across the North to form Republican clubs in support. Among the crowd was local brickmason John W. Hull, who observed Lincoln as one of the "humblest" men he "had seen in many a day."[1]

Lincoln was in Chicago attending the sessions of the U.S. District Court as counsel for the defendants in the "Sandbar" case, involving rights over sandbars along the Lake Michigan coast. He accepted the invitation to speak on his antislavery and political views from Mayor Elisha Ferry of Waukegan and Illinois state senator Henry Blodgett. Hundreds gathered for the meeting in Dickinson's Hall. John Hull recalled that the "sledge-hammer force of [Lincoln's] logic" had a great effect on those in attendance as he spoke about the nation being "half slavery and half freedom, and . . . no government divided against itself in such manner could stand." The *Waukegan Gazette*'s editor, James Y. Cory, wrote that seeing "Old Abe . . . really does one's soul good."[2]

Lincoln won the nomination for president at the Republican National Convention in Chicago, May 16–18, 1860, and the Wide Awakes, a pseudo-militaristic political organization, stumped for his campaign. The closest company of Wide Awakes to Newport Township's Stateline Road community was in Millburn. Other towns had notable clubs, including Libertyville, whose chapter won a prize banner for its large membership. The structured militaristic style of the Wide Awakes appealed to Northerners, who had been troubled by the partisan volatility of the 1850s. Historian Jon Grinspan noted that these young men in their teens, twenties, and thirties, "equipped with uniforms and torches[,] sent an ominous message to those already apprehensive about the Republican party's antisouthern attitudes." In September, abolitionist and U.S. representative from Illinois Owen Lovejoy, the brother of Elijah P. Lovejoy, who had been killed for his stand against slavery, spoke at a "Grand Republican Mass Meeting" in Waukegan. Most remarkable about

21

this gathering was the countywide orchestration of a procession of Wide Awakes and citizens carrying torches. Though Ed Murray declared himself a "staunch" supporter of the Republicans, it is unknown if he participated.[3]

In the November presidential election, Abraham Lincoln swept Lake County, securing 71 percent of the total 3,364 votes cast. In the election, Irish Catholics overwhelmingly supported the Democratic Party. Illinois voted for Lincoln by nearly 51 percent of the vote over Stephen A. Douglas. The Republican Party's and Lincoln's opposition to the spread of slavery in the western territories resonated strongly with Northerners.[4]

By the end of the year, the stability of the Union came into doubt, as Southern states began to secede, starting with South Carolina on December 20. A *Chicago Tribune* editorial focused on the "miserable secession business" and how Democrats were calling for Republicans to "make 'great concessions'" to end the crisis. As it happened, the North had been making concessions for nearly a century, beginning with the Three-Fifths Compromise of 1787, which gave disproportionate representation in the House of Representatives to Southern slave states over free states. Lincoln himself had sought compromise in his platform, proposing a limit to slavery's expansion, not its abolishment. The saber rattling of the South was felt in the North.[5]

As war approached, communities came together at Union meetings and in their support for Lincoln. Ed Murray, John Taylor, and many of their neighbors attended the meetings. These immigrant men strongly supported free labor over slavery, the outcome of which would greatly affect their own prosperity. The South's refusal to accept Lincoln's election and its insistence on the right to secede were direct challenges to Northerners' views on the national union and the outcome of the 1860 election.[6]

It was spring 1861, and though John Taylor had retreated to the barn at the John Murrie homestead for solitude, there was no escaping the news of the first cannon fire of the War of Rebellion. Word of the fall of Fort Sumter and President Lincoln's call for seventy-five thousand militiamen for three-month service reached Waukegan on April 15 by telegram. The message that secessionists were attempting to destroy the United States spread across the countryside by newspapers and riders on horseback.[7]

The North was ignited by a rush of patriotism, uniting native and foreign-born Americans in the excitement. The *Kenosha Times* ran a call to action on its front page: "To Arms! To Arms! Citizens! Freemen! Men with American Hearts! Your Union, which you have been wont to glorify, is assaulted; the Star

Spangled Banner which you revere is polluted with insult."[8] The wording of this piece strategically appealed to all male citizens with "American Hearts," whether native or immigrant.

Meetings were organized at a dozen points in the county. As Charles Partridge recalled, Democrats and Republicans alike made "stirring addresses and declaring their purpose to stand by the Union." The following day a war meeting was held at the courthouse in Waukegan. With pro-Union cheers and the sounds of a fife-and-drum band, men volunteered "amid much excitement and enthusiasm."[9]

On April 18, a meeting was held at Waukegan's Dickinson Hall, which was filled to the rafters with men eager to strike back at the South. The year before, the hall had welcomed Abraham Lincoln, and now citizens were being called to arms by President Lincoln. Attorney Isaac L. Clarke brought the war assembly to order, and within a few hours $1,000 was raised and 85 men enlisted to form a company for the Chicago Zouave Regiment. These men sought to emulate Lincoln's friend, Col. Elmer Ellsworth, who had made the Zouave militia a national sensation.[10]

A similar meeting was held in John Taylor's old stomping grounds in Millburn on April 22 at the Congregational church. The *Waukegan Gazette* published a letter from the meeting: "The insides of the Meeting House crammed to its utmost capacity . . . the doors thrown open . . . men of all parties heartily joining. We raised nine volunteers in no time. It was resolved that a bounty of Ten dollars be given to each Volunteer and it was further resolved that we pledge ourselves to provide for the families of married men who volunteer."[11]

The men enlisted for three-month service in the 12th Illinois Infantry, also known as the 1st Scotch Regiment. They joined Capt. J. R. Hugunin's company at Chicago, which was accepted by Gov. Richard Yates at Springfield. Though two volunteers had a familial association to John Taylor, he was not swayed to enlist. There were plenty of men to fill Illinois's quota of six regiments set under the president's order. A month later, many more companies had organized in Illinois than could be accepted, and Governor Yates ordered they disband and return home, including the men of the Waukegan Zouaves. It was a situation seen in many northern states due to an inability to arm so many men. The *Waukegan Gazette* reported encouragingly, "We wish our patriotic friends [in Newport] who are volunteering could have assurances that their services would be accepted. . . . We advise them however to keep up their organization, get all the men to join the Company that will do so, and meet regularly for drill that in case it should become necessary . . . they will be ready at a moment's call."[12]

Ed Murray supported the government in Washington, D.C., but did not offer his services. He had a growing family and farm, and the general consensus of the neighborhood and the nation was that the war would end quickly. Murray showed his support by attending Union meetings at the local schoolhouse where the Newport Brass Band played "Yankee Doodle" and the de facto national anthem, "Hail Columbia." A number of men enrolled their names for the formation of a rifle company. John Taylor wrote to his cousin David Minto, "We have weekly meetings to aid in the cause. Though not many volunteers have gone from Newport still they are doing well with their means. Besides they have formed a militia company . . . [and meet] for the purpose of drilling."[13]

The *Waukegan Gazette* encouraged enlistment and published a poem titled "Waukegan Volunteers."

> The south they have opened their cannon,
> Its thundering noise we can hear;
> We have done with Mr. Buchanan;
> Hurrah for the brave volunteer!
> Now Waukegan boys, are you ready
> To write down your names without fear;
> With your hand unnervous and steady;
> Three cheers for the brave volunteer.[14]

Republicans, Democrats, and men throughout the North began to unite in the common cause to preserve the Union. Historian Mark E. Neely Jr. noted that prominent Illinois democrat Stephen A. Douglas "rushed to pledge fealty to the Union and to denounce partisanship." In a speech to the Illinois legislature on April 25, 1861, Douglas stated, "It is our duty to defend our Constitution and protect our flag."[15]

In spite of a swell in unity, the Irish were still scrutinized. A neighboring farmer of the Maddens, Mark Daley, published a letter in the *Waukegan Gazette* responding to "reports that I favor the movements of the Secessionists of the South." The Irish-born Daley was a naturalized U.S. citizen and professed that he "cared more for the preservation of the Union than for the extinction of African slavery." Daley was in line with most citizens who initially did not consider emancipation in the effort to save the Union. He saw slavery as a "local question," following Stephen Douglas's thinking of popular sovereignty, which advocated that settlers of territorial lands be allowed to determine whether they would join the Union as a free or slave state.[16]

Irish support for the Union was based on many factors. America was the Irish exiles' refuge from poverty and oppression, and they would fight to preserve this new home. But as historian Susannah Ural Bruce explained, they feared that "zealots . . . would abolish slavery and destroy the federal union in the process." They were concerned about abolitionism's influence on the Republican Party, believing that Republicans wanted them to fight to free the slaves who would then compete for the low-paying jobs the Irish struggled to keep. Tired of defending their position amid the sectional politics and nativist rhetoric of the times, many Irish settlers would have agreed with Daley.[17]

For Loughlin Madden Jr., there was no rush to enlist. He was gainfully employed as a farm laborer, eliminating the need for the pay, and at seventeen he was a year too young for service (although there were numerous cases of eager young men lying about their age on enlistment forms). One of Madden's neighbors heeded the call to arms. In August 1861, Andrew McFadden joined the 37th Illinois Infantry, making him part of the early wave of local volunteers and one of 175 enlisting with that regiment from Lake County. McFadden's Irish-born mother had recently died, so without her to discourage him from enlisting and no longer needing to support her, McFadden was more easily swept up by the patriotism that was encouraged by Irish newspapers, politicians, and religious leaders. Some Irish preferred units with Irish officers, but McFadden chose a unit recruiting locally rather than the 23rd Illinois Infantry, popularly known as the Irish Brigade, organizing in Chicago. As historian Don H. Doyle explained, many Irish felt compelled to "[take] up the sword in America to prepare for the struggle against the British waiting to be waged back in Ireland." They saw themselves as American, but their hearts remained in Ireland, concerned for the continued oppression and suffering of its people. This dual allegiance was criticized sharply by native-born Americans.[18]

During those first months of the war, life continued largely unaltered for the Stateline Road community. John Taylor worked on the farm of fellow Scotsman John Murrie and began to take an interest in his employer's eldest daughter, Nancy "Nannie" Murrie.[19] He worked alongside Ed Murray, James Murrie, and Billy Lewin, and on occasion encountered Loughlin Madden Jr. taking produce to market. They shared the commonalities of their British heritage, occupation as farmers, and support for the Union (although none had enlisted). Considering that only 19 men from Newport Township, out of a total of 521 enlistees from the county, enlisted in 1861, there was no great pressure to sign the rolls. With Illinois's quota met, the urgency and ability to enlist had gone, but as the war progressed, so did the length of service. Taylor's cousin Andrew White with the 12th Illinois wrote, "They tried to get men for three years yesterday, but they did not get 5 out of Company K."[20]

Over the winter of 1861–62, John Taylor taught at the Biddlecome School where Ed Murray was a trustee. John wrote to his brother, "I am getting along amazing well they seem to respect me well. They think I take a different method of teaching from any of their former teachers. . . . One of my Directors . . . complimented me highly said he never saw the school house look so neat and orderly." Teaching was a great first step for a young man eager to make his mark. John was expected to instruct in reading, arithmetic, geography, and American values. His acceptance as a role model for the community's youth was a testament to his integration into society, but he had yet to achieve the "prize of the age"—citizenship.[21]

In early 1862, the Union saw its first major victories when Brig. Gen. Ulysses S. Grant captured two forts on the Tennessee and Kentucky border in quick succession: Fort Henry on the Tennessee River (February 6) and Fort Donelson on the Cumberland River (February 12–16). The Federals had realized the importance of controlling major rivers in the Western Theater to the ultimate defeat of the Confederacy. But soon the intensity and realities of war would change the nation. Word came of the Union victory at the Battle of Shiloh at Pittsburg Landing, Tennessee (April 6–7). The scale of the loss of life— nearly twenty-four thousand killed, wounded, or missing—was unimaginable. Nothing like it had been seen before. Northerners and Southerners alike were shocked. According to Charles R. Bowery Jr., executive director of the U.S. Army Center of Military History, "The Northern press portrayed Shiloh as a senseless bloodbath" and placed the blame squarely on the shoulders of the newly promoted Maj. Gen. Ulysses S. Grant. Letters flooded the White House asking for Grant's dismissal, but President Lincoln knew Grant's value and stood by him, stating, "I can't spare this man; he fights."[22]

Grant's victories dealt a devastating blow to the South and were a key to controlling the strategic geography of the Western Theater and to bringing about the Union's ultimate victory. But the battle brought a new realization that no single military maneuver would end the war, and that there could be many more battles like Shiloh to come. In response to the news of the battle, the Chicago Sanitary Commission (a branch of the U.S. Sanitary Commission) sent a plea to Lake County citizens to take a more active part in contributing to the relief of the boys who served. The women of Waukegan's Methodist church created the Soldiers Aid Society of Waukegan, which maintained consistent support through the remainder of the war.[23]

The war was ever closer in the hearts and minds of Northern civilians, who followed its progress and setbacks in weekly newspapers and letters home from the front. In June 1862, Union forces made a bold move to end the war by attempting to capture the Confederate capital of Richmond, Virginia, in the Peninsula Campaign. In a series of battles between June 25 and July 1, known as the Seven Days Battles, Maj. Gen. George B. McClellan's Army of the Potomac was driven back from Richmond by Confederate general Robert E. Lee. On the heels of the disastrous seven-day campaign, President Lincoln called for three hundred thousand men on July 2 and an additional three hundred thousand on August 4, making it clear that the fight was far from over.[24]

Don H. Doyle noted that "both sides began the war by denying slavery to be at issue." By that second summer of war, the Union began to embrace what other nations already understood: that "the Civil War was indeed Liberty's War, a war to destroy slavery." As historian Gary W. Gallagher explained, abolitionists understood that "a longer war increased the likelihood that slavery would not survive."[25]

The need for more regiments was apparent, but the threat of a looming draft and the incentive of bounties paid to recruits encouraged men to volunteer. As historian Wayne N. Duerkes noted, in the first two years of the war, "Illinois mustered over eighty-thousand men into Federal service . . . over one-quarter of all military-age males from northern Illinois enlisted." During the summer of 1862, Lake County recruited 412 men, enough to fill four companies, but to form a regiment ten companies were needed. It was discovered that Jo Daviess County had only six companies, and neither Lake nor Jo Daviess Counties were able to ally with adjacent counties without conceding a major part of the field and staff officers. As it happened, U.S. representative Elihu B. Washburne of Galena (Jo Daviess County) and Illinois senator Henry W. Blodgett of Waukegan (Lake County) were personal and political friends. Through their intervention, the two counties, although geographically separated by over one hundred miles, were in the same congressional district and thus brought together.[26]

Through regimental negotiations it was decided that the 96th's colonel would be from Jo Daviess County (Thomas E. Champion), since that county was providing the majority of the men, and the lieutenant colonel would be from Lake County (Isaac L. Clarke). Clarke had been an associate principal and teacher at the Waukegan Academy from 1848 to 1850 where abolitionist ideals were encouraged. In 1850 he went to California with gold fever, and on his return he became a lawyer. It was common for Union troops and their officers to have no military experience, making Clarke's professional background and local connections acceptable credentials to lead men to war. The *Waukegan Gazette* touted Clarke's war contribution, stating, "[H]e abandons a lucrative professional business and the comforts of home; but duty calls and he obeys."[27]

Recruitment of Pollock's Company

In July and August 1862, Charles Partridge observed that "recruiting went forward with great rapidity." Like canvassers on the campaign trail, men took to the stump, pleading with those of military age to enlist and to emulate "the heroes of the 15th and 37th Regiments," in which over 250 Lake County men had enlisted the year before. Nightly the mustering drum was heard, and citizens gathered in every village, township, church, and schoolhouse. One advertisement in the *Waukegan Gazette* declared, "Now is the last chance to VOLUNTEER!" eluding to a possible draft and to the climate of patriotism surrounding recruitment.[28]

John K. Pollock of Millburn was a key recruiter for a company of men in what would become Company C of the 96th Illinois. Born in New Hampshire, Pollock came to Lake County with his Scottish-born parents in the fall of 1839. His father, Robert, was an influential charter member of the Millburn Congregational Church, and a founding member of the county's antislavery society. Robert Pollock would not live to see the destruction of slavery, but his son took up the mantle, recruiting dozens to the cause and leading them to war. The meeting to organize Pollock's company was held at the courthouse in Waukegan and was attended by a large group of citizens and soldiers. It was at this meeting that Pollock was elected captain, and he would remain the senior captain of the regiment for twenty-one months. A local man who heard of Pollock's promotion stated, "If the Capt. thrashes the Rebels as well as he did grain he will do."[29]

Edward Murray was in the harvest field when Pollock came to call. Visitors were welcome in this sparsely populated area along Newport Township's State-line Road, but it must have occurred to Murray that there was some urgency to Pollock's visit for him to cut across his fields rather than drop in on him at home. It was the first day of August 1862. The war was on everyone's minds, and this particular caller carried a pencil and parchment.[30]

With his floppy hat shielding his blue eyes from the sun, Murray turned to Pollock and shook his hand as they stood amid the crops. Pollock explained that he was raising a company to fight the traitors who threatened the Union and wanted Murray to sign the rolls. It was not a simple decision for Murray—a thirty-four-year-old married farmer—but Pollock, who was just a year younger and a prominent member of the community, needed Murray as a role model for the younger men. After some conversation about the need to crush the Rebellion and assurance that it would be a month before he needed to report for duty, Murray added his name to Pollock's list.

With Ed Murray's name on the muster roll, Pollock walked across the road to find John Taylor and his brother James working in John Murrie's fields. Such scenes played out innumerable times across the North as the Union rolls were filled that summer. Though exposed to abolitionist ideals, James Taylor noted that his reason for enlisting was "to put down the Rebellion, and defend the Government of the U.S.," and John wanted to be acknowledged as a "good American Citizen." Other influences were the looming draft, encouragement from clergymen, respect for John Pollock, and even a desire to impress women friends and family.[31]

On August 15, William Lewin, James Murrie, and Loughlin Madden Jr. added their names to Pollock's rolls. There was comfort and pride, and perhaps a measure of peer pressure, seeing neighbors and friends on the list. Though some immigrant soldiers felt the need to prove they were loyal Americans and worthy of citizenship, Don H. Doyle explained that many "saw themselves fighting for broadly understood principles of liberty, equality, or democracy that transcended any particular nation." For Murrie, it was not slavery but "patriotism and love of country [that] forced him to abandon the plow."[32]

When Loughlin Madden Jr. signed the rolls, he did so knowing the fine record of the 23rd Illinois's Irish Brigade and the service of his friend Andrew McFadden with the 37th Illinois. President Lincoln's appointment of the Irish revolutionary Thomas Francis Meagher as general made it clear that Lincoln understood the sociopolitical importance of over one million Irish living in the United States. These positive signs of Irish value and a chance to prove their loyalty gave many Irish the impetus to enlist. By adding his name, Madden became one of the more than 144,000 Irish-born soldiers who fought for the Union. As Doyle noted, "Whether they fought for Ireland or America, or some transcendent notion of republicanism . . . [t]he Irish and sons of Irish constituted almost 12 percent of the Union."[33]

Wayne N. Duerkes found that during this period, "with their sense of nationalism attacked . . . communities across northern Illinois became hotbeds of patriotism and Union. . . . The national standard and other patriotic banners appeared suddenly at every house and business." Amid this emotional surge of patriotism, Edward Murray's elderly mother made an American flag that was unfurled at the Murray homestead as a tangible symbol of their Union support.[34]

At thirty-four, Ed Murray was older than the average recruit and had a wife and several small children. Moved by the sacrifice Ed and his wife were making, matriarch Nancy Riley Murray made an American flag as a tribute to their adopted homeland and their devotion to see it remain united. Mother Murray made the distinctive choice to stitch thirteen stars on the field of blue, rather than the thirty-four stars of the U.S. flag, symbolically evoking the unity and spirit of the original colonies and the American Revolution, which was very much a part of public discourse. As Duerkes explained, both immigrants and native-born men "cast themselves as the heirs of the revolutionary generation and as the protectors of liberty and freedom."[35]

The *Waukegan Gazette*'s editor, James Y. Cory, echoed the Murray family's sentiments and highlighted the drain it was to send so many men to war: "Our people . . . are anxious to wipe out the deep stain which this war of slavery has forced upon our nation's history. . . . They go out to do or die in defence of the Union. . . . Many of them leave their families in circumstances not the most desirable; yet they obey the call of the Government. . . . Let not those who have volunteered be forgotten—let not their families suffer."[36]

On the Appointed Day

After signing the rolls, men remained at home to get their affairs in order and work on their farms as long as possible. The state authorities understood that the harvest must be completed. With enlistees spread over miles, notices were circulated to call men to muster. The notice for Pollock's recruits was published in the *Waukegan Gazette* on August 30, 1862: "Attention Company!! Every member of Captain Pollock's Company is hereby ordered and required to report themselves to him in person at the city of Waukegan, on Tuesday, the 2nd day of September 1862, by 10 o'clock a.m., for the transaction of such business as may come before them."[37]

Edward Murray recalled, "James Murrie, J.Y. Taylor, Wm. B. Lewin and Loughlin Madden came with me on the appointed day and met in Searle's hall," Waukegan. The five men had grown to know and to trust one another. They shared a common background as immigrants, farmers, neighbors, and Union supporters. This familiarity made for a comfortable and loyal group, who could support each other through the trials that lay ahead. Madden's Irish Catholic upbringing starkly contrasted with the British Protestant background of the other men. The fact that Madden was included in this group attests to their mutual trust and determination to save the Union. It also represented the wartime solidarity that brought Protestant dominations together and accepted Catholics and Jews. Historian Ryan W. Keating noted that the "enthusiasm" of immigrant volunteers indicated how well "these men and their communities understood the truly unique nature of the American republican experience and their relationship with their adopted nation."[38]

Undoubtedly, preserving the Union was their primary motivation for enlisting. Duerkes concluded that "[r]ural northern Illinois men focused on the oppression that the South had forced onto the country" and not the "defense of black liberty as a reason for war or enlistment." Another 96th Illinois enlistee, George Hicks, reflected that many "volunteered from an imperative sense of duty to their country and to the cause of humanity." There was also a sense that by volunteering they were accepting their duty as men in defending their home and country.[39]

On the morning of September 2, the small band of men, dressed in everyday attire of trousers, long-sleeved cotton shirts, hats, and boots, met at Murray's home. When they arrived at the county seat to form Pollock's Company, they were joined by sixty-five men from around the county. Murray's group must have felt a pride of cohesion, representing Newport Township, and also reassurance at meeting friends and neighbors, with whom they quickly developed a strong esprit de corps based on their geographic ties to Lake County.[40]

Pollock's recruits consisted of about 42 percent foreign-born volunteers. This was the third largest group of immigrants in the 96th Illinois. Companies A and F from Jo Daviess County had the greatest density of immigrants with 46 percent and 52 percent, respectively. Of the total men, immigrants consisted of 23 percent of those recruited in Lake County and 33 percent of the total from Jo Daviess County.[41] Overall, the regiment—totaling 1,046 men—consisted of 71 percent native-born and 29 percent foreign-born enlistees.

Most immigrants serving in Illinois regiments did so in non-ethnic units. Clearly, the 96th was not a regiment with a distinctive ethnic identity, of which

Illinois had five—two Irish and three German. At its organization, the staff officers and noncommissioned officers were Yankees with two exceptions: Quartermaster Stephen Jeffers of Hanover, Germany, and Quartermaster Sgt. William S. Bean of England. Many foreign-born men were promoted quickly, including Edward Murray, attesting to the acceptance and success of immigrants in these counties and the bond they formed as a unit. Most foreign-born men volunteered for the same reasons as their Yankee comrades did: patriotism, preservation of the Union, bounties, social advancement, and adventure. As Duerkes explained, many of the immigrant men also felt the need to prove that they were "loyal Americans worthy of citizenship."[42]

Murray remembered: "After the signing of the roll . . . I now realized that I was a soldier and could not come home without a permit." The men began drilling exercises on the courthouse grounds and McKay's one-mile racetrack. Just two years earlier, John Taylor and his brother, now drilling at his side, had celebrated the Fourth of July here watching horse races.[43]

Patriotic ladies presented each soldier with a needle book known as a "house-wife," which included thread, a needle, and buttons for the men to do their own mending. This small gift represented one of many shifts in gender norms the men had to make. They were about to depart from their domestic circle where women cared for the family's health and well-being.[44]

On September 4, 1862, the regiment's last day in Waukegan, Captain Pollock was presented a sword and sash by Rev. L. Hawkins on behalf of the citizens of Millburn. The *Waukegan Weekly Gazette* reported, "Pollock . . . appreciated fully their kindly feelings toward him and his command, and hoped he should never disgrace his name, his country or the sword they had so kindly given him."[45]

Camp Fuller, Rockford, Illinois

Early on the morning of September 5, 1862, Pollock's Company was given the order to "fall in." The normal two-rank line was formed and the roll called. The list of noncommissioned officers, having been carefully prepared by Captain Pollock and Lts. Addison B. Partridge and William M. Loughlin, was read. Among those promoted to corporal were Edward Murray and James Taylor.[46]

With cheers to the Union, the flag, and the friends at home, the company marched to the Chicago and North Western Railroad depot where they were joined by the three other Lake County companies, who had been drilling in town. The companies had not yet received their letters but would become

Companies B, C, D, and G.⁴⁷ The men were bid a tearful farewell by family, friends, and sweethearts, who came from all parts of the county to wish them Godspeed. The men were showered with the fanfare and patriotism appropriate at the departure of troops.

Among the enlistees in Pollock's Company standing on the train platform was the Taylor brothers' cousin, David J. Minto. His mother had given him a Bible and later lamented, "I do trust you will be very Careful of your health & when you have a few minutes to spare you will read a Chapter or 2 in your Bible and ask your Heavenly Father to keep you in that Wondrous Way that leadeth into life & try to bare with patience all the Privations you may be called to endure." Another of Millburn's young men, George E. Smith Jr., joined Capt. A. Z. Blodgett's Company D. He recalled: "We bid each other adieu at the depot. And I took my seat in the cars for Rockford, and with our hats swinging out of the car windows . . . on our way towards Rebelldom expecting to return again . . . at furthest at the end of 6 months."⁴⁸

Amid the farewells, Corp. Ed Murray received a thirty-day furlough to "straighten up" his affairs and thrash his crops. Married men were given preference for furloughs, and with agriculture the main occupation of the county's residents, its importance was understood. "I was permitted to come home and finish up my harvesting." Murray took his leave after the train left the station at seven o'clock in the morning, going home with the responsibility of securing his family's welfare. To be a good soldier he needed to ensure his family's stability, which he did by renting his farm to Henry Furlong, who had worked for him for two years and was married to Anne Madden. "I sold my horses and wagon, renting the farm for the term of three years unless I returned sooner."⁴⁹

Meanwhile, the train took Murray's companions to Chicago where they were called in line and sworn into service by Lieutenant Hunt of the regular army. They went on to Rockford, where they arrived at two o'clock and walked through muddy streets to Camp Fuller, which had been established as a training ground the previous month. They joined the 96th Illinois's six companies from Jo Daviess County, and also the 74th, 92nd, and 95th Illinois.⁵⁰

It was dinnertime and the men were hungry, but the drum beat to fall in, and the men obeyed. They formed a hollow square and eagerly met their counterparts from Jo Daviess County. As historian Mark H. Dunkelman explained, the new recruits arrived at camp "imbued with community pride and led by respected townsmen." The Honorable Allen C. Fuller, adjutant general of Illinois, mustered in the men of the 96th Illinois. Charles Partridge of Pollock's Company recalled, "With hands upraised to Heaven, swore to serve [our] country for 'three years unless sooner discharged.' . . . It was a memorable meeting as that body of nearly one thousand gallant men gathered for the first time and became a Regiment."[51]

Although their county seats of Waukegan and Galena separated them by 150 miles, the volunteers from Lake and Jo Daviess Counties quickly felt a kinship as frontiersmen. Indeed, the two groups had similar occupations as farmers, carpenters, clerks, teachers, lawyers, and blacksmiths, the only exception being the lead miners of Jo Daviess County. Even the mix of native-born and foreign-born enlistees was similar in each group. The regimental history noted, "Officers and men from the two counties eyed each other closely, but each seemed pleased, and from that moment it is doubtful if there was ever a regret expressed or felt that the combination of Lake with Jo Daviess had been formed." Normally, regiments were formed within communities of close proximity, creating a common bond through place and experience, but the "union proved congenial," and the men forged an immediate bond.[52]

Within a few short days, the men had gone from drilling on the courthouse grounds to rushing to the depot and onward to Chicago to be mustered into service, arriving the same day in Rockford. They learned to drill, follow orders unhesitatingly, clean and load weapons, and to eat poorly cooked army rations. Coming from rural farm communities, they also faced the unusual circumstance of living with thousands of strangers and being exposed to disease and the elements. In spite of this, their greatest personal hardship was homesickness.[53]

After roll call on the morning of September 6, company letters were written on slips of paper and drawn by each captain. "A," however, was assigned to Capt. George Hicks's company, since it was the first company recruited and organized. Captain Pollock drew the letter "C," and it was announced they would be the color company. As Partridge remembered, he and his comrades, including Taylor, Lewin, Murrie, and Madden, let out a hearty and enthusiastic cheer, "feeling proud of their position." This designation further bonded them. Attached to Company C was the color guard composed of a sergeant and six to eight corporals for hazardous duty. The color company was expected to be the first in line whenever the regiment formed, and the color guard could not break and run in retreat during a battle or the regiment would follow. Soldiers were known to defend to the death a regimental flag to keep it out of enemy hands.[54]

About one week later, Ed Murray joined his companions at Camp Fuller. Murray wrote, "I bade adieu to my father and mother, brothers and sisters and last of all to my dear wife and my six small children. I did not realize until now that I might never see them again."[55]

On September 17, Enfield rifle-muskets (from England) and accoutrements were issued to the companies. The 96th was considered fortunate to secure new Enfields when many of the regiments only had old Austrian or Belgian muskets. On September 20, clothing from the assistant U.S. quartermaster at Philadelphia was issued. Each soldier received a dark blue dress coat, sky blue pants, woolen shirts and socks, cotton drawers and felt hats, and shoes if needed. The men swapped clothes to get the right fit, and if that was not enough, there was usually a tailor among them to make alterations. For Company C, German immigrant Joseph Schweri was a tailor by trade. Tailors were excused from duty and set about properly fitting the men's new clothes. With their uniforms issued and fitted, Ed Murray recalled that they were ordered to box up their "citizens' clothes and send them home."[56]

The 96th's hats were the black felt 1858 model Hardee hats issued to army regulars, and not the blue kepis worn in most other units. The regimental history recounted that for a western regiment that already had an "unusual proportion of very tall men," the black hats made them even taller and more distinct. "Our clothing is pretty good," wrote Company B's Evangelist J. Gillmore. "We have hats instead of caps. The hats are high crown but when trimmed & with the feather, eagle, letter (B) bugle & the 96 they look pretty well." Later, some in the 96th adopted the kepis. Historian Robert I. Girardi recognized that "[n]othing made a young farm lad . . . feel more powerful than being armed and equipped as a soldier."[57]

In the following days, light blue overcoats were issued along with knapsacks, haversacks, and canteens, completing each man's outfit. The men received a forty-dollar county bounty and twenty-five-dollar government bounty for enlisting. Bounties were a great incentive to volunteer, helping to ease some of the burden of having men gone from the farms. Loughlin Madden sent his twenty-five-dollar bounty to his brother Christopher. For many immigrant soldiers, the war meant more than bounties and adventure. They wanted to save the republic and be recognized as American citizens.[58]

Every day the regiment drilled for two hours at forenoon and again in the afternoon. They dressed in full uniform, carrying their knapsack (with overcoat neatly rolled and strapped on top), haversack and canteen, cartridge box, belt, and gun—the whole outfit weighed about sixty pounds. Murray called it the "most tiring work I ever did yet there was something inspiring and grand to see and be one of a thousand all in uniform, marching with drums beating and flags flying and going through the maneuvers of a field fight." Murray and his Stateline Road comrades were among the approximately 48 percent of soldiers in the Union Army who were farmers, and were quite accustomed to hard manual labor.[59]

A Photograph for Posterity

With the influx of thousands of men to Camp Fuller, photographers set up shop to meet the demand of those who wished to commemorate their service and send a lasting image to their loved ones. Once Ed Murray and his companions shed their civilian clothes for soldiers' uniforms, they were transformed in appearance and attitude. The magnitude of the task before them and pride in their new identities as soldiers prompted the friends to record their bond as comrades in arms. The photograph demonstrated each man's bond to the other, and to their friends and families with whom the image was shared.[60]

In addition to the portrait with his Stateline Road comrades, John Taylor posed for a portrait with men from the Millburn area: Andrew T. White, David J. Minto, and Chase Webb.[61] Both groups were important to Taylor. He had enlisted with the Edward Murray group, with whom he had developed strong connections through work, church, and Union meetings. The Millburn group consisted of his closest friends and cousins and represented his roots in Lake County. Whether he posed for more portraits that day, including one with his brother James, is unknown.

These small portraits were cherished, and feelings of pride and a longing for home prompted many to create a memento for the family. Nineteen-year-old Loughlin Madden Jr. took an individual portrait. Dressed in uniform, Madden stood at attention in a dark blue single-breasted frock coat, holding his Enfield musket on end. The image was hand-colored, with gold paint added to buttons and buckles. Perhaps most remarkable is Madden's small grin and expressive eyes, which evoke pride and commitment. Madden's feelings of responsibility for his family back home and perhaps even those left behind in Ireland were strong factors in his decision to wear Union blue.[62]

In camp, the men had just received their uniforms and were basking in their transformation when news came of President Lincoln's intentions to free the slaves. Months earlier, Lincoln had read his preliminary proclamation to his cabinet, but he decided to wait for a Union military victory to issue it. On September 22, 1862, following the victory at Antietam, Lincoln signed the preliminary Emancipation Proclamation, officially alerting the Confederacy that unless hostilities ceased within one hundred days, he intended to free all persons held as slaves in states actively seeking to break away. Although Lincoln was convinced of the moral evil of slavery, he took the process of emancipation slowly. There were constitutional constraints, but most critically Lincoln had to calculate Northerners' support of the war, and he was apprehensive that they would not accept a war to emancipate enslaved African Americans. Peace Democrats, also known derisively as Copperheads, were vocal in the North and already calling for peace and a Union with slavery intact.[63]

As Don H. Doyle explained, the Union cause began to embrace the expectation of foreign governments, whose support the North needed, that the war was indeed "a war to destroy slavery." Lincoln understood that to maintain a cohesive war effort he needed bipartisan support, and he framed the emancipation as a means of hobbling the Confederacy. For the 96th, "the action of the President was most heartily endorsed" by its officers and regular soldiers alike. Historian Gary W. Gallagher noted that soldiers and civilians supported the emancipation as a method to "restore the Union . . . rather than as a grand moral imperative."[64]

On October 1, the 96th Illinois's Col. Thomas E. Champion received word that they would soon be heading to the front. Confederate forces were moving in Kentucky and threatening Cincinnati, Ohio. The colonel gave Captain Pollock permission for three men in his company to go home and see their loved ones, and then to meet the regiment in Chicago. Pollock chose Ed Murray, knowing he had left a wife and small children behind. Murray was handed a pass and told to hurry or he would not make the train. He borrowed two dollars for train fare from Loughlin Madden and ran to the Chicago and North Western depot. The train took him to the old Union Depot in Chicago where he caught a late train north, which he requested to stop at the state line. It was late on the night of October 4, and Murray walked six miles on the dirt and gravel road to surprise his sleeping family by his unexpected return home. The next morning, the Murrays went to Baptist services where Edward saw his neighbors and relatives. "I felt a little pride in my uniform of Blue with soft hat and feather, with brass bugle and 96 number in the front."[65]

On October 8, Murray's friends and family accompanied him in horse-drawn wagons to Waukegan to take the train to Chicago. "I was to join my regiment going to the front to see some of the realities of war." Murray was aware that since adding his name to Pollock's list, the single bloodiest day in American history had been fought at the Battle of Antietam on September 17 with an estimated 3,654 dead and over 22,717 casualties. He could also look to the war's Western Theater where Union successes in 1862 at Fort Donelson (February 11–16), Shiloh (April 6–7), and Corinth (October 3–4) provided victories that buoyed the morale of Federal troops.[66]

This tearful farewell would be the last time Murray would see his loved ones for over a year. "I took final leave of my friends and my wife and as we pulled out I stood on the rear platform and waved my handkerchief until they were lost to view."[67]

Captain John K. Pollock, Company C. *Bess Bower Dunn Museum of Lake County, Lake County Forest Preserves.*

Sergeant Edward Murray, Company C. *Al Westerman.*

Corporal William B. Lewin, Company C. *Al Westerman*.

Sergeant James B. Murrie, Company C. *Partridge*, History of the Ninety-Sixth Regiment.

Private Loughlin Madden Jr., Company C. *Bess Bower Dunn Museum of Lake County, Lake County Forest Preserves.*

John Y. Taylor, Company C. *Partridge*, History of the Ninety-Sixth Regiment.

James M. Taylor, Company C. *Partridge*, History of the Ninety-Sixth Regiment.

Seated: Andrew T. White and David J. Minto; *standing:* John Y. Taylor and Chase Webb, Company C. Photographed at Camp Fuller, Rockford, Illinois, 1862. *Bess Bower Dunn Museum of Lake County, Lake County Forest Preserves.*

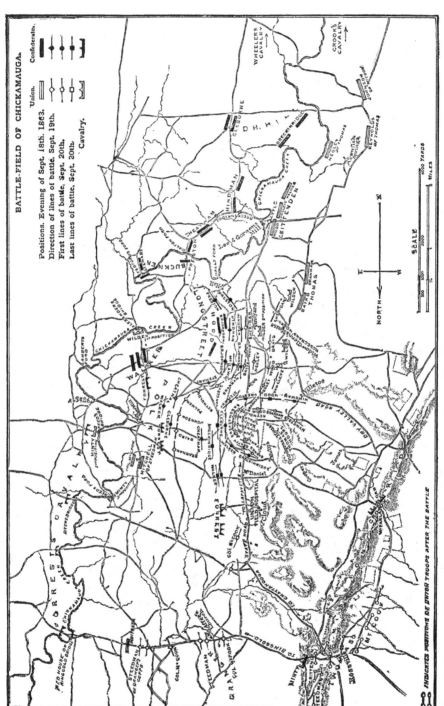

Map, *Battle-field of Chickamauga. Partridge,* History of the Ninety-Sixth Regiment.

"Battle-torn regimental flag of 96th Illinois Infantry Regiment," J. H. and
C. E. Porter, photographers, Waukegan, Illinois, circa 1865. *Library of Congress,
Prints and Photographs Division, Washington, D.C.*

George E. Smith Jr., Company D. *Partridge*, History of the Ninety-Sixth Regiment.

Susannah D. Smith Minto.
Bess Bower Dunn Museum of Lake County, Lake County Forest Preserves.

3. ❖ A Cheer for the West

On the rainy morning of Wednesday, October 8, 1862, the 96th Illinois left Camp Fuller and marched to the Chicago and North Western Railway depot. Their orders were to proceed at once to the defense of Cincinnati, Ohio. The citizens of Rockford and friends and family from home turned out in great numbers, waving flags and giving a cheer: "God bless you, boys!"[1]

The troop trains arrived at Chicago about five o'clock, and Edward Murray rejoined his comrades shortly thereafter. The farewells were not complete—friends of the regiment had been advised of their schedule and were in Chicago to greet them. The visitors went up to the cars and presented specially made lunches. The men also had time to write letters home or to purchase articles needed to complete their outfits. After consolidating two trains and attaching three engines, the regiment started for Cincinnati at half past nine o'clock in the evening. "In our trip from Chicago we passed through many villages and small towns," Ed Murray wrote in his memoirs. "There was a perfect ovation in each, the platforms being crowded with people to see the soldiers and waving of handkerchiefs and the cheering we received . . . gave us enthusiasm."[2]

The men were extremely sleep-deprived when they arrived in Cincinnati—many were too excited and played pranks on those who tried to doze. The train pulled into the depot quite late, and the men ordered out. They formed in two ranks on the sidewalk and stood for about an hour waiting for orders. Murray wrote, "I thought I should drop." Irritated from lack of sleep and general frustration, the men used profanity against their officers, but they had arrived unannounced, and the provost marshal could not be found to tell them where they should go. Finally, they received their orders and walked through the well-lighted streets, reaching the Ohio River and crossing it on a pontoon bridge. On the other side, the troops arrived in Covington, Kentucky, where they reported to Maj. Gen. Gordon Granger, commander of the Union Army of Kentucky, to which the regiment was attached.[3] They were assigned to a position in the batteries in front of Covington and Newport, Kentucky. That summer, Confederate forces under Lt. Gen. Kirby Smith had invaded Kentucky and threatened to move on Cincinnati, the "Queen City of the West," which was connected to the nation by railways and steamboats. If Cincinnati fell, the Union Army would lose a vital supply route, and Smith's Confederate Army of Kentucky would have a good position to advance on the industrial cities of the North.

Kentucky was officially neutral at the beginning of the war, but after a failed attempt by Confederate lieutenant general Leonidas Polk to take Kentucky for the Confederacy, the legislature petitioned the Union for assistance and thereafter came solidly under Union control. Slaves composed approximately one-quarter of the Commonwealth of Kentucky's population, and many Unionist Kentuckians saw nothing wrong with the "peculiar institution." Murray wrote, "Now we were in the land of slavery and we could feel the contrast between freedom and slavery by just looking across the Ohio River into Cincinnati where the streets were all lighted. Here in Covington all was dark and desolate." As historian James M. McPherson noted, from an "antebellum free-labor ideology" the South appeared "mired in backwardness and ignorance."[4]

The regiment marched a couple of miles to Newport over hilly and dusty roads. The march seemed much longer due to their extreme fatigue and heavy loads, and some of the men lay down on the roadside and slept until morning before rejoining their comrades. At this early stage of soldiering, they were not seasoned to the hardships of marches, and they straggled for relief. Those who completed the march were grateful when the column finally arrived in an open field and word passed back through the line that this was their camp. In a spirit of unity, they named the camp "Champion" in honor of Col. Thomas E. Champion, who was already "winning the high regard of his men."[5]

Ed Murray made it to camp, throwing himself on the ground with a blanket over him and sleeping until dawn. When he woke he saw "about 1,000 men scattered over an old trodden camp ground. Not a spear of grass. Each one covered with a blanket. I wish I could draw a picture of that scene as it impressed me at that time."[6]

For breakfast they boiled coffee in tin cups and ate hardtack and pork. Afterward, they worked to pitch their canvas A-frame "wedge tents." The sound of metal stakes being pounded into the ground resounded throughout the camp, mixed with men's laughter as they tried to put up their tents for the first time. James Taylor wrote to his sister, "[W]e live in tents down here since we got to be migratory beings. Our tents are only about 7 feet square and 7 feet high, six in a tent. Close packing ain't it."[7]

Four of the five men from Ed Murray's group were tentmates: Murray, Loughlin Madden Jr., Billy Lewin, and James Murrie. Filling out the six-man tent were Henry Cutler and Henry Bater. Curiously, John Taylor did not share a tent with the Ed Murray group with whom he had enlisted. Instead, John and his brother James shared a tent with George L. Stewart, William Bonner Jr., George C. Dodge, and Samuel W. Dodge. James described their group as "[a] first rate set of boys full of fun fight frolic and mischief and not a rough one among us."[8]

The mix of native-born and foreign-born men sharing tents illustrated a familiarity and mutual background as farmers from the same geographic area. Historian Stephen D. Engle observed that in the military Northerners began to grasp the "ethnically diverse nature of their Union." German volunteers represented the largest group of foreign-born enlistees in the Union Army, estimated at two hundred thousand. However, the disrespect and prejudice they endured prior to the war followed many into service. In the 6th Kentucky Infantry, a Western Theater regiment, many Germans were recruited from Louisville and had urban occupations, while the native-born volunteers were rural farmers. Historian Joseph R. Reinhart explained that the 6th Kentucky's commander, Col. Walter C. Whitaker, "had no love for foreigners," and the Germans were treated "like second-class citizens" by most of their native-born comrades.[9]

The 96th Illinois was part of Maj. Gen. Gordon Granger's Army of Kentucky, which was assigned to the Third Division under Brig. Gen. Absalom Baird and the Second Brigade under Col. John C. Cochran of the 14th Kentucky Infantry. The brigade was composed of the 99th Ohio; the 96th, 92nd, and 115th Illinois; and the 14th Kentucky. On the evening of October 15, while on dress parade, Brigadier General Baird rode up to observe the men. He complimented the 96th's officers and volunteers on their "soldierly bearing," and was surprised that they had been in service barely six weeks.[10]

On October 16 Ed Murray was promoted to sergeant, and with it came sleepless nights on watch and his first real duty as a soldier. Sergeant Murray, along with two corporals and eight privates, was detailed to take command of Fort Shaler, a hilltop earthwork fortification. The battery was named for Dr. Nathaniel Burger Shaler, a prominent Newport, Kentucky, physician, who offered his family's vineyard for the defense of the city. There were two heavy siege guns mounted on trucks inside the round earthwork and a magazine of some fifty kegs of powder. Murray personally had to carry and air out the sensitive kegs every day in his stocking feet. Square nail heads or cleats on the bottom of the men's brogans could produce sparks, which might set off the powder.[11]

Tension was high in those early days of soldiering, the men anxious about meeting up with Rebels. At 11 o'clock on the evening of October 16, shots were fired by the pickets at one of the batteries, and the drum beat to arms, calling the regiment out on the double quick. Chaos ensued as the men frantically stumbled about their tents. John Taylor recalled that they grabbed "the first suit of clothes and accoutrements they could get hold of." Taylor ended up wearing George Dodge's pants and William Bonner's coat. When the all clear was given, they went back to their tents and had a good laugh. However, the citizens and authorities at Covington and Cincinnati did not find the incident humorous. The alarm had been taken up by other camps, reaching the city and causing a fair amount of anxiety. The regimental history noted that the civil authorities believed that Colonel Champion had devised the incident to test the "promptness and coolness" of his officers and men, and they demanded "the head of the officer who started the alarm." Had they been successful in removing him, it would have deprived the 96th of a fine commander.[12]

Back in northeastern Illinois on the night of a new moon, several young ladies gathered to do their part for the war effort. Sarah White, Jane Hughes, Nannie Murrie, and Mary Murray, who were attending the Waukegan Academy, met at a boarding house where Sarah and Jane were lodging. The young women sat by candlelight in their printed cotton dresses with "some patchwork to make a quilt for the soldiers." Sarah White recollected the evening in a letter to her cousin David Minto, noting that John Taylor's sweetheart, Nannie, was one of the quilters. "You see we are doing all we can for the good of our poor sick soldiers who are far away from home and have no kind Mother or Sister to watch over them." Sarah's letter heartened Minto. Letters linked men to their family and friends at home, comforting them with the assurance of being remembered and fostering steadfastness as they faced the hardships of a soldier's life.[13]

On October 19, the regiment received orders. It was divided, with Lt. Col. Isaac L. Clarke taking Companies A, E, F, G, and H to the front via the Falmouth Road to escort a commissary supply train of over one hundred wagons. On the 22nd, under the command of Col. Thomas E. Champion, Companies B, C, D, I, and K marched to Covington, Kentucky. On the morning of October 25, the men woke to find four inches of snow on the ground, which they enjoyed before it melted.[14]

The regimental history noted that less than two months into their enlistment, life as soldiers was "beginning to tell on the men." There was a good deal of adjustment needed to tolerate army rations, sleeping on the ground, and being exposed to the elements and disease. When Colonel Champion and his companies departed from Covington on October 29, "each Company left a half dozen or more of their number in the various hospitals in the neighborhood." Many expected the farm boys from rural areas to fare better under the hardships of military life, but their lack of exposure to "crowd disease" ultimately made them more susceptible to illness. The men who had grown up in urban areas, accustomed to living with a great number of people, had built immunity to many diseases. Armies, as it turned out, were like large cities. At this early stage in the war, camp sanitation was notoriously poor and quickly led to thousands of cases of diarrhea and dysentery. Also, within a few months, men began to suffer from scurvy due to a lack of vitamin C. To supplement their army rations and preserve their health, they foraged for fruits and vegetables. Many felt that since they were in enemy country they could do as they pleased. "I must say I never took part in destroying things," Edward Murray wrote. "I used to think if an army passing by my house destroyed things as was done here, what a desolate place it would be."[15]

The first of November was quite warm as the men endured a seventeen-mile march. When they came to a halt that evening near Jones' Tavern, the command was approached by two Confederate deserters, James Kenty and John McGill. Officers of Company C enlisted the men, but many of the Illinois troops criticized that decision. The recruits proved to be good soldiers.[16]

At seven o'clock on November 2, Companies B, C, D, I, and K marched six miles before camping on Eagle Creek to obtain additional rations. A gristmill near the camp was started by a group of men, including Sgt. Ellis Schooley, an experienced miller in Company C's ranks. Four hundred pounds each of flour and cornmeal were ground and issued to the men. The mill's steam whistle drew the attention of the neighborhood and of Georgetown, attracting enslaved men who sought liberty. Despite President Lincoln's intentions at the onset of the war that the Union did not intend to interfere with slavery in the South, the arrival of Federal troops quickly opened paths for enslaved people to find refuge. Union officers diverged on how to react to the fugitives, depending on their personal attitudes toward slavery. Some officers returned slaves to their masters, while others set them free. In February 1862, when federal troops entered Tennessee, the restoration of the Union and not the emancipation of the enslaved was the dominant Northern policy. This sentiment was echoed by Maj. Gen. Henry Halleck, commander of the Department of Missouri. In a restatement of his General Orders No. 3, he directed that no fugitive slaves "be admitted within our lines or camps" and emphasized "that we come merely to crush out rebellion and to restore . . . peace and the benefits of the Constitution and the Union," not "to oppress and to plunder." Halleck wished to extricate the army from the issue of slavery.[17]

As Union troops arrived in areas with large numbers of enslaved people, particularly in the Western Theater, Halleck's policy of exclusion reached a breaking point. By the time the 96th Illinois was formed in the second summer of the war, the Union had shifted, as Don H. Doyle explained, toward embracing "a war to destroy slavery . . . and in defense of democratic principles." Many officers were adopting more emancipationist policies, routinely confiscating the slaves of rebels and employing them. Relief for the overworked Union soldiers and the eagerness of fugitives to reach Federal lines and find freedom proved irresistible to Federal armies. Historian Kristopher A. Teters explained that this dynamic made the Union Army "the primary instrument by which emancipation became a reality on the ground." There were instances when Union officers were sued for confiscating slaves. However, the officers of the 96th were careful not to entangle themselves in lawsuits with slaveholders seeking to recover their "property" by ensuring that suspect citizens were excluded from entering their camp. According to the regiment's history, "Nearly all [its officers] were radically opposed to slavery," and any fugitive seeking "refuge in the camp was protected."[18]

Several men from Eagle Creek, Kentucky, who sought freedom stayed with the 96th Illinois. One of these men was James Joice, who was employed as a cook and valet for 1st Lt. Addison Partridge. A New Englander by birth, Partridge was known as an abolitionist. Joice endeared himself to the regiment when he assisted Company D's Lt. Caleb A. Montgomery and his men on a foraging expedition as its "pilot." Joice took the soldiers to a plantation where there was a potato crop. The lieutenant stopped at the house to notify the occupant that they were short on rations and if he was a "loyal citizen a receipt would be given so that he could collect pay" for the potatoes. The soldiers went with Joice to gather the vegetables while the lieutenant made the man repeat a long oath of loyalty to the Union. A second foraging party from Company C brought back "thirty chickens, ten turkeys, a lot of ducks, four bushels of potatoes, a churn full of syrup and twenty quarts of honey."[19]

On November 4, the regiment came together with Lieutenant Colonel Clarke's five companies, already at Lexington, and marched out to meet Colonel Champion's command and escort them into camp. After less than two months, the men of Lake and Jo Daviess Counties had bonded and felt a mutual pride in their regiment. Captain Pollock noted, "Arrived at Lexington good Roads but water scarce." The brief remark on the lack of water was in fact a huge concern for both armies due to the severe drought in the region. On the other hand, the dry roads allowed for ease of travel.[20]

While in the Lexington area, Edward Murray and others had time to take in their surroundings. Murray wrote that he saw "slave pens which I had read of in *Uncle Tom's Cabin* and the auction block where many a poor slave had been sold to the highest bidder." Harriet Beecher Stowe's novel personalized enslavement and its horrors, galvanizing the abolitionist movement and opening the eyes of average Northerners. Murray and his comrades were now confronted with the reality of hundreds, even thousands of oppressed people, which they had only read or heard sermons preached about. Charles Partridge noted that at a public sale in Danville, Kentucky, the "strange spectacle of human beings on the auction block" greatly affected the soldiers of the 96th. As Teters explained, these firsthand experiences helped many soldiers recognize "the brutality of slavery" and change their minds on emancipation.[21]

By its own calculation, the 96th Illinois assisted more enslaved people in escaping than many other regiments. Nearly all of its officers "were radically opposed to slavery." Enslaved people who sought refuge in the camp were protected. Such clarity of purpose was not immediately embraced by other Union Army officers. Teters observed that by the second half of 1863, "many officers who had initially opposed emancipation . . . had come around to this position, and it was pragmatism more than principle that had gotten them there." Antislavery regiments, such as the 96th Illinois, set an example for others to shelter African Americans seeking freedom. In one instance, Murray thought there would be a fight between slaveholders and the regiment as they left camp with some fugitives protected at the center of the battalion. He wrote, "The order was to load and fix bayonets and off we started . . . with flags flying and drums beating we went through the city. But no one made a move at rescue. We were what you would call an abolition regiment and would not give a colored man up if he wanted to go with us." The 92nd Illinois from the area of Freeport was also described as an "Abolitionist Regiment" in light of their active concern for the welfare of enslaved people in Kentucky.[22]

Murray was progressing from a man with antislavery sentiments to one taking pride in what he described as an "abolition regiment." The war to preserve the Union was morphing into a war for emancipation and for the rights of all men, black and white. The soldiers' transformation was a result of firsthand experiences, which, according to Gary W. Gallagher, "influenced attitudes about slavery and race, building support for emancipation." Federal troops, as historian Chandra Manning explained, also believed that President Lincoln "shared their vision of the war's cause and purpose," even though some of the folks back home did not understand. Through their wartime experiences of seeing the physical abuse of enslaved people, soldiers became convinced "that slavery must be destroyed in order to win the war and redeem the American Republic from sin."[23]

Just two months into their service, the men of the 96th were experiencing a change in their perception of the war's purpose and in their own ability as soldiers. From November 1862, they were pushed very hard to drill either in squads, companies, or as a regiment. The regimental history noted, "Perhaps at no other point was more rapid progress made in acquiring military knowledge." Historian Paddy Griffith observed that regiments threw themselves "furiously into the task . . . the erstwhile civilian was soon brought to a high standard of knowledge in his new calling as a soldier." Drilling created discipline and obedience, and built a unit's esprit de corps. George Smith wrote to his sister Susannah "Susie" Smith in Millburn, "[T]hem old knapsacks made our shoulders sore as biles we were so sore all over . . . am all feeling first rate and tough as bears except some were rather footsore."[24]

On November 13, the regiment left Lexington, Kentucky, and marched through Nicholasville and Brooklyn. They arrived in Harrodsburg on November 15 and pitched "Camp Clarke," named in honor of Lt. Col. Isaac L. Clarke. At Harrodsburg they had their first encounter with uniformed Rebels, who had been captured at the Battle of Perryville on October 8. In his autumn invasion of Kentucky, Confederate general Braxton Bragg narrowly defeated the superior Union Army of Maj. Gen. Don Carlos Buell at the crossroads town of Perryville. This was the largest battle fought in Kentucky during the war. Bragg retreated back into Tennessee to the vital communication center at Chattanooga, essentially ensuring that Kentucky would remain in Union hands for the remainder of the war. The men were curious about the prisoners and described them in the regimental history as "defiant and saucy, and as quick to enter into an argument on behalf of 'Southern rights' as were their Yankee visitors."[25]

The regiment remained at Harrodsburg for two weeks, scouting, drilling, and standing guard. On November 20, Colonel Champion was directed to send two companies to Danville about ten miles south. He selected Companies C and I for detached service and assigned them to quarters in the Baptist church. The Taylor brothers wrote to their sister that the brick church was "very comfortable quarters." One of the greatest challenges for soldiers was exposure, as they labored almost entirely outdoors. The church provided more protection from the elements than they had enjoyed since leaving home.[26]

The two companies were responsible for preserving order between both armies convalescing in the city. Duties included preventing Rebels from escaping, enforcing travel restrictions within the town (everyone needed a valid pass), and providing military escorts for the funerals of Union soldiers from Buell's army. Partridge noted that Company C was also "obliged to scout and picket outside the city, and more than once were called out, expecting an attack from Rebel cavalry hovering in the vicinity." The Confederates effectively used their cavalry raiders to make things as unpleasant as possible for the Federals.[27]

Despite being weary from their duties, the men had time to forage, see the sights, and enjoy the company of friendly locals. John and James Taylor's Thanksgiving was "an all killing big feast at one of the best Union ladies house in the town of Danville." On November 29, Companies C and I were relieved at Danville by the 92nd Illinois. They marched about a half mile outside of town to rejoin the regiment, which had come from Harrodsburg to camp there. The new camp was named "Camp Baird" for Brigadier General Baird.[28]

About fifty men had been left in the hospital at Harrodsburg due to illness, a substantial number of them with measles. The first death in Company C came on December 3, when Henry H. Swan died from measles. Long before these men faced battle they faced death, and death by disease was perceived as less honorable than dying on the battlefield. To ward off illness, each man had to understand the environment and conditions in which he lived and take the initiative to care for his and his comrades' well-being. They were far from the comforts of home and the traditional care given by mothers, sisters, and wives.[29]

From its organization the 96th Illinois suffered from measles, mumps, smallpox, tuberculosis, pneumonia, typhoid fever, diarrhea, and dysentery. The preponderance of disease in camp was succinctly expressed by George Smith of Company D: "Disease with its strong hand is taking more Prisoners every day than there could be taken at the point of the Bayonet." During the war, two-thirds of all soldiers' deaths were caused by disease rather than bullets. Those first few months in camp proved fatal for many as they faced a myriad of contagions, which affected nearly half of "green soldiers." Added to the risk of disease were the unsanitary conditions created by latrines dug too close to camps, near kitchens, and near streams where the soldiers bathed and got their drinking water. It was not yet understood that fecal contamination led to the outbreak of diarrhea and dysentery. Instead, as historian Ira Rutkow explained, the illnesses were blamed on "eating unripe fruit or uncooked vegetables," or sleeping in wet clothes on the damp ground.[30]

Another concern that plagued the men was vermin such as lice. Frequent bathing and washing clothes in boiling water killed lice, but when troops were on the march they rarely had time for this. John Taylor proclaimed that it was possible to remain vermin free, and he shared details of one such infestation with his sister: "The way we got these vermin was when Billy Lewin, Geo. Dodge and David [Minto] came back to our tent from hospital. They brought a goodly supply of the animals with them for a spell we was troubled and I may say literally covered and like to be eaten up by them . . . in taking a little pains we keep clean of them altogether." Taylor's efforts at self-care made him something of an expert at eradicating insects. Though he was not aware that certain insect bites affected human health, he was mindful of the discomfort they brought.[31]

On December 10, a portion of Confederate colonel John H. Morgan's 2nd Kentucky cavalry was rumored to be in the vicinity. This created some anxiety since Morgan had made a name wreaking havoc on the Union Army in Kentucky. Camp Baird's picket line was doubled, and Charles Partridge recalled that preparations were made to give Morgan a "warm reception should he see fit to pay the camp a visit." Captain Pollock's Company C was ordered to Danville, and Sergeant Murray's small banded group was quick to organize, falling in on that cold winter night. They marched into Danville to guard a building where ammunition was stored, anticipating that they would face the infamous cavalryman. Fortunately or not, Morgan and his cavalry did not come.[32]

On Christmas day, George Smith and his fellow "Millburn boys" spent time with friends in Company C. They "had all the roast turkey, apple pie, sauce and biscuit and butter we wanted." That evening the regiment's dress parade was cut short when they were ordered to Lebanon, Kentucky. Unknown to most of the men, Maj. Gen. William S. Rosecrans's Army of the Cumberland had left Nashville to confront General Bragg at Murfreesboro, Tennessee. The next morning, reveille was sounded by four o'clock. After breakfast, Ed Murray and his companions set about pulling up the wooden floors from their tents and piling the floorboards, boxes, and tables onto blazing fires, destroying these camp conveniences so that the enemy could not use them.[33]

By six o'clock they had formed in line, and the regiment moved out. Rumors had it that Morgan was in the vicinity, threatening a garrison at Munfordville, and the Federals were headed there in support. When they set out the weather was fine, and they marched over a macadamized road made of compacted layers of gravel on a cement bed. They almost always traveled dirt roads (which turned to mud after rain), making this a rare privilege. Within a few hours the sky opened up, and the men were soaked by the downpour. Captain Pollock wrote in his report, "[M]arched 17 miles in a drenching rain."[34] About four o'clock that afternoon, the men halted to set up camp in a muddy field.

Due to the rain, mud, and cold, the march was hard and became even more frustrating when they were ordered back to their old camp, which they had destroyed the day before. Evidently, the Rebel Morgan had sent false dispatches to Major General Granger, precipitating the march to Lebanon. The wet march and ruined campsite demoralized even the most cheerful soldiers.[35]

1863

The New Year began in turmoil within the Federal army. President Lincoln's Emancipation Proclamation had taken effect on January 1, 1863, freeing all enslaved people in the Confederacy. The proclamation only applied to Southern states in rebellion, not to loyal states and territory holding enslaved people within the Union. The intention was to cripple the Confederacy's use of slaves to support their armies and home front. Historian Susannah J. Ural noted, "The proclamation caused the war to evolve from a conflict to preserve the Union to a bloody struggle to abolish slavery and reunite a nation."[36]

Most Federal soldiers had taken little notice of the preliminary announcement of the proclamation on September 22, 1862. When word reached them that it had taken effect on January 1, there were those in Illinois regiments who loudly denounced the president and deserted. During January and February, the 96th Illinois lost sixteen to desertion, or as Orson Young of Company D described his brother's desertion, "French leave." Some deserted because they could not accept the change in the war's purpose from fighting to save the Union to fighting to free slaves. According to Teters, this conflict was also true in the officer ranks, where "continuous and often acrimonious debate over emancipation [left] officers . . . divided on the very meaning and purpose of the war." Despite the dissent, emancipation as a practical measure to restore the Union by freeing the enslaved and thereby denying the South its major source of labor was overwhelmingly supported by white Union soldiers and civilians as a means to victory.[37]

In the fall 1862 elections, Peace Democrats had garnered more success than expected, gaining support in the wake of the North's disillusionment with the war. Historian Mark E. Neely Jr. explained that when Democrats took their government positions in January 1863 and "pressed opposition policies in state governments, particularly in the Illinois legislature," demanding the retraction of the proclamation and establishment of a peace commission to end the war, the nation was shocked. The growing discontent was most worrisome to soldiers in Illinois regiments, who had not been allowed by their state to cast absentee ballots and now had idle time in their winter quarters to stew on the politics playing out at home. A movement of Illinois regiments denouncing "the bitter partisan spirit that is becoming dangerously vindictive and malicious in our state" lasted from January 20 to April 22, 1863.[38]

The officers of the Second Brigade (including the 96th Illinois) met on March 2 to address the issue, writing resolutions supporting the president and denouncing the peace movement in the North. The Copperhead movement, as it was known derisively by Republicans, was strongest in Illinois, Indiana, and Ohio, the three states that supplied the bulk of the fighting men in Kentucky and Tennessee. As historian Jennifer L. Weber concluded, many Union soldiers resented the "lack of support for their efforts" and believed that antiwar comments "undermined their ability to carry out the war successfully." The belief that the war had been extended because "conservatives were . . . speaking against it" rallied most of the fighting men behind the proclamation and created an "anti-copperhead backlash."[39]

One of the brigade's resolutions declared, "We emphatically assure all traitors at home, that not until we have undergone a seven years' struggle (if need be) will we cease this contest, and not until we have experienced such sufferings as were bravely endured at Valley Forge will we begin to murmur." Some fifty-five Illinois infantry regiments, four cavalry regiments and four batteries of artillery participated in the movement. Most of the resolutions contained threats. The 82nd Illinois regretted not being closer to home "to have an opportunity of liberating the halls of our capitol, from this detestable scum." The 96th Illinois's warning shot to the antiwar Democrats wished that the "damnable traitors in the North may be brought to a terrible justice, 'that hemp be not created in vain.'" The resolutions were presented at a dress parade, and one newspaper reported that the 96th Illinois voted in favor of the resolutions "without a single dissenting voice." Years later, the regimental history corrected the record: "The ayes were numerous and enthusiastic, but, strange to say, not universal."[40]

While many came to view the Peace Democrats as "traitors," historian Frank L. Klement noted that "all who opposed any of President Lincoln's politics" were labeled by "a variety of smear terms . . . 'traitors,' 'secessionists,' and 'Copperheads.'" The Democrats as the "loyal opposition," Klement continued, "had the responsibility of keeping the Lincoln administration" in check and "of being the guardian of civil liberties." The conservative Peace Democrats contested the social and governmental changes "the war imposed upon the country," including the creation of a "centralized national government" and the emancipation of slaves.[41]

Support for the president reverberated in letters home. George Dodge of Company C, the grandson of prominent abolitionist Rev. William B. Dodge, wrote, "When we get home after destroying slavery and the rebellion. 'Hurrah for a Union without slavery.'" Orson Young supported the Emancipation Proclamation, "if carried out right." He clarified that he "came here to fight for the union, slavery or no slavery. If we can weaken the power of the south by taking away their slaves I say do it. . . . I think that any man that is not willing [to] have slavery destroyed to save the union is no union man." For Young, emancipation was a war measure to debilitate the south by "taking away their slaves." He mailed a printed copy of the brigade's preamble and resolutions to his parents, writing on the back: "This was got by our officers of our brigade and voted by the men they express my mind as well as I could tell it." Union soldiers, Chandra Manning explained, "serve[d] as advocates of emancipation," knowing it was "necessary to save the Union, but also because they now recognized that it was necessary to make the Union worth saving." This made them pragmatists and not abolitionists. Many Union soldiers understood slavery to be morally wrong while also opposing racial equality. Such attitudes were the norm in nineteenth-century America, and yet these men still did the right thing by supporting the president's proclamation and being the force that freed enslaved people.[42]

Amid the tension that the Emancipation Proclamation created among some Federal troops, the men took heart at Rosecrans's victory at the Battle of Stones River (December 31, 1862–January 3, 1863). The 96th was ready to support Rosecrans, but it had not been called to help in the fight, although some soldiers had friends with the 74th Illinois who had been there.[43]

The 96th kept on with its drilling and camp entertainments. John Taylor and Andrew White "got their hands on a little old fiddle" and took lessons from Ed Murray. With Murray's parents having emigrated from rural Ireland to the industrialized city of Glasgow, Scotland, Edward was influenced by a blending of Irish and Scottish fiddle playing. He livened up the camp as he taught his comrades Scottish tunes played with snap and energy. James Taylor noted, "I tell you our tent resounds sometimes with music most divine, especially when either of them gets to trying to tune the old thing."[44] Their inventiveness to break up the monotony of camp life was good for morale.

From January 10 to the end of February 1863, Billy Lewin was absent from the muster roll, "sick in hospital" at Danville, Kentucky. The majority of sick men had digestive issues—bowel complaints had a mortality rate of about 10 percent and were the war's number-one killer. The month of January ended with the death of Lt. Caleb Montgomery from "inflammation of the bowels." News of his death created a "profound sensation in the ranks." He had been a good and popular officer and had made an impression with his infamous potato foraging party just two months earlier.[45]

On the last day of January, the 96th Illinois with Granger's corps embarked on steamers escorted by gunboats down the Ohio River to the Cumberland River. The ultimate goal was to join Rosecrans's Army of the Cumberland as reinforcements, which they did on February 7. Murray described the experience as "one of the grandest sights that was my privilege to see." The voyage of the "magnificent fleet of steamers" wound its way up the Cumberland River. "Regimental colors were unfurled, and when the weather was not too cold the decks were fairly blue with officers and soldiers." When they reached Nashville, the troops had traveled nearly 550 miles by steamer. Such grand moments in the life of the Union Army resonated deeply with the men, who wrote vivid accounts to loved ones back home. The impressionable Jannet Minto wrote to her brother David, "You say that the rebels only have to hear that the 96th is coming and they skedadle like good fellows. I am glad if they are afraid of you & hope that they always will be & skedadle every time you try to catch them."[46] Clearly David had boasted of his regimental pride, and from his experience thus far, it seemed that the Rebels were indeed *skedaddling* on word of the 96th's approach.

Throughout the winter and into the spring of 1863, David Minto struggled with erysipelas, a contagious disease of the skin and tissue. John Taylor visited him in hospital, and George Smith described him as "reduced to a mere skeleton." He was discharged for disability on April 11, and an older brother came to take him home. The losses to disease ravaged the regiment at every level. In February 1863, 1st Lt. Addison Partridge resigned his position after being unable to recover from "camp disease," brought on by the notoriously unsanitary conditions in camp. On his journey home, Partridge was accompanied by James Joice, who as his personal servant assisted him in camp and looked after him when he became ill. Though many African Americans who sought freedom encountered racism from Union soldiers, the two men formed a connection, and owing to Partridge's honorable nature, he genuinely wished to help Joice start a new life in Illinois.[47]

Soldier self-care and better camp sanitation could have prevented the deaths of Lieutenant Montgomery and Pvt. Henry Swan and the losses to illness of 1st Lt. Addison Partridge and Pvt. David Minto. Through 1862, the sick and wounded suffered while medical services struggled to build an infrastructure to deal with the overwhelming number of soldiers in need. Historian Margaret Humphreys noted that, in time, military hospitals were indeed constructed, which "could be . . . place[s] for effective healing." In spite of these individual losses, the regiment was ready to march at a moment's notice. George Smith wrote: "We have been expecting to be called upon . . . I under stand that we are to be kept as a reserve in case of a fight when the others fall back we are the ones to pitch in and if we do face the enemy I hope that we shall face them with a stern reliance in the God of battles."[48]

After his success at Stones River, Major General Rosecrans focused on reinforcing his army, allowing it to recuperate and gather supplies in preparation for his brilliant Tullahoma Campaign. The success of this campaign would ensure Federal control of Middle Tennessee and open the way to Chattanooga. Both the Federals and Confederates halted operations over the winter due to poor road conditions. Once spring arrived, the armies began to test each other. By March the roads were less muddy, allowing for more military operations.[49]

The men were anxious to be of use to Rosecrans. John Taylor wrote, "[A]s the boys say 'if we do not get our chunk wiped out by the rebels' we will probably live to be respected and acknowledged as good American Citizens. Hope so." It was the hope of many of the foreign-born men that wartime service would gain them improved social status and acceptance. By mid-1863, young Taylor had formed strong opinions about the war effort and the Union's leadership. "I should think 'Old Abe' would improve the time and power he has in getting in plenty of men in to the field, for it is evident that only overpowering numbers that the rebels can be subdued."[50]

Although the men of the 96th were eager to be on the frontlines, they continued at the rear of the army's operations, and on occasion were told to be ready to move at a moment's notice. They came under enemy cannon fire for the first time when a few shells from the front exploded near them while Major General Granger's command pursued Confederate cavalry commander Gen. Earl Van Dorn across the Duck River. The regiment's duties included building fortifications at Fort Granger in Franklin, prompting the men to grumble that they would rather be shooting Rebels than digging pits. They also did picket duty and guarded a bridge on the Nashville and Decatur Railroad.[51]

To complicate matters, the regiment continued to suffer from scurvy and other illnesses, which were compounded by a multitude of factors out of their control, including where they camped, when they marched, and what supplies were available. The scurvy was partially resolved, noted Partridge, by the efforts of officers "who made an urgent request for potatoes, cabbage, and other edibles." During this early point in the regiment's service and while they were "in easy communication with the North," the men received boxes from home filled with butter and fruit and items not provided in their rations. The boxes cheered the homesick men and gave the women at home a chance to care for their loved ones. When George Smith received a bag of dried fruit from his sister, he wrote, "Every thing came as safe and nice as though you would have handed it to me out of your hand." Susie Smith also sent paper, envelopes, thread, pepper, and currants.[52]

Historian Kathryn Shively Meier explained that some newspapers scolded soldiers for their "juvenile dietary preferences" and proclaimed that "their morbid cravings for improper food" led to "poor bowel health." This disapproval was in part due to a bias that volunteer soldiers were not as disciplined as regular army soldiers. The critics failed to consider that many men were hungry from a lack of healthy rations. Hardtack could be filling, but it lacked nutritional value. The men were also homesick. Receiving food from home, even dried fruit or jam, was enough to buoy a young man's spirits and remind him of how much he was loved and missed.[53]

While at Brentwood, Tennessee, twenty men from the regiment along with men from the 78th and 92nd Illinois were selected for Company B of the Pioneer Corps, part of the newly formed Pioneer Brigade. Established by Major General Rosecrans, this select group of soldiers performed toolwork, repaired roads, and built small bridges. Although pioneers had long been a part of the American army, Rosecrans understood the need for a special brigade due to the demands of fighting in the Western Theater, where the army's supply lines often stretched for hundreds of miles through rough terrain. Without a steady stream of goods, an army could not stay in the field. The 96th's 1st

Lt. William M. Loughlin, a master builder, was placed in command of this company. This group was immediately assigned to the construction of Fort Granger on the right bank of the Harpeth River near Franklin.[54]

On April 10, Confederate major general Van Dorn made what William Loughlin called "a spirited attack on our forces" with cavalry and artillery. This was to be the First Battle of Franklin (also known as the Battle of Harpeth River). George Dodge wrote, "Our guns from the fort and battery opened on the rascals. . . . That scared them so that they ran off and we were started after them." John Taylor summed up the Rebel cavalry's action: "charged in and skedaddled out at a mad gallop."[55]

Col. Smith D. Atkins's brigade with the 96th leading marched across the Harpeth River in pursuit of the retreating forces. George Dodge recalled, "We walked faster than I was at all disposed to, for one or two hours without stopping to rest." After crossing a pontoon bridge, Dodge saw a dead man lying on the grass. "It was a hard sight to me, even if he was a rebel." Farther along they saw a dead soldier from the 40th Ohio with a cap over his face. "These sights are unpleasant but we are here, and have come here with the intention of killing as many rebels as we can, unless they will submit, and I haven't changed my mind yet. . . . Ain't I patriotic?" Taylor noted that "[s]ome of the skirmishers on the left wing of our brigade exchanged shots with them but our right never fired a shot. We laid in line of battle behind a stone fence till about ten o'clock. . . . [I]f it had been a clear day we could have seen all the fun."[56]

From the end of April through June, the regiment was detailed to chopping wood, guarding prisoners, building fortifications, drilling, and picket duty. The 96th's heavy concentration of farmers with common work habits were well conditioned to spend days laboring. This was not necessarily satisfactory work, for after a time many of the men questioned their value in the war effort. When not on guard duty, the men took pleasure in bathing, an activity they heartily endorsed. John Taylor had a "jolly old time" in the waters of the Harpeth River. "After walking down to the river we felt somewhat warm and so we sat down on a rock on the bank and were amused by the maneuver of some 200 or 300 men from different regiments who were enjoying themselves in the water Bathing, Diving, etc . . . full of glee." When they were fortunate enough to find water for bathing, the men were also more inclined to wash their clothes, greatly improving hygiene.[57]

On June 8, there was a partial reorganization of the corps, with the 96th becoming part of the First Brigade of the First Division of Granger's Reserve Corps of the Army of the Cumberland. Two days later, a grand review was held by Major General Granger with upward of thirty regiments of infantry and six batteries of artillery. The regiment's history recorded it as the "largest and most imposing review in which [they] had taken part." It was also tedious for the men.[58]

Near Triune on June 11, the men gathered to be paid, but skirmishing with the enemy began, and the regiment was ordered into line. The paymaster left quickly and the men fell in just as enemy shells whistled overhead. Company A was sent to the front as skirmishers. The regiment remained in line for six hours with shells passing close to their lines, but they sustained no losses. Those less exposed to the gunfire were quite envious of Company A, which had exchanged shots with the enemy. However, all the men "began to feel quite like veterans," since this was the closest they had come to a battle.[59]

The Tullahoma Campaign (June 24–July 4, 1863)

The main body of Rosecrans's army had made no general movement in months. Rosecrans and Bragg had been strengthening and fortifying their positions since the Battle of Stones River. Rosecrans's main army remained at Murfreesboro, with additional forces at Franklin and Triune, and Bragg's headquarters were at Tullahoma, with infantry at Shelbyville and Wartrace. Rosecrans had no intention of directly attacking Bragg's fortifications. Instead, he planned a flanking operation to force Bragg to retreat from his earthworks or battle away from his lines. As historian Christopher L. Kolakowski explained, on June 24, "[a]fter 169 days of rest, the Army of the Cumberland was again on the march."[60]

The 96th Illinois's part in the campaign would be a support role at the rear. They marched, or rather plodded, through muddy roads, occasionally hearing cannon fire. Thinking they would be engaged with the enemy when this happened, they stood on the picket line, but they did not enter into any skirmishes. They guarded a wagon train, a critical task in the constant struggle to maintain the army's supply lines, and were detached to escort 489 prisoners from Walnut Grove to the rear, with guns loaded and bayonets fixed. Billy Lewin wrote home about the regiment's role: "Our place is to keep a few miles in the rear of the advance to support them if the enemy is too strong for them." Each day they marched until nearly midnight while pursuing the enemy, and on one rainy day they slogged through the mud and "waded creeks to our waists in water."[61]

On July 3, the last day of the campaign, the regiment marched to Wartrace through a heavy rainstorm to guard several bridges on the Nashville and Chattanooga Railroad. News that Bragg had retreated, relinquishing Tullahoma to the Federals, rather than fought put the men in high spirits. They shouted and sang merrily at the successful conclusion of the campaign. Rosecrans wrote, "On the 4th of July, we had possession of both the enemy's entrenched camps, and by the 7th, Bragg's army was in full retreat over the Cumberland Mountains." Rosecrans had conquered the region between Murfreesboro and the Tennessee River in eleven days with only 570 Federals killed, wounded, captured, or missing. The Confederate losses were estimated at nearly five thousand. As historian Michael R. Bradley noted, it was the "least bloody major campaign of the war."[62]

The Army of the Cumberland received dispatches from Secretary of War Edwin M. Stanton announcing that, after a six-week siege, Vicksburg had surrendered to Maj. Gen. Ulysses S. Grant, giving the Union control of the Mississippi River. Archibald J. McCreadie, serving with the 37th Illinois, wrote to David Minto at home: "Vicksburg is taken at last by the feds so Waukegan can selibrate [sic] its full without any danger of being disappointed." The dispatches also carried news of Brig. Gen. George G. Meade's great victory at Gettysburg. There was "the wildest joy" in the Army of the Cumberland.[63]

Stanton's telegraph to Rosecrans included a question: "You and your noble army now have the chance to give the finishing blow to the rebellion. Will you neglect the chance?" An enraged Rosecrans immediately responded, "You do not appear to observe the fact that this noble army has driven the rebels from Middle Tennessee, of which my dispatches advised you. I beg in behalf of this army that the War Department may not overlook so great an event because it is not written in letters of blood. I have now to repeat, that the rebel army has been forced from its strong [e]ntrenched positions at Shelbyville and Tullahoma, and driven over the Cumberland Mountains . . ."[64]

"To all appearances The Backbone of Rebels is broken," wrote George Smith to his sister. "Also the hind legs and are now crawling about looking imploringly into Uncle Sams face and crying out, dont dont, hit me anny more."[65] Perhaps Smith should have addressed his letter to Secretary Stanton instead.

Rosecrans's masterful Tullahoma Campaign placed the Federal line sixty miles closer to the ultimate goal of Chattanooga. With a population of twenty-five hundred, Chattanooga was a key rail center and the Confederacy's hub of communication between the East and West, a strategic target. Unfortunately, the significance of the victorious Tullahoma Campaign was overshadowed by bloodier engagements in other theaters of the war.[66]

At home, the women of the Soldiers Aid Society continued to respond to the suffering of their soldiers by making quilts, sheets, and rolled bandages and collecting donations of every variety, including shirts, towels, books, soda crackers, bottles of currant wine, jars of pickled cucumbers, and cash. Hannah Clarke, secretary of the local Soldiers Aid Society and sister-in-law to the 96th's Lieutenant Colonel Clarke, published a notice in the *Waukegan Gazette*: "Solicitations . . . for old clothes suitable for dressing wounds, or making bandages. . . . The funds of the Society are now exhausted and it is earnestly hoped that the Strawberry Festival, which will occur as soon as the berries ripen, will be born in mind by every one who has any sympathy for or a desire to aid, those who are suffering and dying for us."[67]

Union meetings were held throughout Lake County, many in protest of the boisterous calls by Peace Democrats to end the war. This anti-Copperhead backlash generated capacity crowds in town halls and schools. A brass band greeted Unionists at the Libertyville town hall with rich patriotic music. Methodist minister Rev. I. E. Hibbard gave a "soul-stirring prayer," and "[h]is invective upon the poor Copperheads of Libertyville was simply—terrible."[68]

While Unionists at home ensured support of the war and its soldiers, the 96th continued unabated with picketing and chopping wood. Health concerns such as diarrhea and dysentery were still a problem, or as John Taylor put it, "the general complaints with the boys sick just now." He included his brother and James Murrie as "both having a severe spell of sickness." Taylor wrote to his sister Mary from Franklin, Tennessee, about his "state of health." He described himself as "not very sick . . . only a bad cold settled on my lung." After chopping timber in the chilly weather and rain he "caught cold." As it was common for soldiers to think that the environment influenced illness, they particularly associated chills, fevers, and sweating with exposure to rain. Considering that Taylor and his comrades had yet to see battle, the enemy they were most concerned with was the environment. Kathryn Shively Meier described it as "the weather, climate, seasons, terrain features, flora, and fauna that they could not avoid."[69]

Taylor reported his symptoms to the regimental surgeon, but prior to the war his sisters would have looked after his health. Americans in general had little contact with doctors, and family members, especially mothers, sisters, and wives provided care for the sick. As Meier explained, women acted as nurses and "often proved the dispensers of [medical] knowledge, sometimes . . . compiling their own recipe books of remedies."[70] The men now had to rely on themselves and their comrades for care and adapt to the military's medical system.

The surgeon attending to John Taylor made up "some powders" and told him to "lay still" and "keep warm all day." When Taylor went to see him again, he was instructed to "get into a tent where there was a stove and wash myself with warm water . . . and not to get any more cold on me if I could help it." According to Meier, a soldier's personal ability to care for himself was often "superior to official army health care . . . considering how poorly disease and treatment were understood."[71]

Not all soldiers were sympathetic to their sick comrades. George Smith noted, "If ones sick and grunting around no one seems to care for him, its get out of the way you whining Puppy. One might just about as well be dead as to be sick here." Although the men were generally good about looking after one another, it was not surprising that some became desensitized to the "whining" given the large number of sick.[72]

The men were constantly trying to supplement army rations, and their diet improved when summer fruit was available. "Apples and peaches are all the go at present," wrote John Taylor. "They are plenty . . . bring about a dollar a bushel in camp. I have bought several batches and sold them again. Peddled them through camp." Taylor's entrepreneurial spirit provided him with extra cash to afford the staples and small luxuries that made his life as a soldier more comfortable. The men had expenses and even debts in buying clothing, food, and sundries. Considering that payday was frequently late and sutlers charged notoriously high prices, efforts like Taylor's were a necessity. Taylor sent some of his income home to his sisters to offset costs in sending supplies to him and his brother.[73]

In mid-August, the regiment marched through Tullahoma and reached camp on the banks of the Elk River near Estill Springs. In addition to their usual picketing and guard duties, the men found time to swim. James Taylor wrote that "John has got to be quite a swimmer." Their cousin Alex Thain (Company D) taught James to swim by tying "a couple of empty canteens under my arms to keep me above water . . . we had a good deal of sport."[74]

While encamped at the Elk River, the men were heartened by the presence of colored troops on the opposite side of the river. John Taylor wrote, "They take great interest in drilling—and I believe they learn faster than we did. The regiment is armed and very well drilled—and no doubt will soon be in the field." Taylor's praise of the African American soldiers rings of sincerity, but it also stemmed from a belief that organizing these men into regiments would bring the war to a quicker end.[75]

The one-year anniversary of the regiment's muster-in (September 5), had George Smith exclaiming, "Here we are still!" He wrote to his sister asking if she thought the 96th had "failed to doo our duty." Like Smith, John Taylor was questioning the value of their service. "We being in the Reserve Corps will hardly see much fighting unless a big one should come off." During their first year of service, the 96th had played an essential yet less conspicuous role guarding the line of communications and supplies to keep the army operating at the front, but it had not been in a heavy battle. Taylor wrote, "The old 96th has had some very narrow escapes from fight and it seems as if we were destined not to see one."[76]

The Army of the Cumberland had been on the move since August 16, when the struggle for Chattanooga had commenced. On September 6, the Reserve Corps received its orders to hurry south to reinforce Rosecrans as he pressured Bragg to evacuate Chattanooga. The next day, all the men in the 96th who could be spared from guarding the rail lines headed out to march over the Cumberland Mountains to Stevenson, Alabama. James Taylor was among the convalescents sent by train to Stevenson. His brother John was left behind to guard the railroad. "Being on guard away from the Regiment with six men at a water tank on the R.R. we were not relieved until the regiment had been on the march for some time—so we got on board the first freight train that came along . . . thus getting rid of over two days marching among the mountains."[77]

Historian David A. Powell explained how the Union Army secured Chattanooga: "Rosecrans turned to maneuver. Feinting north of the town, Rosecrans crossed his main body at Bridgeport and Stevenson and moved due east to threaten Bragg's supply line, the Western & Atlantic Railroad. The plan worked brilliantly."[78] Early on September 8, Bragg evacuated Chattanooga to avoid being trapped. After Bragg's withdrawal, Rosecrans did not expect to meet up with him again.

On September 10, the regiment left Stevenson and camped near Bridgeport, Alabama. After marching for four days over the rugged Cumberland Mountains, the first thing they did after stacking their guns was to wash off the dust and dirt in the Tennessee River. The entire command of two to three thousand troops stripped off their clothes and plunged into the river.[79]

James Taylor was transferred to the Bridgeport convalescent camp due to severe diarrhea and weakness. Over the course of the year, James had repeatedly been treated by the regiment's surgeons for ailments such as colds, sore throats, headaches, and persistent diarrhea. When the 96th left Bridgeport the morning of September 12, the Taylor brothers faced their longest separation as John headed out with the regiment, crossing the Tennessee River on a pontoon bridge. Camp was on the south side of the river, but before they could finish constructing bunks, they got word that they were headed to the front. All extra baggage, including tents, knapsacks, and blankets, were packed and sent back to Stevenson, with Company C's Captain Pollock in charge of the equipment.[80]

The regiment endured a forced march, September 13 and 14, across Lookout Mountain to Rossville, Georgia. The regimental history recorded, "The Regiment was near the rear of the column, and as there were several hundred wagons ahead of them loaded with twelve days' rations and large amounts of ammunition for the command, progress was very slow." They covered a distance of forty miles over mountainous roads in less than thirty-six hours. John Taylor described the conditions: "We marched till dark at night when we bivouacked and got some supper and laid down to take a nap on this earth. At half past ten or eleven we were roused up and ordered on . . . we made some very slow marching til daylight across those rugged mountains."[81]

Charles Partridge recalled in that first year "excellent discipline had been maintained, and the men had been getting ready. Now it was to know—and that right speedily—of what material it was composed, and whether it should do honor to the hopes of those who had sent it forth to battle." John wrote to his sister Isabella: "We the Reserve Corps . . . hold ourselves in readiness to march. . . . Yesterday we could hear cannons all along the lines in the direction of Town. Yesterday deserters came in very fast, faster than I ever saw them before." The cannon fire and deserters foretold of the conflict to come. The 96th Illinois was about to face its greatest challenge at Chickamauga, Georgia.[82]

4. Brave Boys Are They

"Chickamauga! Though long years have passed since that name was hurled into history from the smoking throats of a hundred cannon and a hundred thousand muskets, yet the hand trembles and the pen falters as the word is written."[1] And so begins the 96th Illinois's account of their single most important engagement of the war.

After skillfully maneuvering Bragg out of Chattanooga, Rosecrans pursued the Confederates despite his own forces being scattered. He believed that Bragg was retreating toward Rome, but when Maj. Gen. James S. Negley's division encountered a large Confederate force at Davis's Crossroads on September 10–11, Rosecrans realized his mistake. It was now clear that Bragg had halted twenty-six miles south of Chattanooga at LaFayette, Georgia, where he was expecting reinforcements from Mississippi and Virginia. Bragg was determined to reoccupy Chattanooga. David A. Powell explained that Rosecrans needed "to recombine his scattered forces. Both sides spent the next week maneuvering, but Bragg was unable to prevent the Federals from uniting at Lee and Gordon's Mills." In this process, the 96th Illinois arrived at Rossville Gap on September 14. For several days they were allowed to rest, but they heard "distant cannonading" which kept the men on high alert.[2]

During this period, there was nearly a mutiny when foragers went outside the picket lines and Major General Granger had them tied up by their thumbs. John Taylor noted the lack of provisions at Rossville: "Lots of our troops are on short rations here at present. We thought we would live like fighting cocks after we got into Georgia or Alabama—but there is no great plenty here yet." Inadequate rations forced men to forage even in dangerous circumstances to stave off hunger. Charles Partridge of Company C felt the men faced a "peculiar hardship" because troops marching ahead of the 96th had "drawn" most of the fruits, vegetables, and chickens for themselves. Capt. George Hicks and other officers of the 96th demanded the release of their men. A crowd of soldiers gathered, and officers stepped forward from other regiments. Granger faced the men using profanity and threats, but once Brig. Gen. James B. Steedman pressed the issue, the men were released.[3]

On the morning of September 18, the opening engagement of the bloodiest battle of the Western Theater began along the banks of West Chickamauga Creek, where Union cavalry delayed the Confederates' crossing at Reed's Bridge. With only three regiments of cavalry and a total of 973 men, Col. Robert H. G. Minty held off repeated attacks from the much larger forces of Confederate brigadier general Bushrod Johnson's division of infantry and Brig. Gen. Nathan Bedford Forrest's cavalry. Union mounted infantry armed with state-of-the-art Spencer repeating rifles fought off the Confederates in a daylong fight, but the Northerners eventually retreated. This was the start of the Battle of Chickamauga, fought September 18–20, 1863, between Major General Rosecrans's Army of the Cumberland (fifty-eight thousand men) and General Braxton Bragg's Army of Tennessee (more than sixty-six thousand men). The conflict was named for Chickamauga Creek, which meanders near the battle area in northwest Georgia.

The same morning that Minty's cavalry was attacked, a portion of the 96th Illinois (including Company C) moved out of Rossville on Ringgold Road to McAfee Church. John Taylor wrote to his sister from Rossville in a tone so carefree it showed a lack of knowledge of the peril he would soon face. "To pass time and inform you of our how and whereabouts I now seat my-self with this fancy sheet—pen and ink. I am well and feel as hearty and strong as need be."[4]

The men reached the wood-framed McAfee Church about noon, where they stacked their guns and ate dinner. After five o'clock they were called into line and marched down the road without an advance guard or guns loaded. Partridge recalled that the command assumed that since the Second Brigade had just "come in over the road without a fight" there was no danger. The troops entered the heavy timber lining the road and came to the Little Chickamauga stream. Brig. Gen. Walter C. Whitaker and his officers watered their horses in the creek while the men crossed on a log to keep their feet dry when "like lightning from a clear sky, the sharp crack of a rifle rang out, and a bullet whizzed past [Whitaker's] head." The offender was a Rebel sentinel, who had been startled while making his coffee.[5]

Ed Murray recalled that "General Whitaker fearing that the rebels had a battery planted so as to sweep the road with grape and canister, called out" and cleared the men from the road. The general shouted commands, and

Colonel Champion called "Attention!" and gave the order for the men to load their muskets at will, deploying Companies D and F. The regimental history recorded that the first to start across the road was Cpl. Elisha Haggart, but the moment he "emerged from the bushes he fell, his brain pierced by a bullet." Several minutes later, Capt. Asiel Blodgett of Company D was struck by a bullet in his shoulder, but he soon rejoined his company. The men advanced, Murray wrote, and "sharp skirmish ensued, lasting about forty-five minutes . . . we drove the enemy about three-fourths of a mile."[6]

After the enemy retired from their front, the regiment camped near the Chickamauga. This was the 96th Illinois's first engagement in the prelude to battle. Throughout the chilly night, the men lay in line clutching their rifles while their teeth chattered. No fires were allowed due to their proximity to enemy lines. Ed Murray and his comrades could not even warm themselves with a cup of hot coffee.[7]

Fighting began in earnest on the morning of Saturday, September 19, near Chickamauga Creek. The battle extended over miles of territory through dark forests and farm fields, the creek itself deep and tree-lined, and bordered by rocky banks. So much of the battlefield was concealed by the dense terrain that senior officers had an unclear perception of their commands and the enemy's movements. The battle had begun, but the 96th Illinois remained in the area of McAfee Church, and the rest of its available men came up from Rossville. At three in the morning, they were placed north of the church on a ridge at the left of the road where they stayed for twenty-four hours. Almost half of the 96th's men were sick, presumably from the previous night's chill, but most remained with the command.[8]

Although other regiments in the brigade's line (84th Indiana, 40th Ohio, and 115th Illinois) took part in heavy skirmishes that day, the 96th Illinois did not. The regimental history noted that the "tide of battle did not cross the road" to where they were positioned. The thunderous sound of cannon and crack of musketry was heard by the Reserve Corps, but there was no way for them to know the battle they would face. As they lay guarding Rossville Gap at the extreme left of the line, Partridge recalled the men telling "big stories as to how the boys at the front were gobbling up the entire Rebel Army." They were "spoiling for a fight," half hoping to be spared and half anxious that they would again have an inconspicuous role and not share in the battle's honors. In their first year of service, the men of the 96th had grown accustomed to long marches, outdoor living, and distant cannon fire, but they were still green when it came to battle. With the pounding thunder of artillery calling, they wanted more than anything to "see the elephant" and prove their manliness.[9]

It was another cold night for the men as they slept on pine boughs without wool blankets or tents. Partridge described them "shivering and wishing for morning." By midnight the cold and discomfort had them up kindling small fires in a ravine at the rear of the line. In the predawn, Ed Murray and his comrades ate breakfast and steeled themselves for the work ahead. It was now the morning of September 20, and the *Official Records* (*OR*) noted that "the sky was red and sultry, the atmosphere and all the woods enveloped in fog and smoke." The 96th Illinois was about to receive its baptism of blood.[10]

The regiment sent 419 men into battle on Sunday afternoon. At enlistment, Captain Pollock's Company C totaled ninety-three men. Now only thirty-five were fit for battle, and Pollock was not there to command them as he had been sent to Stevenson with the camp and garrison equipage. Company C's command fell to nineteen-year-old Lt. Charles W. Earle, a veteran of the 15th Illinois. Among the company's ranks at Chickamauga were four of the five men who had enlisted together: Sgt. Edward Murray, Cpl. John Taylor, Cpl. William Lewin, and Pvt. Loughlin Madden. Absent was Cpl. James Murrie, who had been in the hospital since September 6 with one of the digestive illnesses that plagued the men. Murrie wrote to John Taylor, informing him that he was "getting better," but he did not rejoin the company until the end of November.[11] Though none of the men were eager to face death, they wanted to prove their courage in a fight with the enemy. It was difficult for Murrie to hear of the battle afterward, and this was especially true for James Taylor, knowing he was not at his brother's side for the fight.

Near McAfee Church, Company A's Capt. George Hicks spoke with Lt. Col. Isaac Clarke about his pride in the men's skill in drilling, discipline, and "soldierly bearing," but he feared it "would be absolutely worthless, if now, at the supreme moment . . . of battle, we should fail." Lieutenant Colonel Clarke responded, "I have no fear for our men. They will do their duty, every man of them. And I have no fear for myself. I shall go into this fight, and go through it, and come out of it all right." Officers often felt their manhood and honor were on trial, and so were particularly anxious to put themselves to the test.[12]

To the frustration of Company C and the entire Reserve Corps (fifty-four hundred men and three artillery batteries), they waited all morning on the twentieth for orders. Officers and men grew impatient, but, as Partridge remembered, they spoke only in subdued tones, "as if in the presence of a great peril." They were within earshot of a fight while "guarding a wagon road on which there was no enemy." Captain Hicks recalled, "The sun got up high in the heavens and poured down its rays straight and hot upon our heads, and the pealing thunder of guns was incessant."[13]

The Reserve Corps's last orders from Rosecrans the night before were to defend Rossville and support Maj. Gen. Alexander McCook and Maj. Gen. George H. Thomas where possible. Reserve Corps commander Major General Granger reported after the battle: "At 10:30 a.m. I heard heavy firing, which was momentarily increasing in volume and intensity on our right, in the direction of General Thomas' position." With fighting just a few miles to the south, the reserves' position seemed only good for protecting the Rossville Gap and keeping the road to Chattanooga open. As the morning waned, the gunfire in the distance grew louder. There were no new orders, and Granger wavered between holding his position or going to support Thomas. Granger noted, "[B]eing well convinced, judging from the sound of battle, that the enemy were pushing him hard, and fearing that he would not be able to resist their combined attack, I determined to go to his assistance at once."[14]

At a little past eleven o'clock, Granger hurried to the support of Major General Thomas, four miles distant. Steedman put Whitaker's First Brigade (made up of the 96th and 115th Illinois, the 40th and 89th Ohio, the 22nd Michigan, the 84th Indiana, and the 18th Battery of the Ohio Light Artillery) on the march for the Lafayette Road. The 96th Illinois was given the lead. The march was rapid through woods to Lafayette Road, stirring up heavy clouds of dust while trying to avoid an encounter with Confederate cavalry. Behind them was Col. John G. Mitchell's Second Brigade (78th Illinois; 98th, 113th, and 121st Ohio; and Battery M of the 1st Illinois Light Artillery). Granger left his remaining five regiments and an artillery battery under Col. Daniel McCook at the McAfee Church, following Major General Rosecrans's original orders to keep the route to Chattanooga open.[15]

The *OR* recorded that they marched en masse "with alacrity and enthusiasm" and came to a Union divisional field hospital near Cloud Spring. The hospital had been used by the left wing of the Union forces and fallen into Rebel hands. A number of Rebel soldiers guarding it were captured. Near the hospital, the men glimpsed a long row of Union dead and realized the nature of the bloody work nearby, increasing their pre-battle nerves. They passed to the right of the hospital and, as their history noted, hurried through "a terrible snarl of tangled vines," continuing on the double-quick across an open field. Confederate major general Forrest's dismounted cavalry and artillery galloped into the field at the left and unlimbered its guns within four hundred yards of the 96th. Partridge wrote, "The soldiers saw the puffs of smoke and heard the hiss of the shells." Soon the "air seemed full of iron" and the ground "seamed and furrowed."[16]

Since this was not where they were most needed, the commanders re-formed the lines and hurried the men forward. They traveled almost con-tinuously for two hours, cutting across open fields as a safer and more direct route to Thomas toward Snodgrass House. Half the time the men marched at the double-quick. Ed Murray and his comrades were exhausted from the demanding speed of the march and lack of sleep the previous night. Thirsty from exertion and the hot sun beating down on them, the men were given few water breaks, but there was solidarity in hardship and knowing it was time to prove their individual and unified courage.[17]

At last, Granger's men came through the woods and onto a field within sight of Snodgrass House on a hill. Little did they realize that their presence caused a mix of hope and fear in the very man they had come to reinforce. Major General Thomas observed "troops approaching from the north through the fields" and commented, "If that is the enemy we're lost; if the Reserves, the army is saved." The clouds of dust made it impossible to distinguish if the uniforms and flags were of friend or foe. Thomas sent a staff officer to meet the advancing line, who signaled that these were reinforcements. Relief poured over Thomas.[18]

Major General Rosecrans reported after the battle: "Fortunately, Major-General Granger, whose troops had been posted to cover our left and rear, with the intellect of a true soldier and a general, hearing the roar of battle on our left, and being beyond the reach of orders from the general commanding, determined to move to its assistance."[19]

About two o'clock, Thomas and Granger shook hands. Historian David A. Powell explained that the arrival of the Reserve Corps "could not have been timelier, blunting another Rebel flank attack in the nick of time." Johnson's *Battles and Leaders* recorded that Granger informed Thomas that "[m]y men . . . are just the fellows for that work. They are raw troops, and they don't know any better than to charge up there." During their hurried consultation, the thunder of battle continued on the far side of Snodgrass Hill. The Reserve Corps officers were informed of the events of the morning. Faced with repeated Confederate assaults, Rosecrans had worked to shift men to the hard-pressed left. Chicka-mauga's heavy woods concealed a Federal division, causing one of Rosecrans's staff officers to report that there was a gap in the Union line. Without veri-fying this for himself, Rosecrans ordered Maj. Gen. Thomas Wood to shift his division, inadvertently creating an actual gap. Wood followed Rosecrans's order in spite of "deep misgivings" that it was based on flawed information.[20]

Powell concluded, "The real problem was that in the space of a quarter of an hour, General Rosecrans set virtually the entire Union right wing in motion. He did so in the face of a powerful enemy already attacking his left wing, and who at that moment was preparing to attack his right wing." A supporter of Wood's, Col. Emerson Opdycke of the 125th Ohio reported, "These disconnected and fatal movements . . . were [all] in progress . . . when Longstreet attacked. . . . Disaster was the immediate and inevitable result."[21]

The breach was exploited with deadly force, with Major General Hood leading parts of Confederate lieutenant general James Longstreet's corps of seventeen brigades from Virginia. At 11:30 a.m., Longstreet ordered the charge. According to Dr. William Glen Robertson, "Hood's column struck a segment of the Federal line that was momentarily devoid of troops." The Confederates slammed through, routing the panicked Union soldiers and driving one-third of the Union Army from the field, including the Army of the Cumberland's commander, Rosecrans. Partridge confirmed the "disastrous break" in the lines occurred "not long after eleven o'clock or almost at the moment that the Reserves left McAfee Church." It was across this field of battle that the 96th Illinois had marched as they came to Thomas's aid. "The air was full of smoke, the fences and fields burning in many places. . . . Wounded men were frequently met, and dead bodies lay here and there, giving evidence that the ground over which the columns were passing had been the scene of a hot contest."[22]

The situation was growing critical, and as Partridge described, Longstreet was "preparing to swing in his Division[s], like a ponderous gate, and completely envelop Gen Thomas's army. A half hour more and the movement would be complete." It was at this moment that the Reserves "arrived, hot, dusty and fatigued with the long march at double-quick."[23] Rosecrans, along with one-third of his army, retreated back to Chattanooga, leaving Thomas as the senior officer on the field to take control of what was left of the army. Thomas's troops held their ground at Horseshoe Ridge, a strong defensive position.

Ed Murray, John Taylor, Billy Lewin, and Loughlin Madden barely had a moment to catch their breath, wipe the sweat from their brows with shirt sleeves, and wash the dust from their throats with water from their canteens.[24] Their hearts pounded with the knowledge that it was time to prove their mettle to themselves, their comrades in line, their regiment, and their loved ones at home.

> *They met old Longstreet and his host,*
> *Of whom the rebels all do boast,*
> *On Chickamauga's battle plain,*
> *And fought till half their men were slain.*[25]

A relieved Major General Thomas reported, "This opportune arrival of fresh troops revived the flagging spirits of our men on the right, and inspired them with new ardor for the contest. Every assault of the enemy from that time until nightfall was repulsed in the most gallant style by the whole line." Whitaker's and Mitchell's brigades under Brigadier General Steedman were moved into position, and the 96th Illinois formed the extreme right of the line against the enemy in the gorge and on the ridge. With the 96th were the 115th Illinois in the center and the 22nd Michigan on the left of the first line. In the second line were the 40th Ohio on the right, the 84th Indiana in the center, and the 89th Ohio on the left.[26]

Skirmishers were sent to the right, guns inspected, and men counted. Whitaker's brigade moved forward in a double line, with the 96th Illinois, 115th Illinois, and 22nd Michigan leading. Steedman at the front on his horse gave the order to charge. The exhausted men ran forward with a united cheer that relieved tension and intimidated the enemy. Historian James M. McPherson explained: "Yankees yelled just as loudly [as the Rebels], though in a deeper pitch."[27]

The men sprinted uphill nearly four hundred yards to the crest of the ridge. Partridge noted, "A series of little ravines were passed, and the soldiers broke into a double quick. Ascending a longer ridge, there came the pattering of shots, like the first drops of a shower; then the ragged, tearing report of an irregular skirmish volley; then the constant, deafening roar, as regiment after regiment took up the deadly work." As the 96th reached the crest, the Confederate line was in full view just sixty yards below them. With fixed bayonets, the Union line attacked. "Through the smoke and bushes [Rebels] could hardly be seen, although the guns belched forth a terrible fire seemingly right in their faces."[28]

> *Yet there they stood on that battle field,*
> *At the cannon's mouth and would not yield,*
> *While the air was thick with shot and shell,*
> *On, on, they charged with a deafening yell.*[29]

Dozens of soldiers in blue fell in the first few minutes as they "pressed on down the slope, with a wild cheer, bounding over logs and stones, through the hollow and up to the crest of another ridge." Col. Thomas Champion's horse was struck twice, and men dropped all along the regimental line. "A hundred officers and men must have fallen in that first half hour."[30]

The *OR* records that the "conflict was terrific," and the Federals drove the enemy back "near half a mile." Ed Murray recounted, "Our Colonel, our regiment being the first in line of battle, three other regiments being in the rear, gave the command: Forward, double quick march, with a yell and we went with a will. But the Rebs had their pickets out watching and they commenced firing a gun here and another there all along the line." For the first time, the men of the 96th were faced with taking another man's life. As historian Jonathan M. Steplyk explained, with no previous battle experience, these citizen-soldiers had been tending their crops only the year before and now were expected to "overcome natural and cultural inhibitions" to kill. The smoke-filled battlefield provided some barrier to seeing the result of their work.[31]

The 96th's Colonel Champion reported, "We charged the enemy's left in the face of a murderous fire of infantry and artillery at short range, and maintained our position until every regiment on our left and in our rear had given way." With their first shots fired, the men felt a physical release from their pre-battle anxiety. Sergeant Partridge noted that he "had not the least sense of fear," and through the fight "there was a wild, hurried excitement that I remember but as a dream." Captain Hicks recalled an "exaltation of feeling" that lifted him "above the plane of all ordinary sentiments." In this state of "supreme duty," Hicks barely glanced at his corporal who was shot and "fell lifeless." He pressed on without "the slightest feeling of pity, or sympathy, or any gentle, kindly emotion." In this way, the men were able to "repress the unbearable horror" of battle.[32]

Ed Murray recalled that in the charge "[t]hey hit some of our men, but we did not stop until we got to the top of the rise when we were ordered to fire at will, and there was a Rebel battery right in front of us, supported by infantry and they poured galling fire into our ranks. Our lines were broken and the boys got behind logs and trees, as protection." In the midst of battle, instincts took over from training, and officers' commands were drowned out by the deafening sound of muskets and cannons firing.[33]

"Lie down!" was shouted along the line. The men's exhaustive drill practice, now almost second nature, kicked in full force. Hearing the command, they kept close to the ground to protect themselves from the hail of minié balls and fired their Enfields while lying down. Partridge wrote, "How furious the rattling clangor of musketry, without stop, without a moment's pause. . . . How unceasing the whistling of the bullets tzip! tzip! tzip! . . . Ever and anon would be faintly heard the soldier's muttered cry, 'Oh!' or 'I'm hit!'" Historian Drew Gilpin Faust explained that troops that formed in close ranks lessened "soldiers' self-doubt and inhibitions about killing—as well as any desire or chance they might have to flee." In this way, "Men acted as part of a whole, which both removed an element of agency from the individual and encompassed him within the pressures and solidarity of the group."[34]

The 96th Illinois advanced and were soon hundreds of yards out in front of any other Federals. Lieutenant Colonel Clarke was the only officer still mounted. Partridge recalled that Clarke had led his men up Horseshoe Ridge and "sat calmly on his horse near the left of the Regiment, speaking words of cheer to the men as they met the terrible fire."[35] A moment later, Clarke was shot through the chest. He was helped from his horse by a small group of men and taken to the rear on a blanket.

> *Before the charge brave Clarke did cry*
> *My boys that starry flag stand by*
> *But soon amid the awful roar*
> *His manly voice was heard no more.*[36]

Sgt. Thomas J. Smith of Company I was sent with Lieutenant Colonel Clarke and remained with him until his death two days later while crossing the Tennessee River in an ambulance.[37]

In the thick of the fire, the left of the regiment began to recoil, and someone shouted, "Fall back!" Colonel Champion attempted to counter this command, but he realized the brigade line was broken and the regimental line could not be kept. To remain would mean annihilation or capture. Champion gave the order: "Keep in line. Keep your colors!" As the Confederates pressed, the disorder of the retreating troops increased, but Ed Murray could not retreat with his unit. When the lines had broken, Murray stepped about three paces to the front, fired his gun, and stepped back. "Balls were flying through the air like hail storm," he recalled. Finding himself in a dangerous place, he dropped to the ground to load his musket as he had been trained. After loading his gun, Murray rolled onto his left side to get a cap from his cap box and was "struck between the shoulders near the right side of the spine so as to completely paralyze my lower limbs and rendering me perfectly helpless while the battle continued." It was at this moment that the 96th fell back.

Murray was now stranded, "it being too hot a place for our boys, they had to fall back, reluctantly leaving me where I lay."[38]

Color Sgt. Mathias M. Bruner (Company F) also fell wounded, and Color Cpl. John W. Swanbrough (Company G) caught the Stars and Stripes before they hit the ground. Flags were powerful symbols, and color bearers and color guard held a place of honor and danger. They would rather die than have the colors fall or be taken. The vividly colored flags led the regimental line in an attack and rallied the men in retreat. Swanbrough had the regimental flag's staff shot twice in his hands, but he ran backward with the national and regimental flags to where Colonel Champion, Brigadier General Steedman, and Colonel Mitchell were rallying the men.[39]

With the enemy halted at the ridge where the first charge had been made, the Federals had time to regroup about five to six hundred yards away. Falling back, the 96th broke into two groups, one led by Colonel Champion and the other by Captain Hicks. Champion was rallying his men when he learned that Whitaker was wounded, which left him in command of the brigade. He asked Swanbrough to carry the colors farther up the ridge as a visual rallying point. The corporal's courage inspired the men as they gathered around him and formed the line.[40]

In the midst of rallying his men, Capt. George Hicks was approached by a staff officer in a manner of "intense excitement."

"Captain! Why in thunder don't you form this Regiment?"

Unaware of the events that had unfolded in the command, Hicks replied, "I am forming my Company, sir. Where's Colonel Champion?"

"He's taken command of the Brigade; Whitaker's wounded."

"Well, where's Colonel Clarke?"

"Why, don't you know? Clarke was killed at the first fire!"

Hicks had no time to process the loss and made quick work to rally the regiment: "Comrades, you have made one charge—a gallant charge. On yonder hillside lie the bodies of your fallen comrades. Forward to avenge their deaths!" The men responded with a cheer and again moved to the front.[41]

Col. Thomas E. Champion recalled in the second charge that "[w]e repulsed the enemy after about twenty minutes' desperate fighting. We then moved to the left of the battery and again charged the enemy, driving him down the ridge running nearly parallel with our first line nearly half a mile, until we received an enfilading fire from the Eighty-fourth Indiana and One hundred and fifteenth Illinois Volunteers, and were compelled to retire."[42] The 96th had been in the line of friendly fire.

The battle on Horseshoe Ridge raged with occasional intervals until dusk. Partridge explained: "Sometimes there were two lines, but by some strange fate, the Ninety-Sixth was always in the front one." Dozens of men had been shot, including Ed Murray, John Taylor, and Billy Lewin. They were not among those "lying silent in death," but Murray was paralyzed on the field, and Taylor and Lewin were making their way to the rear in search of a field hospital.[43]

The regiment's extensive drill training had given them the skills and confidence to march in line and load and fire their rifles, and the esprit de corps they had nurtured gave them the steadfastness they needed in the face of great danger. The command held the ground where it had gallantly fought Longstreet's veterans, and it only left the line when night closed the battle. The men of the 96th, and Company C (the color company) in particular, had responded promptly to every order to advance, no matter the danger. According to Partridge, they understood "the desperate need of the hour" and that it was imperative that they "hold the line till night should come to the rescue of the remnant of an army still fighting with Gen. Thomas."[44]

Historian Steven E. Woodworth described the scene as night began to fall: "Thomas made his difficult fighting withdrawal in the face of the repeated Confederate attacks . . . his tired troops marched northward through the darkness to the sound of Rebel yells back at the battlefield." While Thomas withdrew toward Rossville, the 96th Illinois and 121st Ohio remained, responding to the irregular skirmish fire that continued for a time. They were the last organized body to leave the field. Captain Hicks recalled, "Never did I long for sunset as on that Sunday at Chickamauga."[45]

Sgt. Edward Murray's Ordeal

With so much loss and suffering that day, the experiences of Sgt. Edward Murray stand out. During the initial assault on Horseshoe Ridge in which Lt. Colonel Clarke was mortally wounded, Murray was also wounded.

The 96th could advance no farther. As they fell back, William Lewin came close by Ed Murray. "Billy will you help me off the field?" Murray asked.

"Are you hit, Ed?"

"Yes."

With compassion for his fallen comrade, Lewin threw his rifle over his right shoulder and reached down. Murray caught Lewin's hand with both of his, but he could not be moved. He was "a dead weight" with "no power to help myself."[46]

"I can't lift you, what will I do?" Lewin asked. Looking over his shoulder he saw the tide of battle coming. "Here are the Rebs right at me."

"Run Billy, I am all right," Murray said. Lewin ran and Murray was left in the enemy's hands. Moments later, Lewin was grazed by a "bullet slightly cutting his head and plowing a deep furrow about ten inches in length along his back," disabling him for the remainder of the battle.[47]

The line of Rebels quickly passed Murray, and a battery swung into position less than seventy feet from where he lay. As the battle raged, Murray worried for his comrades. Even in this dangerous position, Sergeant Murray's thoughts drifted to his men. Two more lines of Confederate infantry passed over him, and then the Federals rallied and the Rebels retreated. "Almost the entire afternoon was occupied with charges and counter charges, the Regiment alternately advancing and falling back, driving the enemy only to be driven in turn."[48]

Amid the frenzy of battle, Murray was helpless to act. He spent that afternoon between the lines, "exposed to the fire of both friend and foe." While he lay on his back with his hands across his chest, he was struck in the left shoulder by another minié ball. The ball came out near the elbow on the inside of his arm, and since he could not move his arm, he thought it was broken. Another ball hit him on the "flesh part of my hip," and a fourth "hit his tin cup."[49]

Toward dusk the Rebels had rallied, pushing the Federals back. The Confederate lines passed over Murray, and one Rebel stopped and picked up Murray's gun, "which was a very nice one." Battlefield salvage of weapons was common by soldiers on both sides. The Rebel took Murray's cartridges and left his old gun in place of Murray's Enfield.[50]

It was nearly dark and a soldier dressed in blue came along. "Partner, will you help me off the field?" Murray asked.

"Is that you Ed?"

Murray recognized the voice of Henry P. Barnum.

"I can't Ed. I am wounded myself." Barnum was "badly wounded through the face." After he left Murray's side, he momentarily became a prisoner as the Rebel line passed him.[51]

Later that evening, Murray heard the Rebels "making the woods ring with their hurrahs and the Rebel yell." They had captured a number of prisoners and flags. When the celebration quieted, Murray heard the buzz of conversation and activity in the Rebel camp. "I had time to think of my home and loved ones and whether I would ever see them."[52]

That night, Ed Murray's thoughts were distracted by a soldier some distance from him, calling out for water at the top of his voice. Two Rebel soldiers came out of their camp and gave him water. They saw his thighs were broken and picked him up carefully, carrying him to a campfire and laid him down. Then they went to another wounded soldier and picked him up, taking him to the fireside. Next, they came to Murray and asked if he was "fit." Murray told them he was paralyzed, and they carried him to the fire and laid him down. The agonizing sounds of the wounded prompted many a soldier to take pity on his enemy.[53]

In his injured state, Murray was afraid of being too close to the fire with leaves on the ground. On the march over the battlefield that day, he had seen wounded Union soldiers burned up because they were unable to get out of the way of fires. With some urgency, Murray got the Rebels to brush all the leaves away. They asked him if he had a blanket, which he did not. One remarked that it was "too cold . . . to lie there without one." He went to find a blanket but was not gone long, for "there were so many dead lying around." He returned with a thick, soft woolen blanket, but it was butternut in color. Murray knew it had come from a Confederate soldier, but thanked him "very kindly" all the same.[54]

"That was a night stamped on my memory that can never be erased as long as life lasts. I was in no pain whatever. I knew everything that was transpiring about me and yet I lay there perfectly helpless with my thoughts centered on my far away home and my loved ones and how, or when, or if ever I should see them." Memories of his life in Illinois flooded Murray's mind as he thought of his wife Nancy, their young children, and the farm that he had labored so hard to build. The realization that he could die in this place without his family around him to hear his last words was impossible to accept. It was a long night not knowing his fate and listening to the suffering of soldiers left on the field. In the distance, the whistle of a locomotive at Ringgold announced trainloads of Confederate troops arriving to the front. On hearing that whistle, Ed Murray prayed for his own survival and that of the Union Army.[55]

By ten o'clock on the night of September 20, the Battle of Chickamauga was over. The defeated Army of the Cumberland was forced to leave the field, abandoning their dead and wounded. The men of the 96th fell back and were constantly in search of their comrades, as the day's fighting had separated many from the regiment. Captain Hicks and his remaining men eventually encountered Colonel Champion's party. Together the groups formed a line. "Never mind your Companies," Colonel Champion said. "Let us get into line, somehow what there is left of us! . . . Dress up on the colors!" There were few comrades left, and the colors were in tatters from minié balls and grapeshot, but the men formed their last line of battle before leaving the field in case of any attack.[56] No more shots were fired.

The men were numb from battle and faint from loss of blood, fatigue, and dehydration, and yet most had to walk—or shuffle—miles back to camp. As Partridge described it years later, there were many scenes of "devotion manifested by comrades for their wounded friends . . . men were carried in blankets for miles . . . they were borne upon the back, or two comrades would support a third between them," all the way until they made camp at Rossville.[57]

Partridge observed that the men, "dusty" and "powder-grimed," were so hoarse from exhaustion and lack of water that they could "hardly speak above a whisper." They gathered around campfires, sipping coffee and eating a bit of hardtack, "the sensibilities of the mind and heart stunned by the dreadful work." Now that they had a moment to pause and were relatively safe, they began to contemplate what had been won and lost. With devastation and despair around them, the soldiers had time to reflect on their actions in battle, their own survival, and concern for comrades left on the field.[58]

For the thirty-five men of Company C, Partridge recorded that "twenty-five had been hit, and nearly every one of the remaining ten had bullet-holes through his clothing or accoutrements." Among Company C's wounded were Ed Murray, Billy Lewin, and John Taylor. Loughlin Madden, the only man from the Newport Township Stateline Road group who came through the battle unharmed, feared for his comrades as he searched the camp for any word of them. With so many missing, not knowing whether they had died or were wounded and lying on the battlefield brought worry and sadness. In a single afternoon at Chickamauga, the 96th Illinois lost 225 men killed, wounded, and missing, vastly outnumbering their losses from sickness, disease, and desertion during the course of their first year of service. The magnitude of this sudden and traumatic loss was difficult to comprehend. In the heat of battle, the men had to carry on—kill or be killed—but now miles from the battlefield they "discussed the incidents of the day in undertones." They "were sad, for so many were gone."[59]

During the fighting, troops had charged the enemy with fixed bayonets. Most of the men of the 96th Illinois had never been in a skirmish, let alone a battle, and taken another man's life. Facing an enemy in hand-to-hand combat made it even more difficult to kill. A soldier looking into his enemy's face made killing personal and instinctively repulsive. Drew Gilpin Faust explained that for the God-fearing men in the ranks, killing "violated fundamental biblical law." One justification for their violent acts that eased their conscience was the sin of slavery.[60]

Charles Partridge was forthcoming about his battle experience: "While crossing the open field where the shells were bursting all around us, I at first felt a disposition to dodge. When we heard the hiss [we] would drop down. I did so two or three times, but growing indifferent I paid but little attention to them. When we made the charge, I had not the least sense of fear and was actually surprised when I was hit. When we fell back, I first felt afraid. One shell burst close to me, throwing dirt and bark all over me and wounding two or three of our boys." He admitted to being afraid, but only "at first" when they fell back, bearing out the vulnerable position of retreating troops and an assertion of bravery in the face of great odds.[61]

They were also aware that "[a]ll of the dead and many of the severely wounded were lying unprotected and uncared for on the battlefield." The field was not theirs, and the inability to care for their wounded brothers-in-arms and bury their dead weighed heavily on their hearts. Victorian-era death customs were centered on the family at a loved one's side to care for them and hear their final words. Faust explained that the war upended these traditions and their "most fundamental assumptions about life's value and meaning." George Smith anticipated that in days to come "when I get to thinking about it I will choke and tears of gratitude come into my eyes to think that one of us after feeling such a storm of lead and Iron should have escaped, but such is the chances of every battle."[62]

The next morning's roll call made it all too clear. Partridge grieved: "[H]ow heavy had been our loss." The 96th Illinois had been in the front line and at the right where the danger and work was greatest. "It had charged the most frequently, penetrated farthest to the front, held its advanced positions longest, and was always slowest in falling back." In Granger's Reserve Corps, the highest losses were sustained by units in Whitaker's First Brigade. The 96th Illinois had the third highest percentage of losses at 54 percent killed, wounded, or missing. The 89th Ohio suffered a 65 percent loss, and the largest losses were sustained by the 22nd Michigan at 85 percent. Though other units had larger losses, the 96th's regimental history declared its losses "the heaviest of any Regiment in the Reserve Corps." It was not unusual for regiments to vie for recognition, and one way to achieve that was to glorify the number of its dead. As Faust explained, for the veterans, "deaths became a measure not of defeat but of victory."[63]

The 22nd Michigan's devastating loss was felt so keenly that for thirty years its survivors searched for the regimental colors lost at Chickamauga. In 1895, while in Washington, D.C., veteran James Greeson found a book with an inventory of property captured at the surrender of Richmond in 1865, which listed "two flags of the 22nd Michigan Infantry." By an act of Congress, the flags were returned to the regiment's veterans at their reunion in Pontiac, Michigan, on September 4, 1895.[64]

With its fighting force depleted by more than half, the men of the 96th steeled themselves against indulging in "emotions of grief." The survivors were relieved they had made it through the fire. Capt. George Hicks expressed that they understood they needed to brace themselves "to meet the peril of another day. The danger to our army with the cause of our country closely linked to that army's fate was still imminent." James M. McPherson noted that soldiers, "at some level at least, *meant* what they said about sacrificing their lives for their country."[65]

That night after he reached camp, Lt. Col. John C. Smith of Company I (promoted after Clarke's death) wrote to his wife Charlotte: "Love every one of the 96th for they have done nobly. No Regt on the field have done better." Most soldiers were volunteers, and many northern soldiers fought with patriotic fervor. Like Smith's, their letters and diaries were filled with great awareness for what was at stake. McPherson explained, "This was, after all, a *civil war*. Its outcome would determine the fate of the nation."[66]

Especially troubling for the men of Company C was the loss of William Bonner, a tentmate and friend of John Taylor. Bonner was "shot through the body" in the first charge on Horseshoe Ridge and never seen again. In the chaos of the battle, he was "left upon the field," but no one could confirm his death. One comrade's report made it back to Bonner's family stating that William had been propped against a tree, still alive, but when his friends went back to tend to him, he was gone. Sgt. Charles Partridge echoed this scenario: "Some thought that Bonner was mortally wounded. He was carried a short distance back when the boys left him to make a charge." The regimental account stated, "doubtless dying within a few hours." Since no body was found, he was reported missing.[67]

Months later his whereabouts were still in question when Billy Lewin wrote, "I have not seen any one that has seen or heard any thing of Wm Bonner since the battle of Chickamauga." For many years, family and friends clung to the belief that Bonner had survived and would return home. Their hearts leapt each time a lone man came walking down the road, stirring up dust and their hopes. Bonner's demise was never satisfactorily explained, and his final resting place remains unknown. Drew Gilpin Faust wrote that not knowing their loved one's fate "left a 'dread void of uncertainty' that knowledge would never fill."[68]

News of the battle reached comrades who had not been in the fight. James Taylor had been transferred from the convalescent camp at Bridgeport to the hospital at Stevenson to make room for the incoming wounded. He wrote in his diary on September 22, "Learned in the evening papers that our division had done splendid fighting. Feel very anxious about the results among the boys especially John."[69] It would take nearly a week for James to learn that his brother had been wounded, and a full three weeks before he heard from John directly.

Chickamauga was by far the deadliest battle fought in the West. It was second only to Gettysburg (July 1–3, 1863) in the number of lives lost during the entire war. General Rosecrans's army suffered a staggering 16,215 casualties. The Confederates had more than 18,454 casualties, their dead and wounded intermingled with Northerners on the field. Throughout the afternoon, Longstreet's repeated assaults on Horseshoe Ridge were repulsed. The Union lines held thanks to the determination of Major General Thomas. Thomas ordered a general retreat only after nightfall. For his fierce resolve to hold the Union position, even after his commanding officer had left the field, Thomas was thereafter known as the "Rock of Chickamauga."[70] Despite the Confederates' greater losses, this was their largest victory in the Western Theater. It soon became a strategic loss when the Federals were allowed to escape to Chattanooga.

After the fight, Thomas praised Steedman and the men of his First Division: "You have saved my Corps." The 96th's Captain Hicks recalled, "That was a deed worthy to be proud of." Partridge recounted that during that dreadful afternoon, the 96th Illinois "stood out, manfully, as if courting death . . . while the dread storm of shot and shell raged over the timbered ridges, and the hills and valleys reverberated with the roar of battle."[71]

The *Nashville Daily Union* reported, "A tremendous effort has evidently been made by the expiring rebellion to destroy Rosecrans's army, by concentrating against it a force too large for him to resist with the least probability of success. . . . They rushed upon our gallant army like an avalanche; but it seems to have been an avalanche dashing against a mountain."[72]

The Reserve Corps was praised for its "heroic action" on Sunday afternoon. Partridge wrote that the 96th as part of the reserve had "fought more than three times its own numbers." It had "hurled itself against the solid lines of the enemy," and despite terrible odds, it remained on the field until nightfall, allowing Thomas to withdraw his forces.[73]

In his post-battle report, Colonel Champion stated that the "[o]fficers and men behaved with great gallantry." He made special note that "the most conspicuous in rallying and encouraging the men" were Capt. George Hicks, who led the regiment after the loss of Lieutenant Colonel Clarke, and Lt. Charles W. Earle. Earle was wounded twice but never left the field. Brigadier General Whitaker took note that the "Ninety-sixth Illinois, Colonel Champion, fought with bold impetuosity, efficiency, and gallantry." And Major General Rosecrans wrote, "Never, in the history of this war at least, have troops fought with greater energy and determination. Bayonet charges, often heard of but seldom seen, were repeatedly made by brigades and regiments in several of our divisions."[74]

The County of Lake was also rightfully proud of the men of the 96th. The *Waukegan Gazette*'s editor James Y. Cory, an outspoken abolitionist, wrote, "There is no better fighting material in the Union army than that which has gone from Little Lake." Charles Partridge echoed their bravery: "The boys of Company C did as well and I think better than any others for they all kept together around the colors. . . . Six out of eight of the Color Guard were killed or wounded. The flag staffs were shot to pieces and the pieces brought off by Corporal Swanbrough of Company G."[75]

In a grand patriotic gesture, the Lake County Supervisors appropriated fifty dollars "towards purchasing new colors for the 96th Regiment." A few citizens of Waukegan as well as Jo Daviess County raised additional funds. The *Waukegan Gazette* reported, "The colors will soon be on their way to the regiment and in return we shall receive two of the four battle torn flags of the glorious 96th. They will be souvenirs of the war and of the prowess of the Lake County boys which our people will highly prize."[76]

5. ❀ The Faded Coat of Blue

"**O**ur forces were not routed," the editor of the *Waukegan Gazette* emphatically stated on September 26. After "gallantly [driving] the enemy with heavy loss," the 96th Illinois as part of Granger's Reserve Corps "fell back to their present position in good order, and are now considered impregnable" at Chattanooga. "Rosecrans, with his splendid western army, will be completely triumphant. God grant that he may." The following month the paper ran a tribute to Lieutenant Colonel Clarke: "He was an ever watchful and kind friend to his men; in battle he was clear and cool headed . . . amid the terrible storm of lead and iron at Chickamauga, he was as self-possessed and apparently unconscious of danger, as if he had been riding in the streets of Waukegan."[1]

The heroic language used in the *Gazette* was not simply a prosaic method for a community to find meaning in the loss of loved ones. The Civil War was the first time the American press had focused on something other than politics. Newspapers were political entities; their main purpose was to promote one party over another. Consequently, journalists were suddenly at a loss for words, so they turned to the chivalrous language of combat from the Old World to describe the war. Their poetic language belied the modernity of the Civil War battlefield, but the losses and sacrifices were still abundantly clear to readers. Loyal Northerners turned to newspapers and *Harper's Weekly* magazine for news from the battlefronts, hungering for information and opinions on military affairs.[2]

In response to the terrible news of the battle, women on the home front were quick to rally. The Ladies' Soldiers Aid Society planned a dinner and dance at Mother Rudd's in Gurnee. The goal was to raise funds for the "relief of the sick and wounded soldiers . . . particularly from Chattanooga, where so many of our brave boys now lie suffering." The U.S. Sanitary Commission received all of its donations from these local aid societies. Civilians were confident in the Sanitary Commission's efforts and praised the aid and comfort they brought to soldiers. The commission and other female-dominated charities were critical of the military medical services' care of the soldiers.[3]

Ideally, women wanted their soldiers sent home so they could care for them in the customary way. Moving wounded any distance could be detrimental, and army leadership wanted men with minor wounds or illnesses returned to their units as soon as possible. This was accomplished by constructing hospitals near regiments. A furlough system developed, but the vast majority of men could not be sent home. Women found it necessary to advocate for positions as nurses in hospitals where they could provide the care they were experienced in giving. Meanwhile, medical services worked to build the infrastructure necessary to treat the overwhelming number of sick and wounded.[4]

With his own personal resources, Henry Blodgett, the brother of Company D's Capt. Asiel Blodgett, started for the front. Once he reached the regiment encamped at Moccasin Point, he spent several days there and in hospitals, assisting the boys of the 96th and 51st Illinois Regiments and gathering information for the folks at home. Eight days after the battle, Blodgett sent a letter from Nashville to the *Waukegan Gazette*: "The severely wounded are still back at Chattanooga. Col. Clarke's body has been encased and forwarded by express. . . . The men from the 96th are all scattered about, and it is doubtful whether I could find them all without staying a week, as it would take at least that time to go through all the hospitals."[5] His list of the killed and wounded was diligently compiled, as he knew that so many were waiting for news.

Descriptions of the battle continued to arrive through newspapers and letters home. The story of Granger's Reserve Corps coming to reinforce Major General Thomas was given particular attention. Locals understood that Lake County boys were among Granger's troops and gloried in the account of their impressive arrival: "Suddenly a vast cloud of dust was seen to rise above the trees, away to the left, and a few minutes afterwards a long line of men emerged from the woods. . . . Their discipline seemed very perfect, and it was an imposing pageant when, as they came on their banners fluttered above their heads, and their glittering arms flashed back the sunlight through the thick clouds of dust."[6]

Lt. Theodore F. Clarkson of Company D, who was wounded at Chickamauga and recovering at a hospital in Chattanooga, gathered information about the wounded and sent it home to be published in the local paper. Through his reporting, the *Waukegan Gazette* clarified the 96th's role: "The impression has prevailed here to some extent that Granger's corps, in which the 96th reg't was, were held as a reserve and would only be used in case of an emergency. This is an error, for, according to the above authority, this corps was in the extreme front, left wing, and were in the hottest of the engagement nearly the entire time." This emphatic explanation of the 96th's role in the battle was an expression of soldierly esprit de corps and patriotism.[7]

Weeks passed before most families received a letter from their "soldier boy" or one of his comrades. It took sixteen days for Pvt. George Smith to write to his sister in Millburn. "I suppose you have all heard of the fight in which we were engaged at Chickamauga, and are all waiting with beating hearts to hear the result." For Smith, the army's heavy losses were difficult to comprehend. "Every Parent, Sister or Brother is thinking that their own dear son, Brother or Father is purhaps now lying Dead or wounded on the Field of strife." While Smith was one of the few fortunate to have survived nearly unscathed—he had a "bullet mark his foot"—Edward Murray remained in a terrible position.[8]

Confederate general Bragg reported, "Ten Miles South of Chattanooga, September 21, 1863. The enemy retreated on Chattanooga last night, leaving his dead and wounded in our hands. His loss is very large in men, artillery, small-arms, and colors. Ours is heavy, but not yet ascertained. The victory is complete, and our cavalry is pursuing."[9]

As dawn broke on September 21, Confederate troops gathered on the field, coming a short distance from where Murray lay. Murray was incapable of getting out of the way, and he thought he would be killed if there was "another terrible day of fighting." He asked a Rebel officer, "Friend, will you see that we are taken off the field before the fighting commences?" The officer agreed and "raising his hand beckoned with his finger, and shortly afterwards came four men with a stretcher." The Rebel soldiers set the stretcher on the ground, but chose to take a soldier with broken legs.[10]

Long minutes later they returned, and Murray silently willed them to take him, but again they took another man and "left me alone with the dead around me." In daylight, the horror of the battlefield was in plain view, and Murray was in a "terrible suspense" waiting for the stretcher-bearers to come back. His anxiety had a firm grip on his mind as he longed for home. In this vulnerable condition, Murray's only hope was to voice his concerns. "It seemed to me hours when it might have been but a few minutes, for I thought they never would come, but they did, and put me on the stretcher, lifted me on their shoulders and off they went."[11]

Murray was placed on the ground near the chimney of a frame house. There he realized the Confederates had been "collecting the wounded all morning for there were some hundreds lying around on the ground as far as I could see." The woman who lived in the house "gave the wounded every attention her limited means would allow." Murray recalled that "[she] was very kind to me and would come out and sit beside me and visit." She told him how she went into her cellar during the battle, "out of harm's way . . . and her house was riddled with bullets from both armies." It was not uncommon for civilians to aid soldiers, even enemy soldiers. The woman was curious about him, and he shared how he had left everything to fight to save the Union. She brought him chicken broth every day, which was all he lived on while he lay immobilized. "She would often say 'poor fellow, wish you were home,' and I wished so too," Murray wrote. "[B]ut for this old lady and her half pint of broth I must have died."[12]

By the fourth or fifth day after the battle, two Union surgeons came through the lines to assess the wounded. When they reached him, the blood from his wounds had become hard and dry, requiring them to cut his shirt to examine him. "They took a silver probe about seven inches long to try and feel the bullet. But it was not long enough to reach it." He asked them for medicine, but they had none, and considered Murray too critical for care. They left him, saying he "was another poor fellow who could not live long." Many surgeons lacked adequate training and supplies, unable to cope with the overwhelming numbers of war wounded. "That night I thought I should die with the cold," he recalled. "When morning came I saw a piece of white blanket and asked the Rebel nurse if he would get it for me and he helped me up and I got off my blouse and took my knife and cut a couple of holes in the blanket, wrapped it around my body and put on my blouse."[13]

Each night there were several deaths, and each morning the dead were carried to a rail fence nearby and thrown into a pile. The stench was unbearable. Since the Federals had lost control of the field, it was up to the Confederates to bury the Union dead, which they did in mass graves. Several months later, Union troops returned to begin the process of identifying and re-burying their dead.

On Sunday, September 27, one week after being wounded and taken prisoner, Murray and "those that were alive" were loaded onto mule-drawn wagons and taken a long distance over a portion of the battlefield. They were unaware that General Bragg had agreed to hand over the Union wounded, and this was the first step in that process. "Dead men were strewn all over the field," Murray remembered. "Some places five or six or maybe a dozen lying in a heap, just where they fell, and they had been in this position one whole week without burial."[14] There was a lack of preparation—on both sides—for how to handle the great number of wounded and dead.

The wounded were unloaded at a "cow yard" near some tobacco sheds. "The second day I was here," Murray recounted, "one of my comrades named Budman who laid close beside me died." Cpl. Squire W. Inman, or "Budman," was from Antioch, Illinois. He was an acting color corporal at Chickamauga and was severely wounded in one of his legs and left on the field. Though he appeared to be less seriously wounded than most, he quickly began "losing ground, and in a few days, to the surprise of most of those who knew him, he died."[15]

Before his death, Squire told Edward, "I don't know as I shall live to get home and I have a few little trinkets. I wish you would take and give them to my folks." Soldiers who realized their fate often gave instructions for the distribution of their possessions to provide comfort to their loved ones or to exert some final control. Edward agreed, but he told his friend that Inman would make it home before him. The army had no formalized method of notifying families of deaths, and so these pacts became common between men. This exchange gave the corporal some solace in his last hours as Murray became his surrogate family and took the responsibility of the deathwatch. Murray "faithfully complied" with the request and tucked his comrade's personal items in his haversack.[16]

On September 29, a Rebel soldier informed the prisoners that they were being paroled and sent back into their lines. The Rebel wrote down each man's name, regiment, company, rank and state. Then he requested they raise their right hands and swear not to "reveal anything . . . about their army as to numbers or fortifications." To Edward it was a small thing to ask in exchange for his freedom. "I shall never forget the joy I felt at being again inside our own lines with the prospect of getting home."[17]

The Federals sent hundreds of ambulances to bring out the wounded, but Murray was not near the line of ambulances and fretted about being missed. "After a number had been loaded and drove out I felt I must make some exertion, so I rolled over and got on my hands and knees, pulled my blanket and haversack up to me and dragged myself along a little . . . in time got in the way, when two men got hold of me and brought me up to the ambulance. . . . A man . . . gave me a little tin cup [of whisky]. . . . I drank it with relish and it warmed me up and helped to strengthen me for the long ride." He was right to be anxious, since not all of the Union wounded could be carried out that day. Murray was one of 250 men transported on September 29.[18]

After stopping at two army hospitals in Chattanooga and finding them full, the ambulance continued to what Murray described as a depot building.

He was "carried upstairs and laid on a cot in a large hall and two doctors came to me with their nurses, who washed me. The doctors examined my wounds and probed it to find the ball but it was too deep in to reach and one said: 'there's another poor fellow.' They put a clean shirt on me and laid me down on this clean, fresh cot, with white cover and I felt refreshed although I was tired out."[19]

On Thursday, October 1, Murray was moved into a large room with other wounded and placed on a cotton mattress on the floor. He asked the nurse to get a sheet of paper from his knapsack. Then the nurse "raised me up so that I wrote just a few lines telling [my wife] I was wounded, but did not know how bad and would make for home as soon as I could."[20] By then his family was sick with worry, having heard reports of the battle. When his letter arrived in Nancy's hands, the Murrays sent his older brother John to fetch him home.

Not even Murray's comrades were sure of his fate, such was the chaos of the battle and its aftermath. Sgt. Charles Partridge wrote to his father, "Some thought Murray killed, and I doubt if he is yet alive, but he may be."[21]

Having a view of the hallway, Ed Murray watched as people passed. One day he recognized a soldier and called out. Thomas J. Smith (Company I) came into the room and looked down at Murray lying on the mattress and said, "You have the advantage of me."

"Don't you know Sergeant Murray?"

"My God, is that you?" Smith asked.

He shook Murray's hands, and with tears in his eyes he told Murray he was glad to see him. This was the first that any of his comrades knew Murray was alive. They had given him up as killed in the battle.[22]

On October 4, the wounded were boarded onto ambulance wagons headed for the field hospital at Stevenson, Alabama, due to the very real threat of General Bragg attacking Chattanooga. The hospital at Stevenson had been completed at the end of August in preparation of the army's advance. Murray was carried on a man's back and put into an ambulance before being taken across the Tennessee River on a pontoon bridge. Over the next several days, the ambulance train made slow progress over the "roughest road" Murray ever saw. The mountain pass was so steep that Murray described it as "rock climbing up, almost standing on our heads . . . then we would be going down, nearly standing on our feet." The jolting ride exacerbated the men's wounds, but despite Murray's suffering, it "buoyed" him knowing he "was going towards home."[23]

When Murray's ambulance arrived in Stevenson on October 6 or 7, the troops stationed there rushed to see if they knew anyone. Captain Hicks

(Company A) was the first person Murray recognized. The next was James Taylor, who looked in the ambulance and asked, "Are any of the 96th boys here?"

"Yes," Murray said.

Taylor knew Murray's voice, but looking at him said, "I would never have known you."[24]

In the two weeks since being wounded, Murray had suffered blood loss, paralysis, near starvation, exposure to the elements, and a fear that had shaken him to the core. James Taylor was happy to see Ed Murray alive, but his thoughts quickly turned to his brother. Unfortunately, Ed had no news of John. All James knew was that John had been wounded and sent to a hospital in Nashville.[25]

After being shot in the right wrist on the afternoon of Sunday, September 20, John Taylor was incapable of going on with the fight. He was unable to load and fire his rifle, making him useless to his comrades. Charles Partridge explained: "There was no organized force of stretcher-bearers in the Reserve Corps, and only such of the wounded as could walk, or a few who were assisted by their comrades, were able to reach Rossville that night."[26]

The soft lead minié ball that struck Taylor had shattered his wrist, destroying the flesh and muscle and splintering bones beyond repair. The pain of his injury was dizzying, but somehow he made it across the hilly terrain in the midst of acrid smoke and bullets falling around him, and finally out of range to find the white flag of a field hospital. With the great number of injured flooding into the hospital, little time could be spared for any man. Taylor was examined by a surgeon to determine the severity of the wound. The news John received was not good.[27]

A wounded Charles Partridge described the scene at the field hospital: "When I got back about a mile, where the Doctor was dressing wounds, I received some attention, had the ball cut out, [from my hip] and rested perhaps an hour. During that time, it seemed as though all of Co. C. came back wounded." John Taylor and Billy Lewin "came before I left."[28]

The surgeons at the multiple Federal field hospitals were quickly overrun with wounded, and with the Union's retreat from the field, those not in enemy hands were taken by any means toward Chattanooga. "In the retreat every vehicle, baggage wagon, and supply train, as well as the ambulances, were filled with wounded." The hospitals were soon crowded to capacity, and the men had to be moved further still. Partridge wrote, "I walked to our camp in Rossville, where I arrived a little after eight P.M. In less than an hour afterward, the Company, eleven strong, came into camp. Notwithstanding the gloomy circumstances, the boys were quite jovial, each trying to keep up the spirits of the other." Once in camp at Rossville, the men lay down on the ground in exhaustion, hunger, and shock. George Hicks noted, "With the sensibilities of the mind and the heart stunned by the dreadful work of that afternoon, and with physical powers almost utterly exhausted, we were glad to throw ourselves down upon our blankets and obtain rest and sleep."[29]

Partridge remained in Rossville until September 25, when he went on to Bridgeport, Alabama, before finally arriving in Nashville on September 26. His fellow wounded comrades likely followed the same route and timeline. John Taylor reached Nashville by September 26, where he was assigned to Hospital No. 12 at the Broadway Hotel. Meanwhile, at the Stevenson field hospital, James Taylor took to nursing the battle wounded. Due to the number in need of attention and despite his own poor health, James was asked to assist but given little training. In many respects, the wounded were considered an unnecessary burden, since they were no longer able to bear arms. That the sick cared for the sick was an established military principle.[30]

James Taylor had charge of a tent and requested that the surgeon assign Ed Murray to him. Soldiers often took responsibility for one another's care, and Taylor became a surrogate for Murray's family. With the order approved, the ambulance brought Murray to the tent and he was lifted onto a cot. Taylor dressed the wounds and gave Murray "sulphate of morphine" to relieve pain and allow him to sleep.[31] Murray's discomfort continued as the bruises he received coming over the mountains made it difficult for him to find an agreeable position. He suffered night sweats, which required Taylor to change his shirt and bedding.

Between October 10 and 17, John Murray arrived from home to care for his brother. When John came inside the tent, Ed "put [his arms] around [his] neck and sobbed like a child." The emotional reunion, which included news of his wife and children, overwhelmed Ed, who just days before had thought he would never see his loved ones again. John had come to take Ed home, but it was not that simple. The doctor felt that Ed could not be moved in his condition, and so John Murray spent the next three weeks trying to strengthen Ed by procuring fruit and "milk punch"—a medicinal drink made with condensed milk and whiskey, and sometimes sugar and nutmeg—each day to bolster Ed's spirits. John also obtained a pair of crutches, but Ed had no control of his right leg. It was a difficult process for John Murray and James Taylor to help Ed onto the crutches, and Ed found it extremely painful to have one foot and then the other pushed forward.[32]

Back home, friends from the Millburn neighborhood met at John Strang's home for an apple bee, where they pared, cored, and strung to be dried nearly twenty bushels of apples for the soldiers. The *Waukegan Gazette* wrote, "Let the boys and girls of other neighborhoods, emulate this noble example set by those of Millburn. Apples are plenty in the County. . . . [L]et them be dried or made into cider apple sauce and sent to the hospitals." Almost every neighborhood had an aid society, and the apples from Millburn orchards became part of an organized donation to the U.S. Sanitary Commission. A procession of nearly one hundred wagons, ornamented with patriotic inscriptions and flags and loaded with fruit, vegetables, quilts, and bandages was coordinated by John G. Ragan of Waukegan. On October 27, the wagons were driven directly to the Sanitary Fair in Chicago.[33]

On October 19, James Taylor learned the shocking news that his brother's right arm had been amputated. Considering that the arm had not been amputated sooner indicates either John's reluctance or the surgeon's belief that the wound would heal. Minié balls were notorious for shattering bone. Margaret Humphreys explained, "[S]uch wounds, with broken skin and bone in multiple fragments, rarely healed successfully." With his condition worsening, the right arm was amputated on October 8, nineteen days after he was wounded at Chickamauga. The vast number of amputations during the war led some soldiers to call surgeons "butchers." But as Humphreys noted, a surgeon's decision to amputate was based on a belief that "the man would otherwise die from his wound."[34]

John Taylor also suffered from malaria at the hospital, which James referred to as "ague chill." The symptoms were fever and shakes, which were treated with quinine and sometimes whiskey or opium for pain. At the time, the connection between insects (mosquitoes) and disease was unknown, and instead the "bad air" in the hospital was blamed. As Ira Rutkow concluded, the military hospital system "was doing all it could to upgrade the treatment of the sick and wounded," but it was mired in the "medical primitiveness of the times." Men who survived were often permanently impaired by disease and wounds that would not heal.[35]

James Taylor was now in a fit to be reunited with his brother in order to nurse him back to health. James's doctor "[p]romised to send Ed and me off first chance so I could see him." On October 20, James went to Dr. David McKibbin, the surgeon in charge of the Stevenson hospital, to get a pass to Nashville; however, he was denied, despite other patients being sent. The next day James received a letter from his brother "stating his case in a much more cheerful manner than Barnum had." While being treated for his battle wounds, Henry P. Barnum had visited with John in Nashville.[36]

Ed's brother John was able to secure a pass to take him to Nashville where he could be furloughed. When the sick train arrived on October 31, James dutifully prepared Ed to leave. James again spoke to Dr. McKibbin, but his impatience and temper "spoiled the whole," and he was not given a pass. To add insult to injury, James was ordered to return to his regiment for duty. James's last best hope to provide care for his brother was to have John Murray take John Taylor home.[37]

Ed Murray was loaded onto an ambulance wagon and transported to the hospital train, a scene that James Taylor must have watched with mixed emotions. The ambulance was unable to get close to the railroad tracks, requiring John Murray to carry his invalid brother on his back to the boxcar. Two men stood in the door and lifted Ed off John's back, placing him in a bunk reserved for him in the car. John Murray went back to the ambulance for their belongings, but before he could return, the train started to move. To be separated now was not an option after spending weeks restoring Ed's health, so John ran alongside the train, tossing their bags inside, and then clasped hands with the men to pull him into the car. With a sigh of relief, John joined his brother at his bunk for their journey to Nashville.[38]

Murray was assigned to the Cumberland Relief Hospital where he and his brother stayed for nearly a month waiting for his furlough papers. The hospital headed by Maj. Burkitt Cloak, a Kentucky surgeon with the U.S. Volunteers Medical Staff, was located south of Nashville and consisted of wooden pavilions with a capacity of nine hundred beds. Ira Rutkow noted that the pavilion-style hospitals were designed to provide maximum air circulation to negate any "foul air" from "bodily secretions and patients' breathing."[39]

Four days later on November 4, James Taylor wrote in his diary that a "Sanitary agent for Illinois" had inquired about Ed Murray, but had given him no news of his brother. "I think [the agent] is rather negligent when I stayed to help Ed and missed my chance to go north." The situation was regrettable for a faithful soldier whose only request was to be at his brother's side. Perhaps more frustrating was that James knew that John Murray was with John Taylor and had heard nothing. "I think he might drop me a few lines frequently for I threw away some chances of getting up there. John was doing well when I last heard from him but I am very much pained at his continued silence for I know there are plenty around that would willingly write for him."[40]

Although his health was not fully restored, James Taylor left the Stevenson field hospital—as ordered—on November 7 to join the 96th Illinois at Nickajack Cove, Tennessee. Here he was again in the company of Billy Lewin, who had recovered sufficiently from his battle wound to be put on picket guard for three days and nights. After hearing the news from James Taylor, Lewin wrote home that Ed Murray was "getting well fast" and that John Taylor's arm had been amputated.[41]

Determined to fulfill his promise to James Taylor, John Murray made daily visits to Hospital No. 12 to see John Taylor. As it turned out, Taylor's state was "very low," which was common for surgical patients after an operation. Amputations resulted in more complications than successes, as difficulties such as infections were largely not understood. Taylor's low state was compounded by the melancholy of separation from his brother and closest comrades, but John Murray did all he could to bolster Taylor's state of mind by visiting him every day.[42]

John Murray tended to Taylor in much the same manner as James had cared for Ed. He found ways to build Taylor's spirit and health, perhaps by reading to him from the *Nashville Daily Union* newspaper, changing the cloth dressings from his amputation (surgeons bandaged the wound rather than suture it to allow it to drain), or getting him to drink whiskey in lemonade to keep his spirits from falling even lower. Contrary as it may seem, the delay of nineteen days before Taylor's arm was amputated increased his odds of dying. Amputations performed within seventy-two hours of receiving the wound had far better success rates than those undertaken later after "inflammation" had set in.[43]

When the day finally came for the Murrays to head home, John Murray again visited John Taylor, who had not recovered enough to accompany them. It was the morning of Tuesday, November 24, and sadly, it would be their final meeting. With John Murray at his bedside, John Taylor took his last breath. He was just twenty-one years old.[44]

Edward Murray's Return Home

When Ed and John Murray left Nashville on November 24, it was with heavy hearts. John Taylor was the first of Murray's small band of comrades to die. Certainly they had known the risk heading off to war, but now the sacrifice seemed too great to bear. Taylor had enthusiastically done his part to save the Union, but his hopes for a future as an American citizen had come to a tragic and premature end.

The Murray brothers headed to Louisville, Kentucky, by train. There, they took a ferry up the Ohio River and "into our own free country."[45] Edward was exhilarated to be in the North again and making steady progress towards home. In Chicago, they took the last train on the Chicago and North Western.

At two o'clock in the morning on Thursday, November 26—Thanksgiving Day—the Murrays arrived in Kenosha, Wisconsin, the closest station to home. John carried Edward into the depot, setting him on a bench while he went for a wagon at their sister Elizabeth English's house nine blocks away. There was a good deal of excitement on their arrival. Many acquaintances stopped at the English residence to "congratulate" Ed on getting home.[46]

Though Ed was impatient to reunite with his wife and children, President Lincoln had proclaimed this day the first official Thanksgiving. Murray recalled that "nothing would do," but for him and John to "eat Thanksgiving with them." Afterward, a spring wagon was brought up to the house and a mattress put in for Ed to lay down for the ride. Covered in blankets on that cold but sunny day, Ed gazed up at the bright sky, grateful to be among loved ones. News of his return spread, and all along his journey to the Stateline Road community, friends and neighbors poured out of their homes to shake his hand and kiss his cheek, wishing him a happy homecoming.

The first place in the neighborhood they stopped was at his sister Jane Murrie's house. Ed recalled, "They were all out and my little boys"—nine-year-old William and five-year-old Edward—"had come down to meet me. It was a joyful meeting, but still a sad one for me. I felt I was coming home helpless, when I went away strong."[47] It had been fourteen months since he had last seen his family on the depot platform in Waukegan.

Amid the homecoming, the news of John Taylor's death was shared with the Murries, but Edward had not anticipated the grief it would bring. "For my sister's oldest daughter, Nannie, it was sad, as the young man she was engaged to, John Taylor, was dead and when my brother told her that he died the morning we left Nashville, she dropped right down on the ground as if shot." The shock struck the seventeen-year-old as if it was a physical blow. For her, the fear of losing the person she loved—a fear that so many carried during the war—had become a reality.[48]

Her romance with the Scottish lad had been brief. Nannie had become attached to John when he lived with her family as a farm laborer and schoolteacher. Since no letters are known to exist between the pair, Edward Murray's account offers rare evidence of the personal nature of the relationship. Nannie's dreams for their happy future had come to a sudden end. Likewise, the death of a friend was hard to accept, as Billy Lewin, stationed with the regiment at Nickajack Cove, expressed to his friend David Minto: "We were all very sorry to hear of J. Y. Taylor's death."[49]

After the reunion and the wave of emotions at the Murrie homestead, Ed Murray was taken up the road to the front door of his home. There he was lifted out of the wagon. "It was with feelings that can never be forgotten. My wife and the children were greatly affected as well as all in the house. All were greatly excited and in commotion. But oh, how glad I was that I was home again surrounded by my loved ones."[50]

For Nancy Murray, her husband's return brought the welcome duty to care for him in the comfort of their home. She rightly believed she was better suited to nurture and heal him than any military surgeon, but Edward regained his strength slowly. "I was very weak and it did not take much to tire me. . . . It was a long tedious winter to me as I had to be waited on so much." Ed spent much of his time seated on the lounge near the stove to keep warm, and he was prone to fever, coughs, and spitting blood. To strengthen himself, Edward walked across the living room leaning on his wife for support.[51]

Still an enlisted man, Murray had to renew his furlough every thirty days, which required him to see the examining physician, Dr. Benjamin Cory, in Waukegan. In Murray's frail condition, this military requirement was both tiring and troubling. The first time Murray was examined in late December, the doctor was overheard saying that he "might live to spring but it was only a question of time." Murray survived that very cold winter and followed with interest news of his comrades in the 96th Illinois through newspapers and letters from the front. His support of the war had not faltered, but he was a changed man after what he had experienced on the battlefield at Chickamauga. News of battles and of soldiers' deaths weighed heavily on him, as he had seen death and suffering firsthand, some of which he may have caused.[52]

The following spring, in May 1864, Murray received a letter from the U.S. War Department summoning him to the Marine Hospital in Chicago. During the war, the Marine Hospital began accepting soldiers and not just sailors for treatment. On May 9, Ed set off for the hospital "taken under the care" of his neighbor Mr. Wells, who had business in Chicago. By this time, Nancy's attentive care had given Edward the ability to walk a little on his own with a cane. To Murray's astonishment, the doctor told him he would have to go to the front. "I did not see how I could, but he was very short with me and said that was his orders."⁵³ Murray was unprepared for this possibility and had nothing with him. He stayed overnight at the Soldiers' Home, which had been built earlier that year to care for injured soldiers.

The next morning, less than six months since his return home, and as if in a bizarre dream, Murray headed south for Nashville. For the three-day journey, he went by train, ferry, and horse-drawn omnibus. On his arrival, the Provost Guard took him to the convalescent barracks. It was filled with soldiers ordered to the front, but unlike Murray they were hearty and boisterous and playing cards. Exhausted from his journey and unwell, Edward found a corner to lie down on the floor. He had no blanket, and rats ran over him through the night, making it impossible to sleep. The next morning, the surgeon came to select men for duty. Upon seeing Murray, he told him he should have gone to the Cumberland Field Hospital, the same hospital where he had convalesced before returning home.

With no transportation provided, the good soldier Murray set out on foot. His unstable condition required him to rest often. By midafternoon he made it to the Cumberland Hospital, where he was assigned a tent. "As I lay down on my cot, I felt clean worn out and discouraged and as night settled down and all became quiet. . . . I was startled with a rattling in my throat that sounded to me like a person dying." He raised himself up just as the nurse came by and when he coughed, blood gushed from his mouth. The nurse fetched the doctor, who gave him medicine. "With an oath [the doctor] said a man must be a fool to send a man like me down here," where they needed all the cots for the battle wounded. Murray begged the doctor to let him stay until he was stronger.⁵⁴

In a few days, his cot was given to a wounded soldier, and Murray was sent to Nashville where he received orders to report at Louisville. There he stayed at a convalescent camp about three miles outside of town. By Murray's own admission, he was well treated in all the hospitals and given special care by the ladies of the Sanitary Commission.⁵⁵

Murray was eventually ordered to Quincy, Illinois, and the Sanitary Commission gave him two lemons "to use on my journey as it would keep me from drinking too much water." Murray traveled by hospital boat fitted with hundreds of cots "so clean with white and pink covers and nice clean sheets." He arrived at Jefferson Barracks south of St. Louis, Missouri, where he spent the Fourth of July, 1864.⁵⁶

Nearly ten months after being wounded at Chickamauga, Murray had yet to regain use of his legs "to any great extent." He spent his days lying on the porch of the Jefferson Barracks wondering why he was not being discharged and sent home. On July 9, he traveled by hospital boat up the Mississippi River to the military hospital south of Quincy. Here he began to move about, walking a short distance every day, but "his limbs tremble[d]" and he needed a cane to walk. His doctor told him that he would have to be discharged, as he "did not think I would ever be able to do any service." In fact, according to Murray's attending medical officer, the minié ball was still lodged near Murray's tenth rib and caused "severe pain." Murray also suffered from "symptoms of pneumonia such as fever cough spitting of blood." These symptoms were treated at the hospital with strychnine and tonics. Researcher Janet King explained that strychnine was given to soldiers to prevent "collapse" and thought to have a "stimulating" effect, while tonics such as quinine and whiskey were commonly prescribed as stimulants for fevers.[57]

Most remarkable, Murray told his doctor that he "still expectorate[d] portions of his shirt" when he coughed. The bullet had apparently driven a part of his army blouse into his lung, and Murray would occasionally cough up a bit of cloth. Clearly Murray was not a well man, and at last he had found a medical officer who agreed. Dr. Daniel Garrison Brinton, surgeon and superintendent of hospitals in Quincy, reviewed Murray's case and authorized his discharge, noting "partial paralysis of lower extremities. . . . Disability total." Sgt. Ed Murray received his much-deserved discharge on August 19, 1864.[58]

On arriving in Chicago, Murray received his final papers at Provost Headquarters and back pay to July 1, 1863. With over three hundred dollars in cash, Murray went into a clothing store and bought himself a "black suit of clothes and satin vest." He took a late train north but knew he could not get off at the state line, because "there was no way of getting home as I could not walk." So Murray got off at Waukegan and hired a dray wagon driver to take him to the City Hotel. There Murray asked to be taken home, but the staff preferred he spend the night and go in the morning. The thought of one more night apart from his family was too much. Murray repeated his request, and his tone and war-worn appearance won them over. A team of horses was hitched to a wagon, and, by the light of a kerosene lantern and waning moon, Murray was taken home. It was midnight when he arrived home for good. His life as a soldier ended.[59]

Prisoners of War

"The fact is that the army of the Cumberland came pretty near being cleaned out at the battle of Chickamauga," wrote Orson Young of Company D, 96th Illinois. "The rebels turned on us so sudden and in such great numbers that it rather discumfuddled old Rosey [General Rosecrans] for a time but we just barely escaped with our bacon. . . . Our division fought the flower of the southern army. That is Longstreet's corps and with a single line drive them although they were three to one."[60]

The remainder of the 96th Illinois that had survived withdrew to Rossville with the main army. Of the Newport Township Stateline Road comrades who fought in the battle, only Loughlin Madden had come through without injury. At reveille the next morning, it was sobering to count the men assembled for roll call. Despite the heavy losses, Capt. George Hicks warned the men not to "indulge . . . emotions of grief. . . . We were yet on the battle field, as it were, and must steel our hearts to bear, if need be, still further loss."[61]

To cover the retreat of the army to Chattanooga, companies from the 96th and 78th Illinois and 40th Ohio were placed on the skirmish line on Missionary Ridge on the evening of September 21. Loughlin Madden and his remaining able-bodied comrades from Companies C and H stood on picket that evening. The rest of the 96th Illinois marched to Chattanooga, crossing the river to Moccasin Point opposite Lookout Mountain. At midnight, one of Brigadier General Steedman's staff officers was sent to relieve the companies from their picket. The officer either could not find them or—as the regimental history stated—would not proceed to the picket's advanced position after hearing Rebels talking nearby, instead reporting back that the companies had been relieved. In either scenario, the consequences were dire.[62]

At eleven o'clock on Tuesday morning, September 22, the picket's position was discovered by Confederate general Benjamin G. Humphreys's brigade. Second Lt. Charles W. Earle of Company C recalled that they "foolishly attempted to resist the advance of the entire Brigade" and were quickly surrounded and captured. Earle broke his sword and threw it away before it could be taken. "[T]hese Companies were sacrificed—were allowed to be captured—because a staff officer had not the courage to do his plain duty."[63]

A total of two officers and thirty-nine enlisted men were taken prisoner. Loughlin Madden and his tentmate Henry Cutler were among fifteen prisoners of war from Company C. After coming through the horrors of Chickamauga, the twenty-year-old Irish immigrant Madden was now a POW. By midday on September 23, they were marched with a cavalry escort for Dalton, Georgia, the closest railroad connection. From there, the captives rode in boxcars to Richmond, Virginia, subsisting on a few crackers, corn meal, and a small piece of pork.[64]

By the time the men arrived in Richmond late on the night of October 1, they were without blankets and much of their clothing. At each stop along the route when they changed cars or were housed in barracks for the night, the Rebel authorities searched them and took away their overcoats and blankets. At Richmond, they marched from the depot toward Libby Prison with the officers at the head of the columns. After some distance, they were halted and informed that the officers would be separated from their men. Company C's Second Lieutenant Earle was allowed to run back to his fourteen men to bid them "goodbye." Earle gave them Confederate money he had obtained by selling his watch. He was sent to Libby Prison with the other officers, while the enlisted men were sent to "other prisons in the vicinity," including Pemberton, Royster House, Castle Thunder, and Belle Isle.[65]

Early in the war, informal prisoner exchanges were largely done between opposing field commanders to transfer sick and wounded. As the war progressed and greater numbers of men were taken prisoner, a systemic process for exchange was needed. Historian Charles W. Sanders Jr. explained that Abraham Lincoln hesitated to implement an official system, perceiving the exchanges as "recognition of the Confederate States as a sovereign nation." Pressure mounted in the North for a change in policy as the deplorable conditions in Southern prisons became known.[66]

On July 22, 1862, the Dix-Hill Cartel was formalized between the Confederate and Union governments, authorizing a program of exchange. The cartel began well and reduced the great number of prisoners in both the North and South, but after several months the process began to break down. An incident that had a large impact on the operation occurred in New Orleans in June 1862 when Union major general Benjamin Butler executed a civilian for treason for pulling down a U.S. flag and shredding it. Confederate president Jefferson Davis labeled Butler "a felon deserving capital punishment," and U.S. secretary of war Edwin Stanton responded by suspending the exchange of commissioned officers. An even larger point of contention developed when the Confederate government refused to parole and exchange African American soldiers, instead considering them runaways to be returned to their owners.[67]

By the end of 1863 the cartel had collapsed, with each government justifying its position. With the cartel's failure, the prison camps once again began to fill beyond capacity. This was particularly problematic in Richmond, where thousands of prisoners had been brought in anticipation of being exchanged. Charles W. Sanders Jr. explained that with thousands more Union prisoners having arrived, "the capacity to house, feed, and otherwise care for them was rapidly overwhelmed." The crowded conditions were coupled with an ominous trend in prisoner care. During the last half of 1863, those in charge of the prisoner-of-war systems, both in the North and in the South, became hardened to the suffering of the men. Some embraced the idea that retaliating against prisoners was justified due to the mistreatment of their own men in enemy prison camps. Added to this, the Confederate government changed its official policy and no longer provided prisoners with "the same in quantity and quality" as given to their own enlisted men, whom they had always struggled to provide for adequately.[68]

After ten weeks of imprisonment in Richmond, Loughlin Madden and about six hundred other men were moved to Danville, Virginia. The move was in part prompted by pressure from Richmond's citizenry, who feared for their safety, and the realization that the overwhelming number of prisoners could not be fed. Confederate general Robert E. Lee suggested sending as many prisoners as possible to Danville. There, Lee believed, "wood is cheap and provisions are in abundance," and there would be little danger of the prison being raided by the Federal army.[69]

After being marched to the depot and herded into boxcars, the men endured a 145-mile journey to Danville, which took nearly twenty-four hours. They were then marched into six tobacco warehouses that had been converted into prisons. If Madden and his comrades anticipated better conditions than those at Richmond, their hopes were quickly dashed. Each of the three-story buildings held an average of 650 prisoners. A bitterly cold winter was upon them, and the only source of heat was one pot-bellied stove on each floor, with little or no wood to build a fire. Sergeant Hileman of Company H recalled, "The cold was so intense that to keep ourselves warm we would form in a line . . . and double quick around the room, and then lie down and try to sleep."[70]

Rations were insufficient and consisted of corn meal (corn and cob ground together), watery cabbage soup infested with insects and worms, and rice crawling with maggots. "We suffered greatly for water," Sergeant Hileman wrote. Muddy water was drawn from the Dan River for the men to drink and use for bathing. Under these conditions, the men contracted diseases such as smallpox, which spread rapidly through the overcrowded buildings.[71]

On January 6, 1864, Henry C. Payne of Company C died of smallpox. Loughlin Madden also contracted the dreaded disease and was sent to the "Variola Ward" on January 12. Sanders explained that daily wagonloads of corpses were taken "to the burying ground designated for the Federal dead."[72]

Though the prison hospital lacked the supplies and number of surgeons to adequately care for the hundreds of sick, Madden was strong enough to survive. But the worst was yet to come.

The number of prisoners continued to increase in Richmond and Danville, and with no hope for the resumption of prisoner exchanges it was determined that additional prisons needed to be built. A location in Georgia remote enough to prevent military raids and where food and water supplies were adequate was suggested. A site near the Southwestern Railroad was selected, and the construction and supplying of Camp Sumter (Andersonville) began. There were many complications, but that did not prevent authorities in Richmond from sending prisoners before the new camp was ready to receive them. Again, the strain on Richmond's resources and the threat of prisoners escaping pressured authorities to act quickly. On February 9, 1864, a group of 109 officers escaped from Libby Prison by digging a tunnel under its walls, and the very real threat of the U.S. Cavalry attacking the city to free Federal prisoners sent Richmond into a panic.[73]

The first prisoners reached Andersonville on February 27 and immediately noticed its construction was not completed. With each new arrival, the quantity and quality of rations declined, and the water from a branch of the Sweetwater Creek that ran through the site was quickly polluted. The stockade was completed in mid-March, and it now held over seventy-five hundred prisoners with a capacity of ten thousand. The Confederate government considered the supplying of Andersonville a lower priority than filling it with Yankee prisoners, and by late June almost twenty-five thousand prisoners were crammed into an area of approximately eleven acres. A ten-acre expansion of the stockade was completed on the first of July.[74]

The situation was so dire that some men chose death over hopelessness. For those desperate enough, all they needed do was to step into the "deadline." Along the interior of the stockade, nineteen feet from the wall, was a line of small wooden posts with a wood rail on top. This was the "deadline" beyond which the sentries in the "pigeon roosts" placed at thirty-yard intervals along the top of the stockade would shoot to kill. The guards at the prison were not regular army troops as had been requested but untrained Georgia reserves consisting of old men, boys, and convalescents. With discipline lax and their working conditions difficult and unhealthful, random shootings of prisoners—even those not beyond the deadline—became common.[75]

In early April 1864, Madden and his comrades were transported by cattle cars to Andersonville, a journey on which Sergeant Hileman described the prisoners as "more like beasts than men." Madden, who had survived Richmond and Danville along with a bout of smallpox, had clung to the hope of being paroled. Then he arrived at Andersonville where conditions were so deplorable and overcrowded that dozens of men died each day. Thoughts of his family and the lovely Illinois "Irish Hills" he called home were all that sustained him.

While Madden struggled to survive these inhuman conditions, his comrades in the 96th Illinois were with Maj. Gen. William T. Sherman on his Atlanta Campaign, fighting the Battle of Resaca, Georgia (May 13–15, 1864). Billy Lewin, who had been wounded at Chickamauga, had recovered and rejoined the regiment, although his comrades needed to assist him in dressing the "ugly flesh wound" until it healed.[76]

On May 14, the 96th Illinois in a reserve position was rushed by Rebel infantry, and a scalding fire "poured lengthwise of the line." Colonel Champion gave the order to retreat and rally at the breastworks, but the men could not hear his command amid the enemy fire. Instinctively, they retreated for self-preservation, and the majority of the 96th entered a ravine. However, as Billy Lewin described, he and his tentmate Orange Ayers crossed a road "in full view of the enemy with pieces leveled" and were captured. The two were taken to Confederate general Joseph E. Johnston, who inquired about the Union numbers in the engagement. Neither Lewin nor Ayers replied satisfactorily, and they were sent to the rear with the other prisoners on rations of bread and water.[77]

Lewin and Ayers, along with about "sixty other luckless Union soldiers," were taken to Calhoun and then by railcars to Atlanta. After a few days they were "persuaded by bayonets to accept seats in a freight car for that prison . . . recorded as having no parallel in the world's history." Their arrival at Andersonville caused "no little excitement among those of the Ninety Sixth" already at the camp. "They were overjoyed to meet us, but sorry we came." The greeters included comrades from Company C: Joseph Schweri, a German-born tailor; James Kearney, an Irish-born farmer; Joseph Savage, a Yankee; and Lewin's friend from Newport Township, Loughlin Madden. The officers and guards searched the new prisoners, "even running their fingers through our hair." Items taken included knives, rings, pens, watches, and photographs.[78]

Shortly after their arrival, the camp's population reached twenty-four thousand. The pollution-, garbage-, and feces-laden water supply was used by the men for drinking, cooking, and bathing, making them sick with dysentery. Lewin recalled that those "unlucky enough to be a prisoner many months . . .

would be clothed in nature's robes." For shelter the men used parts of coats, pants, tents and blankets sewn together and hung on poles. Others made mud houses or dug holes in the ground. Rations consisted of unbolted corn meal, raw rice and raw beans. "Many could not eat the rations which they drew," and did not have tin cups or pots to cook the rations to make them edible. They "would walk all day, calling aloud, 'Who will exchange bread for peas, rice or meal?'" By the end of July, the lack of fruits and vegetables in his diet and subsequent depletion of vitamin C caused Billy Lewin to suffer terribly from scurvy.[79]

While some doctors understood the importance of vegetables in the diet, many doctors (North and South) were adamant that scurvy was caused by the presence of three factors: physical and environmental conditions, morale and mental depression, and lack of proper nutrition. Over a period of weeks, scurvy caused a gradual worsening of symptoms, resulting in weakened bones, bleeding gums and tooth loss, joint pain, profuse bleeding from the smallest of cuts, fever, and eventually death. In Lewin's case, the disease had "so contracted my limbs as to make it impossible for me to walk but a few steps at a time, and caused me severe pain." In spite of the disease, tentmate Myron Brown recalled that Lewin remained "cheerful, though cramped with scurvy."[80]

A rumor began to circulate that some of the men would be exchanged in thirty days. The "exchange" in reality was a relocation of prisoners out of the Union Army's path. Union offensives led by Major General Sherman were driving south through Georgia, and Confederate authorities feared the Federal cavalry would soon be in striking distance to liberate the prisoners at Andersonville. To maintain order during the relocation, the prisoners were told that they were being paroled. They were also told that only those fit enough to walk would be paroled, but this was in order to move them quickly to rail lines and away from the advancing Federals.[81]

The tantalizing rumor of an "exchange" motivated Lewin to better his physical condition. By a "pure Yankee trick," he had managed to keep his watch during the initial search on entering the prison camp. "Soon I met a soldier selling potatoes and biscuits, all of which were contained in a knapsack. I proffered my watch for the lot and two dollars." Lewin realized this was an important transaction on "which my future existence in this world largely depended." He was quick to close the deal, securing seven and a half dozen potatoes and two biscuits. Very quickly he made a meal of "raw scraped potato." A Confederate doctor had told Lewin that a person with scurvy who ate one large raw potato would prolong his life by a month.[82]

With concern for his friend, Lewin navigated the overcrowded pen—which now held over thirty-two thousand men—the following day to track down Loughlin Madden. Lewin presented Madden with the biscuits, and "Words will not do justice to the kind expressions he made me for this small offering." Madden had endured eleven months of imprisonment, but now at Andersonville he was crippled from scurvy and exposed to the hot Southern sun. In moments of despair, his thoughts returned to his family and the life they had made in America. It was nearly thirteen years since his widowed father made the decision for the family to leave their beloved Ireland to find a life far from oppression and famine in America. Yet when Madden enlisted to fight for his adopted home, he never imagined he would face starvation again. As historian Kerby A. Miller recognized, "The Great Famine seared its survivors with vivid, imperishable memories." And now the famine from which Madden's family had fled had reached its boney hand across the Atlantic to take him back.[83]

Madden gratefully received Billy Lewin's kindness, but by that time his physical and mental state had deteriorated to a point of no return. A comrade remembered, "For a time he kept up, but at last became disheartened and homesick, longed for his friends, and fell victim to scurvy and camp fever." On August 4, Madden was admitted to the prison hospital and died on Friday, August 12, 1864. It was the despair that sealed Madden's fate. Such anguish and heartache compounded the effects of meager and unnourishing rations, scorching sun, and inhuman conditions. Madden's body was taken by Union soldiers on a wagon with other corpses across the compound to the burying grounds. There he was placed in a shallow trench, shoulder to shoulder with hundreds of other Northerners.[84]

For Billy Lewin, the death of his friend, the helplessness of not being able to save him, and the guilt of surviving were imprinted on him forever. Madden's loss motivated Lewin to improve his mobility to meet the requirement for the rumored exchange. Near the Sweetwater Creek, he found a small piece of ground where he exercised and regained his ability to walk.

On September 5, hundreds of prisoners, including Billy Lewin and Orange Ayers, assembled at the prison's gate for the exchange. The men were marched from the stockade to the rail station. Myron J. Brown of Company G wrote that for some it was "more than could be endured by their frail forms. . . . [M]any fell to the ground and were returned to the prison." Lewin and Ayers were among those who made it into the freight cars. Many "confidently expected to be paroled" and cheered when they heard Union guns firing in the distance. After they reached Charleston, South Carolina, and continued on, reality and mournful disappointment set in. Lewin recalled, in a few days "they found themselves inside another Southern prison" at Florence, South Carolina. The men's spirits and energy sank. As with Andersonville, the prison stockade at Florence was not completed when Lewin and his fellow prisoners arrived. The men were marched into an open field and guarded until slaves finished the enclosure in mid-October. By then there were nearly thirteen thousand Union prisoners.[85]

The conditions at Florence were similar to Andersonville, with the addition of cold rains and hailstorms during the winter months, and no firewood or shelters to warm them. Most of the men at Florence had little clothing left, and a large number were barefoot. Rations consisted of cornbread, molasses, and rice, and initially the men were not provided utensils for cooking or eating. Some relief arrived in the middle of October with a delivery of supplies from the U.S. Sanitary Commission, including clothing, bedding, and tinned rations.

Lewin's companion Orange M. Ayers, who had been captured with him at Resaca, had reached his limit. He was in terrible health and, according to Lewin, had suffered "more than death a hundred times." At sunset one day in early January 1865, Ayers shook Lewin's hand and ran. Shots rang out, and Lewin watched, unable to look away, as the bullets "fell harmless at his feet." Ayers disappeared into the dark. The next day, the guards told Lewin that his friend "filled a soldier's grave a short distance from the stockade." Years later, however, it was ascertained by Charles Partridge while compiling the regimental history that Ayers had traveled north and died at Salisbury, North Carolina, days later on January 15.[86] Another month into imprisonment found Lewin in a very low state with "swamp fever." In addition to the scurvy, which he had overcome to some degree, Lewin now suffered from high fever, chills, sweats, and fatigue. Lewin's tentmate, Eli Thayer, also became sick with "camp fever." By now many of the men were preparing to be paroled, as a prisoner exchange had been negotiated between the Confederate and Federal governments. Confederate commanders had begun to parole the very sick, and with Sherman's continued advance, Florence Stockade was closed after four months of operation. Unfortunately, Eli Thayer died just before they were to be paroled. Lewin and two comrades "conveyed [Thayer] to his final resting place."[87]

About February 14, several hundred prisoners along with Lewin were called to the gate. They were marched under guard to freight cars, which took them near Wilmington, North Carolina, at which point they were unloaded. Confederate major general Robert Hoke was prepared to turn over the Union prisoners as part of the exchange cartel, but Union brigadier general John M.

Schofield initially declined. Schofield's forces were approaching the city, and caring for the prisoners would interrupt military operations.[88]

The Union prisoners were unaware of the circumstances of the delay, and, fearing they would be returned to Florence Stockade, Michael Devlin and Myron J. Brown decided to escape. Brown later wrote that they "urged Lewin to accompany us; but Lewin was in a bad condition, and became taciturn, and refused to go with us." Billy Lewin recalled that Devlin and Brown thought "at best I could survive but a few days, as I was very low at the time with swamp fever." At nightfall, Devlin and Brown made it past the guards with approximately two hundred other prisoners.[89]

The next day, Lewin and the remaining prisoners boarded the train for Goldsboro, where they were paroled. In his reduced condition, Lewin could not believe he would "be enroute for our lines." Once Schofield had secured Wilmington, he agreed to receive the captives, and preparations were made. Brig. Gen. Joseph C. Abbott was placed in charge of the parolees, and he immediately sent commissary stores to Maj. Gen. Alfred H. Terry's encampment at the Northeast Cape Fear River, where the prisoners were to be released.[90]

Wilmington was North Carolina's largest city and Cape Fear an important Confederate port and principal distribution center. With its occupation, Union forces secured the river and rail lines, cutting off supplies to Confederate general Robert E. Lee's Army of Northern Virginia. Historian Chris E. Fonvielle Jr. explained that controlling Wilmington aided Sherman's operations by providing him with a "safe haven and a base of supply." The success of the Wilmington Campaign hastened the Confederacy's downfall.[91]

The first Union captives officially arrived at the Northeast Cape Fear River on February 26, and Lewin was paroled on February 27–28. Lewin recalled Brigadier General Schofield and his staff meeting the parolees at the train. As the men disembarked, they passed between a Confederate and Union commissioner of exchange to be checked and counted. Fonvielle explained, a group of guards from Major General Terry's command stood at present arms as the "captives passed into freedom." After a short walk the parolees crossed a pontoon where Lewin described they "received a welcome never to be forgotten." It was at that moment that Lewin realized "our men were expecting us." A band played popular tunes and fellow Union soldiers held signs: "Thrice welcome, comrades," and "Home again."[92]

The soldiers were profoundly affected by the appearance of their freed comrades, and Myron J. Brown remembered their expressions of "great horror" and declarations they could now "shoot Rebels with a clearer conscience than ever before." The paroled prisoners were in varying states of sickness or even on the verge of death. Some appeared as mere skeletons and were so weak a doctor observed they "were in a state of mind resembling idiocy."[93]

Lewin was "overjoyed to be . . . under the folds of the dear old flag." He was given a good army ration, which he relished after months of starvation. The men were then sent to Wilmington where they boarded a steamer and traveled down Cape Fear River around Cape Hatteras to Annapolis, Maryland. There the former prisoners of war received clothing, food, and two months' pay. Lewin and others were sent to Benton Barracks at St. Louis, Missouri, where they arrived on March 14. Four days later, Lewin was given a thirty-day furlough to return home.[94]

The joy of having Billy home was tempered by his shocking appearance. Scurvy, swamp fever, and lack of proper rations had left Lewin emaciated, haggard, and barely able to walk. It reinforced how profoundly his life had changed to see the "alarmed reactions" of his family and friends. His mother Jane and sister Carrie set about nurturing him back to health with home remedies and home-cooked meals. To be at home, in his own bed, receiving his mother's care was the best medicine of all.[95]

In time, Lewin called on Ed Murray. The two men had last seen each other on that fateful Sunday at Chickamauga when Billy was unable to lift a wounded Ed from the field of battle. Lewin had seen Ed in his worst moment and felt the guilt of having to leave him as he fled from the advancing Rebel lines, and now Ed saw Billy broken from months of imprisonment. Lewin also suffered from severe headaches and psychological wounds. Brian Matthew Jordan concluded that "[t]he trials of captivity, the humiliation of starvation, and the omnipresence of death . . . indelibly marked" ex-POWs. Only another soldier could understand the horrors he had been through. Though Ed Murray had not been in a Rebel prison, he had been a prisoner on the battlefield and feared he would never return home. These men knew each other's struggle well.[96]

On April 10, Billy Lewin traveled to Waukegan to be examined by Dr. Benjamin Cory, who had been appointed by the U.S. government to examine "Invalid Prisoners." Dr. Cory noted that Lewin was unable to perform military duty in consequence of "a serious impoverished condition consequent upon long confinement in Rebel prison." Accordingly, Dr. Cory recommended that Lewin's furlough be extended to May 17. Two days later, with his health partially improved, Lewin traveled to Springfield, Illinois. He was sent to the chief mustering officer for Illinois and mustered out on May 24, 1865.[97]

6. ✣ Tenting on the Old Camp Ground

September 22–November 25, 1863

A demoralized Major General Rosecrans retreated to Chattanooga with one-third of his army on the afternoon of September 20, 1863. Despite dispatches from his chief of staff to "get here as soon as possible to organize the army," Rosecrans remained in Chattanooga. It was not until nine o'clock on the morning of September 21 that Confederate general Bragg and his staff became convinced that the Army of the Cumberland had left the field. Additionally, multiple reports convinced Bragg that the Federals were abandoning Chattanooga.[1]

Early on September 22, the remainder of Rosecrans's army, including the 96th Illinois as part of Whitaker's First Brigade, marched through the mostly deserted Chattanooga. The 96th crossed to the north bank of the Tennessee River and camped at Moccasin Point, where Company C was placed on picket duty. The men were exhausted and gutted by their losses, but "morale was higher than ever" as they took up positions and regrouped.[2]

Company C was a shadow of its former self. It had gone into the Battle of Chickamauga with thirty-five men, twenty-five of whom were injured or killed, and then lost fifteen to capture on Missionary Ridge. Of the small band that remained, most were recovering from wounds or illness. About thirty men rejoined the 96th Illinois after Chickamauga, having been detailed to guard a wagon train during the battle or absent due to illness. Billy Lewin, who was wounded at Chickamauga, rejoined the regiment the next day for the march to Moccasin Point. Lewin's injuries made him "too sore and lame" to wear his accoutrements, and he was excused from picket duty the night his comrades, including Loughlin Madden, were captured on Missionary Ridge by Bragg's army.[3]

Company C's Captain Pollock was still on duty at Bridgeport, but Lewin's old friend James Murrie, who had missed the fight due to illness, was once again with him. When Murrie returned to camp, he found Lewin recovering from a gunshot wound and suffering from frequent "dull heavy pains in his head."[4]

Though Rosecrans remained shaken after Chickamauga, the men of his Army of the Cumberland were stalwart in their support of him. On September 22, Rosecrans rode his horse along the line, receiving cheers from the men, including those of the 96th working on fortifications. For the 96th Illinois, whose numbers had been greatly diminished just two days earlier, the sight of their commander restored morale. The men were now veterans of battle and seasoned soldiers who had overcome what Meier described as the "uniquely challenging environment of war." The appearance of the general riding past on his steed bolstered their strength, created a shared sense of pride, and eased the tension of an imminent Confederate attack.[5]

Chattanooga's strategic importance lay in its location on the Tennessee River and its rail lines, which provided a means of communication and supplies to whomever controlled it. Rosecrans feared the Confederates would pursue his army and attack at any moment. He vacillated between defending his position and retreating across the Tennessee River. To bolster Rosecrans's beleaguered army, Secretary of War Edwin M. Stanton, sent troops from the Army of the Potomac. Maj. Gen. Joseph "Fighting Joe" Hooker was designated to lead a detachment of two corps (approximately twenty-three thousand troops) by rail from Virginia to Chattanooga.

Once Bragg realized the Federals were not retreating but entrenching at Chattanooga, he moved his army tentatively toward the city. The Confederate general understood that cutting communication lines into Chattanooga would either starve the Federal army or force it to leave. By securing Lookout Valley, the Confederates controlled the three supply routes—the Tennessee River, the Nashville and Chattanooga Railroad, and a wagon road that paralleled the railroad. The Confederates took up positions on Missionary Ridge, Lookout Mountain, and Raccoon Mountain from where they could fire upon the Federals.[6]

Rosecrans's supplies were at Bridgeport and Stevenson, Alabama, close by rail, river, and wagon roads. Partridge explained that Bragg's position gave the enemy "full control of the short and easy line," forcing the Federals to haul supplies by wagon over a "circuitous route, north of the river, and over a mountainous country, increasing the distance to over sixty miles." This route over Wallen's Ridge was so long that it could not be effectively guarded against Rebel cavalry raids.[7]

Due to dwindling supplies, clothing, and ammunition, the Federals had their daily rations reduced to one-quarter. Partridge explained it was "not to the point of starvation, but to such a degree that we hung on the edge of hunger for a number of weeks." Though still suffering from his injuries, Billy Lewin spent three days and nights on picket guard "with only two crackers and a half to eat during that time." Months afterward, the men referred to Moccasin Point as "Starvation Point."[8]

When Hooker's troops arrived at Bridgeport the first week of October, they could not move on Chattanooga. Robert Underwood Johnson wrote in *Battles and Leaders*, "It would have been folly to have sent them to Chattanooga to help eat up the few rations left there." Instead, the reinforcements gathered in the vicinity, protecting Rosecrans's line of communication and waiting for orders.[9]

Confederate artillery batteries were placed on Lookout Mountain as part of Bragg's strategy to control Lookout Valley. To counter the daily artillery and picket firing from the Rebels, Brigadier General Whitaker's First Brigade was ordered "to occupy heights opposite the Point of Lookout Mountain." This brigade included the 96th Illinois, the 10th Indiana Light Artillery Battery, and the 18th Ohio Light Artillery Battery. Historian Douglas R. Cubbison recognized the decision to place batteries at Moccasin Bend as "conceivably the single most important decision that Rosecrans made during the siege of Chattanooga." The 96th was detailed with construction of the battery fortifications. Partridge noted: "[A]ll were bomb-proofed by the infantry, the NINETY-SIXTH on one occasion working an entire night with picks and shovels."[10] This was familiar work. These men had spent the better part of the year building fortifications.

The 96th was camped several hundred yards from the Tennessee River, nearly opposite the northern base of Lookout Mountain. A short distance behind them was the 18th Ohio Battery, who, beginning on October 5, had daily "conversations" with Rebel artillery. Humorously, Partridge noted, "These occasional dialogues would not have troubled us in the least if the principal parties had kept the conversation exclusively to themselves." Fortunately the incoming barrages were not very accurate, owing to the distance. Cubbison noted that the strategically positioned Union gunners denied the Confederates "free movement around Lookout Mountain" and kept the enemy at bay. Artillery was a key to Chattanooga's defense and relief.[11]

While the situation in Chattanooga was growing more tense, members of Lincoln's administration discussed Rosecrans's usefulness. His failure at Chickamauga had sealed his fate, as Steven E. Woodworth explained: "[A] general who left a battlefield on which his troops were still fighting and fled thirteen miles to the rear simply did not have much future as a general." On October 17, by order of President Lincoln, the Military Division of the Mississippi was created of the Departments of the Ohio, Cumberland, and Tennessee, and Maj. Gen. Ulysses S. Grant was given command of all troops in the Western Theater. This new military organization brought together all the armies of the West.[12]

Grant was given the power to choose the commander of the Army of the Cumberland. Learning that Rosecrans wished to withdraw from Chattanooga—essentially surrendering a valuable strategic position—Grant replaced him with Maj. Gen. George H. Thomas, the "Rock of Chickamauga." At the same time, Grant ordered Thomas to hold Chattanooga "at all hazards." Thomas resented the removal of Rosecrans and the implication that Chattanooga would be abandoned, but swallowed his anger and replied, "We will hold the town till we starve." When Grant arrived in Chattanooga on October 23, he more clearly understood Thomas's remark that there had been but two choices: "one to starve, the other to surrender or be captured."[13]

Charles Partridge recalled that General Rosecrans "withdrew from his position as leader so quietly, that for some days it was not generally known that he had been relieved from command." Rosecrans could not bear to face his troops, and he left before the news reached them. "He was favorably regarded by his men; but the smoke of Chickamauga had clouded his reputation as a commanding General, and, justly or unjustly, he went to the rear."[14]

On Grant's arrival, he reviewed the military situation with what Partridge described as "characteristic promptitude and vigor" and set about opening the "Cracker Line." Grant recalled, "They had been so long on short rations that my first thought was the establishment of a line over which food might reach them." Grant ordered Brig. Gen. William F. Smith, chief engineer of the Army of the Cumberland, to seize Brown's Ferry across the Tennessee River. The plan involved using pontoon boats, which Smith had been building. The victorious fight at Brown's Ferry was the first step in ending the Confederate siege of Chattanooga. It would link Thomas's Army of the Cumberland with Hooker's incoming relief corps, which consisted of veterans of the Army of the Potomac who would open the railroad, river, and wagon roads. In support of this movement, the 96th Illinois with other troops left camp at Moccasin Point with the purpose of forming a "junction with Hooker's column." On the morning of October 28, the 96th crossed the Tennessee River on the newly established bridge.[15]

From their vantage point on Lookout Mountain, the Confederates watched Hooker's progress and feared the Union's supply lines would be reopened. They could not allow this and attacked Brig. Gen. John W. Geary's division of the XII Corps at Wauhatchie on the night of October 28. A continual roll of musketry pierced the night, alerting the 96th and other regiments of the assault. The 96th arrived after the battle ended, but on the march they had been constantly under fire from Lookout Mountain. The significance of the engagement at Wauhatchie was clear. The Confederates had squandered their last chance to prevent the reinforcement of Chattanooga and had lost control of the Tennessee River. The 40th Ohio's history noted, "General Hooker had a firm hold on Lookout Valley, the river was opened to Bridgeport, and Chattanooga was no longer in a state of siege."[16]

The "cracker line" was now open. Soldiers cheered jubilantly: "'Full rations, boys! Three cheers for the Cracker line,' as if we had won another victory; and we had." The opening of the food and supply lines allowed Grant to make plans to attack Bragg, and throughout November Grant moved reinforcements and supplies to the Army of the Cumberland.[17]

On November 1, the 96th marched to Shellmound, Tennessee, where it drew full rations for the first time in weeks. Part of the brigade remained at Shellmound while the 96th Illinois and 40th Ohio were given outpost duty at Nickajack, Georgia. With the threat of a Confederate attack greatly diminished and the new Union supply line from Bridgeport needing to be guarded, soldiers in Whitaker's newly designated Second Brigade of the First Division marched out with their orders. On the way to Shellmound the men stopped at Nickajack Cave, where they were allowed to fully explore its "splendid entrance hall." Taking time to sightsee at this natural wonder buoyed their spirits and gave them a brief respite. The 96th Illinois and 40th Ohio went into winter quarters at Nickajack Cove, on the "left hand mountain," with ample wood and water. These regiments were the only ones to occupy this cove while the others remained in camp near Shellmound.[18]

On November 8, Sgt. James Taylor rejoined his unit at Nickajack Cove. Later that month, James and his comrades from the 96th Illinois, including James Murrie, Billy Lewin and George Smith had the extraordinary opportunity to watch as "Sherman's Corps passed" on the Wauhatchie Road. The impressive line of the victorious Army of the Tennessee, now led by Maj. Gen. William Tecumseh Sherman, was on its way to Chattanooga to reinforce the downtrodden Army of the Cumberland. Partridge wrote, "Everything indicated that Gen. Grant was preparing for an aggressive movement on a grand scale."[19]

Partridge bemoaned the "military powers" that would not let them "settle down to the full enjoyment of our shanty city." On November 19, the 96th drew six days rations and were ordered to be ready to march. Grant was about to take the offensive to end Bragg's siege, which would be Cpl. James Murrie's first important engagement of the war. Sgt. James Taylor was left behind to guard a wagon train of rations.[20]

Initially, when the troops marched from the cove on November 20, they left everything behind, anticipating they would spend the winter there. They went about two miles and stood in the drenching rain for several hours before heading back to camp. Unknown to them, the order for their return was due to a delay in Grant's plans for taking Missionary Ridge. Grant had given the leading role to his trusted friend Sherman, but Sherman's troops were not yet in position. Thomas's Army of the Cumberland was to wait in the wings, because Grant felt they were too demoralized after Chickamauga to be of much use.[21]

With Sherman not ready, Grant decided to investigate the rumors that Bragg's army was withdrawing. As noted in *Battles and Leaders*, the change obliged Grant to "call on troops of the Army of the Cumberland to make the first offensive movement." On the morning of November 23, while the 96th Illinois marched from the cove to Lookout Valley, Grant directed Thomas to "'drive in the enemy's pickets,' and feel his lines for the purpose of finding out whether he still held in force."[22]

Thomas had the advantage of surprise as he led four divisions in his grand offensive on Orchard Knob. Maj. Gen. Thomas J. Wood's troops formed on the plain with thousands of soldiers and bright flags, causing curious Rebel pickets to come out of their rifle pits to watch what appeared to be a parade. It was then that Wood's troops advanced with fixed bayonets, and the Rebels scattered to find cover. Orchard Knob was won. After claiming this advanced position—halfway across the valley to Missionary Ridge—Grant and Thomas had the information they needed: Bragg's army was still present. They agreed to hold this position and soon reinforced it with more infantry and artillery.[23]

Woodworth explained that Grant's intention was to have Sherman's Missionary Ridge operation be the "main event" of his offensive, but "high water in the Tennessee River had broken the pontoon bridge at Brown's Ferry before the last of Sherman's divisions" could cross. Grant now considered Hooker's plan to assault Lookout Mountain, and while it offered Grant "little militarily" in defeating Bragg's army, an attack there could draw attention away from Sherman's movements. Grant ordered Hooker "to make a demonstration, and, if this showed a good chance for success, then to make an attack."[24]

On November 24, the remnants of the 96th Illinois, less than 250 fit for duty, woke to a misty morning. After a hasty breakfast at four o'clock, the men fell in line facing Lookout Mountain.[25]

> *When beneath Mount Lookout's frowning steep,*
> *In the vale of slumber lay,*
> *Fame whispered thus through the bars of sleep:*
> *"Soldiers, awake! Fresh laurels to reap—*
> *Up! Make a historic day."*[26]

"Boys, I have a few words to say to you," Colonel Champion began, seated on horseback as if on parade. "Before night I expect we will have to climb the side of yonder mountain. You all know that at Chickamauga the Ninety-Sixth covered itself with glory. . . . I expect every man to do his duty; I shall try and do mine." For a few moments no one spoke as they began to realize the task at hand, and their eyes lifted toward Lookout.[27]

The plan was for Major General Hooker to make a direct attack on the mountain while a "flanking force," consisting of Geary's division and Whitaker's Second Brigade, scaled the side of the mountain to strike the enemy. As part of this force, the 96th marched up Lookout Valley with mist clinging to their faces and wool jackets as a cover of fog hid them from the enemy's watchful eye. They left their knapsacks and anything that could be spared to lighten their load before crossing Lookout Creek to make their ascent. Because of the high water in the creek, the men "clambered across on an old dam," reaching the right bank at eight o'clock that morning.[28]

Generals Grant and Thomas observed troop movements from on top of Orchard Knob. Grant later wrote, "The day was hazy, so that Hooker's operations were not visible to us except at moments when the clouds would rise. But the sound of his artillery and musketry was heard incessantly."[29]

The regiment ascended Lookout Mountain with no opposition but struggled with the rough terrain of fallen rocks, forest, and deep ravines. Partridge described their climb up the mountainside to where it rose perpendicularly, their line stretching "far down the slope of the creek." Whitaker maneuvered his troops into the front line, requiring the men of the 96th to "face the steepest and roughest ground along the whole line." Before ten o'clock that morning, Union forces began the sweep around the face of the mountain. The 96th's position close to the sheer cliff protected them from the Rebel guns of the upper battery. For a time the regiment's advance went unnoticed, the only sound "the tramping of many feet, and the hard breathing of men unused to mountain climbing." By eleven o'clock, the line of battle was stretched from the palisades to the base of the mountain. Union batteries in Lookout Valley and Moccasin Point began assailing the mountain with fierce artillery fire in advance of the Federals' line. The batteries of the enemy responded.[30]

An enemy skirmish fire developed in front of the 96th, but the regiment pushed on, climbing over rocks with cheers and driving the enemy's advance line before them. Woodworth explained that they were "driving their foes out of a position many had believed impregnable." The regiment had ascended a rising ledge that placed them above the rest of the brigade. They now could look down on Craven's farmyard where the 24th Mississippi's forces had gathered. Partridge wrote that the enemy's works had been constructed to resist a direct attack from below, but the 96th Illinois was in a position to "rake them with an enfilading fire" from above.[31]

Whitaker's brigade reached the east side of the mountain, pushing through the front line and pursuing the enemy. In a "headlong charge over the 'nose' of Lookout," the 96th Illinois proudly came to the aid of the 40th Ohio, who in their eagerness to advance went far beyond the brigade's line and found themselves in the rear of the Rebel line. Partridge recalled the 40th "in danger of being crushed by superior numbers. We threw a whole Regiment of men" at the enemy and poured a "destructive fire" into their ranks. This movement gave the 40th Ohio the ability to rush forward and charge, resulting in the surrender of a large number of the enemy.[32]

The heavy fighting for the 96th Illinois ceased at two o'clock. The brigade's ammunition was nearly expended, and the men were so drained from their "hard climb up and around the mountain" that they were in no condition to pursue the enemy further. Another heavy bank of clouds made further offensive operations impractical. Direct communications with Chattanooga were established and fresh troops dispatched, but these encountered some opposition while crossing Chattanooga Creek. They brought all the ammunition they could carry. Hooker's men were able to fall back out of the line of fire, while the skirmishing continued until nearly midnight.[33]

General Grant telegraphed Washington: "The fight to-day progressed favorably. Sherman carried the end of Missionary Ridge, and his right is now at the tunnel [Tunnel Hill], and his left at Chickamauga Creek. Troops from Lookout Valley carried the point of the mountain, and now hold the eastern slope and a point high up. Hooker reports two thousand prisoners taken, besides which a small number have fallen into our hands, from Missionary

Ridge." President Lincoln responded: "Your dispatches as to fighting on Monday and Tuesday are here. Well done. Many thanks to all."[34]

Poetically referred to as "The Battle Above the Clouds," Lookout Mountain saw the 96th Illinois "wrapped in a seamless mantle of vapor" that at once protected and disoriented them. The 40th Ohio noted, "History will differ as to whether the capture of Lookout was a battle or not. General Grant is reported as saying it was nothing more than a skirmish." The 96th referred to the "rough-and-tumble fight . . . striking in spectacular effect, affording abundant materials for the use of artist and poet," yet many felt that, from a military standpoint, it did not deserve to be called a battle.[35]

Company C noted the day in their official report: "Was in the fight at Lookout Mountain." Company B: "The Regiment assisted in taking Lookout Mountain in which battle the Company had one man killed and one slightly wounded."[36] In part due to the small number of casualties, the victory these men achieved was minimized. Had a heavy fog not concealed their movement, the day could have played out very differently.

The 96th Illinois remained on Lookout Mountain. James Murrie, Billy Lewin, and their companions slept with only sheets to wrap about them and campfires to keep them warm against a cold northwest wind. Weeks later, Lewin wrote about the experience to David Minto: "[W]e had a pretty hard time taking the Mountain charging over rocks and logs and climbing the hill and driving the rebels from their entrenchments."[37]

As the next day broke clear, the wind having swept away the fog, the men realized their position was vulnerable. There was still a chance that a "hostile presence" could be on the rocks above them. They watched and waited for any glint of steel or flutter of flag, but soon felt assured the enemy had gone. What had remained of the Rebel army, Partridge wrote, "withdrew during the night so cautiously and silently that the mountain was in our possession for some time before we became aware of it."[38]

The 96th Illinois and 8th Kentucky were assigned the honor of holding the mountain while the rest of the brigade went with Major General Hooker toward Rossville Gap to assist in storming Missionary Ridge. To mark the victory on Lookout Mountain, a flag was planted on the summit. The 96th Illinois had equal rights to that privilege, but her regimental colors were so "riddled" by the "tornado of shot and shell at Chickamauga" that they could not be distinguished from the enemy's flag. The 8th Kentucky's colors were "new and bright," and Brigadier General Whitaker was a

Kentuckian, so he gave the honor to his native state. Whitaker asked the 8th Kentucky for volunteers, and fifteen men climbed the narrow rocky stairway to the summit.[39]

In spite of the excitement surrounding the ascent, the men watched anxiously, many fearful that the 8th Kentucky's men would be killed by lingering sharpshooters. Partridge declared, "Our eyes were soon gladdened by seeing our flag waving from Point Lookout. Never did it seem so grand as when the sun kissed its silken folds on the apex of that ragged cliff . . . cheer after cheer, which surged around the crest of Lookout, and rolled down into the valley in cataracts of sound. . . . The multitudinous shout of a great army came up to us from below." After their terrific losses at Chickamauga, the sight of the Stars and Stripes atop Lookout Mountain caused a spontaneous and thunderous cheer from the Army of the Cumberland encamped around Chattanooga.[40]

> *Ah! It was good to hear*
> *Our war scarred veterans cheer,*
> *When that Flag of Freedom blossomed in the sun.*[41]

According to Douglas R. Cubbison the Battle of Lookout Mountain "set the stage for the stunning Union victory on Missionary Ridge the next day." On November 25, from atop Lookout Mountain, the men of the 96th Illinois and 8th Kentucky had the privilege to watch Sherman's, Thomas's, and Hooker's armies as they fought the Battle of Missionary Ridge, directed by Grant from Orchard Knob. Partridge wrote, "All the pomp and magnificence of a great battle within easy view, and yet so far removed that all the horrors of wounds and death are eliminated from the scene. . . . But with the close sympathy of comradeship we join in the charge."[42]

The major Federal victory at Missionary Ridge, Partridge noted, "delivered Chattanooga from the presence of the enemy, and shattered their strength." The Confederate Army retreated to Dalton, Georgia, and General Bragg was forced to resign. Woodworth explained that the campaign for the control of Middle and East Tennessee "ended decisively in favor of the Union. Never again would any substantial part of the state of Tennessee be considered Confederate territory in a military sense."[43]

The two regiments held Lookout Mountain until December 1, when they descended the west side of Lookout. The 96th Illinois returned to its shantytown winter quarters at Nickajack Cove.[44]

News of John Taylor's Death

On December 3, James Taylor returned from guard duty in Chattanooga and "found three letters waiting" from Nashville, including one from John Murray. Anxious for news of his brother, James opened Murray's letter to find the devastating news that John had died on the morning of November 24.[45]

That evening James was invited to have supper in Captain Pollock's tent. This setting allowed James the privacy to confront his disbelief with someone who had been acquainted with him and his brother for nearly a decade. Perhaps James reminisced about John's hardiness during their first year of military service, calling him "tough as a pine knot." James, who had struggled considerably with poor health since enlistment, surely envied his brother's stronger constitution. James then visited with Sgt. Henry J. Harriman of Company K, hoping for more details of his brother's last days. Unfortunately, Harriman had not seen John while at Nashville, which disappointed James as he struggled to piece together his brother's last moments.[46] In a letter to his sister Isabella on December 7, James's own words best expressed his grief:

> I was almost expecting it from the fact that I got a letter from him while on Lookout Mountain telling me the Doctor had said there was but little hope of his recovery, but even in that John appeared to think differently, and said he thought he would get well yet. And by this means deceived us all till it was too late for any one of us to see him. I am thankful that John Murray was with him. And that he was not entirely alone among strangers in his last hours. It seems terrible hard. I can't realize it. It seems yet that I can't believe him dead, but that I shall meet him among the friends at home. At least I hope to meet him among the redeemed above at last. I am afraid if this war continues much longer that there won't be a home in the country either north or south, but what has yielded some of its members a sacrifice to [fall to the] God of War.[47]

James's plaintive "I can't realize it" illustrated the inability to accept his brother's death in his own mind. The brothers were extremely close, and not being at John's side made acknowledging his death impossible. James's hope to meet his brother "among the redeemed above at last" indicated his belief that at least in death John was now free from "war and suffering."[48]

Among the condolences, James received a letter from his sister Jane in New Byth, Scotland.

> Oh what that horrid war has cost us. It cost me many a tear before the sad account of our dear brother John reached us. . . . I am very sorry for you. I know you will feel John's death so much you were so closely attached to each other. . . . You have both been heavy on my mind since ever you have been there. And when the sad news of dear John's death came it was so severe I don't know when I will be able to get my mind off it . . . Oh if I only knew how he was cared for. If he had suffered a great deal or if he was prepared for death, all these things lie heavy on my mind.[49]

Richard Thain (Company D) wrote to his aunt Isabella Taylor Low in Waukegan, "I sympathize with you for the loss of your Dear Brother John. It seemed like hearing of the death of a Brother when I heard that he was Dead. But he died in a good cause and I sincerely trust that he is in a Land where there is no War." Though it was several months after John's death when Thain sent his condolences, he affirmed his cousin's death was for a "good cause" and that he had gone to a better place. Such sentiments were typical for those trying to soothe the grief of family members whose loved one died far from home. While his sisters took up the mantel of ritual mourning for their brother, James Taylor had to fulfill his duties as a soldier. The circumstances of war did not allow James to indulge long in his grief.[50]

The men of the 96th Illinois hunkered down for an unusually harsh winter. In their little shanty houses they kept fires blazing against "sharp frosts." In late December, they were pleased by the arrival of a familiar and motherly presence, Mrs. Charlotte Gallagher Smith, the wife of Lt. Col. John C. Smith (Company I). That autumn, Mrs. Smith and her three little boys had headed south from Galena, Illinois, to visit her husband and the regiment, but due to the regiment being at the front, Charlotte only made it as far as Nashville. After Chickamauga, more nurses were needed at the military hospitals to care for the great number of wounded. The regiment's history praised Charlotte Smith for rendering "service as a thoughtful, patriotic woman" and spending her days changing dressings on wounds, helping men eat and drink, and writing letters to their loved ones.[51]

She arrived at the regiment's winter quarters with two of her boys (one died of smallpox at Nashville) and stayed about a month. These family visits had been important to her husband since the first days of his service at Camp Fuller. While it was a luxury few soldiers could enjoy, the troops warmly accepted the family's presence, and Mrs. Smith affectionately came to be known as the "Mother of the Regiment." The regiment had many friends supporting them, but none received a moniker that connected them so intimately. When Charlotte Smith was not with the regiment, her husband sent detailed letters filled with "good spirits and love" from himself and the men. Smith's letters kept his wife informed about her "soldier children," and when she arrived in camp it was as if she represented every soldier's mother.[52]

The troops accepted and respected Charlotte and enjoyed seeing the children run through the camp. The semblance of home and normalcy brought by Smith's wife and sons was a great comfort after the men's recent trials in battle. In their civilian lives they had the care of their mothers and sisters, but the war had thrown them into a strange world devoid of women. The suffering they endured, which was not always shared with their families, was made tolerable by the presence of Charlotte Smith, bringing a bit of home to their camp and in turn easing their homesickness and weariness. The men felt so much gratitude and affection for the Smith family that photos of Mrs. Smith and the two boys, Robert and Samuel, were included in the regimental history.[53]

On January 1, 1864, the 96th Illinois was presented new regimental flags from Lake and Jo Daviess Counties, replacing the colors that had been shot to pieces at Chickamauga. The presentation committee consisted of representatives from Jo Daviess County, but regrettably the Lake County members "owing to some disarrangement of plans . . . were not present." The men appreciated the new silk flags with their gilded lettering but lamented handing over the old flags. "[F]or had they not passed through Chickamauga, and had they not led us over Lookout? We parted with the rolls of glorious rags with regret." The battle-torn flags were charged with the very essence of the battles in which they had fought, making the loss of those flags bittersweet. The regimental flag represented a tangible and visible record of their achievements as bonded members of a tightly knit unit and representatives from their homes in northeastern Illinois. The men "resolved to make our new flags famous when we should enter on another campaign."[54]

Life in winter quarters continued with guard duty and small entertainments. On January 13, James Taylor wrote a letter to Edward Murray, and then Alex Thain visited his tent and played chess. Afterward, Thain taught Billy Lewin and James Murrie "a lesson in Chess," while Taylor baked beans. His health still a concern, Taylor was given a pass to Nashville to be examined. He spent several days "eating well, shopping and going to Church and Theaters." There was no mention in his diary of visiting his brother's grave.[55]

When the regiment left its winter quarters on January 26, 1864, "many a lingering look behind was cast at that strangely built city on the hillside." They again marched over Lookout Mountain, but it was much easier thanks to a macadamized gravel road the engineers and pioneers had built. This time the 96th marched through Chattanooga "with drums beating and the new colors unfurled."[56]

In late February at Tunnel Hill, the 96th faced heavy skirmishing. For a time, the troops were halted at the crest of a wood ridge, and for ten hours the firing never ceased. The Rebels called out tauntingly from the pits: "Chickamauga!" In reply, the Union skirmishers shouted: "Lookout Mountain and Missionary Ridge!" At this engagement, James Taylor's friend, Sgt. Harry J. Harriman, was struck in the head by a bullet and killed instantly. "His death caused great sadness in the command."[57]

In early March, the men rejoiced at the return of Company C's Lt. Charles W. Earle, who had been taken prisoner at Missionary Ridge on September 22, 1863. Earle was among the 109 officers who tunneled under Libby Prison on February 9, 1864, and made their way back to Union lines. The men gave the "intrepid boy lieutenant" a resounding ovation and celebrated for several days. Earle had been fearless at Chickamauga, and though wounded twice, he never left his command of the "color company," as Company C was known.[58]

7. ❊ Bonny Boys in Blue

The Atlanta Campaign (May 7–September 2, 1864)

"Wer bound for Atlanta, Abes blue coats swarm forth front and rear," the 96th's George Smith wrote to his sister. "Old Johnston look well to your greenbacks & that flee thats in your Ear." Smith was one of many soldiers whose values of duty and honor sustained and motivated him as the war raged on. The men needed that deep belief in "the Cause" for the long road to Atlanta that lay ahead.[1]

After Ulysses S. Grant's appointment as general in chief of the U.S. Army and promotion to lieutenant general, Grant designated his principal subordinate Maj. Gen. William T. Sherman as his successor to command the Military Division of the Mississippi. While Grant would attack General Robert E. Lee's Army of Northern Virginia, Sherman would focus on General Joseph E. Johnston's Army of Tennessee. Sherman's goal was to destroy the Army of Tennessee and capture Atlanta, Georgia, the Confederacy's important manufacturing, railroad, and supply center. Throughout the first part of 1864, Sherman prepared for his Atlanta Campaign by concentrating forces and equipping approximately 133,000 troops, including Maj. Gen. George H. Thomas's Army of the Cumberland. Nashville and Chattanooga were turned into Union supply depots for the campaign.[2]

As Sherman's massive army headed on its way to destroy the Army of Tennessee, the 96th Illinois marched at the rear of an "immense wagon train" of thousands of supply wagons pulled by mules. At the start of the Atlanta Campaign, the 96th Illinois had "an aggregate strength of 409 officers and men." Company C had twenty-five men in line and, Partridge proclaimed, "though few in numbers . . . was never lacking in promptness or in pluck." The 96th was in good company. Historian Richard M. McMurry noted that "more than half the units in Sherman's armies were from Illinois, Indiana, and Ohio."[3]

The opening battle of Sherman's Atlanta Campaign occurred at Rocky Face Ridge near Dalton in northwest Georgia, thirty miles southeast of

Chattanooga. Confederate general Johnston had a strong position in the steep ridges of Rocky Face Ridge protecting the Western and Atlantic Railroad, which passed through the mountain by way of Buzzard's Roost Gap (Mill Creek Gap) and which supplied his army. Sherman also wanted this rail line to support his army.

Thomas's Army of the Cumberland positioned itself to make an assault on Buzzard's Roost Gap to keep the main body of Confederate troops occupied defending the ridges. This would allow Maj. Gen. James B. McPherson's troops to move south behind the ridges to pass through the undefended Snake Creek Gap (to reach Resaca).[4] The goal was to cut off the Confederate Army from its base in Atlanta and force it to fight or scatter.

By three o'clock on the morning of May 9, the 96th Illinois was in line. After sunrise, they moved with the division into the valley that lay between Tunnel Hill and Rocky Face Ridge. The 96th's Companies A and B were deployed as skirmishers, followed by Companies G and K. The enemy in an elevated position on the ridges could clearly see every movement and "rolled stones upon them." The regimental history noted the skirmishers did not waver, "going at a run . . . [u]p the steep slope, running from tree to tree, halting a moment behind rocks and then pressing on." The main line, including Billy Lewin, James Murrie, and James Taylor, kept near the skirmishers, "advancing as ordered, sometimes boldly and in line, and again crawling up the steep incline." Despite the constant barrage of bullets, the line held resolutely.[5]

The men pressed into Buzzard's Roost Gap and "gained a position within 50 to 75 paces of the Enemy's works, which position was held under a very severe fire." This "incessant" fire turned the air "thick with smoke." The "rapid and repeated discharges of the muskets" echoed through the gorge. In a position of "extreme peril," the regiment began to run low on ammunition, and the men longed for the sun to set for the battle to end. "It had never seemed to move so lazily since that dread Sunday at Chickamauga."[6]

Clutching their muskets from daybreak until nine o'clock at night, the men had "no opportunity to eat except as they munched hard tack on the skirmish line. . . . Nearly every man had fired from forty to one hundred rounds of ammunition. Their faces were powder-grimed and their clothing stained with the soil where they had hugged the hillside throughout the weary, weary day."[7]

Shortly after sunset while positioned in the skirmish line, James Taylor was struck by a rifle ball in the right "Fore-arm." He wrote in his diary that night with a shaky hand: "I got wounded on top of the ridge just a little after sundown, and was carried back to Tunnel Hill" hospital by men of the ambulance corps. George Smith was among the six "stalwart men" of the 96th Illinois chosen as stretcher-bearers for the newly created ambulance corps. At "great personal risk" during the Battle of Rocky Face Ridge, Smith "carried nearly a score of dead and wounded men from the battle field."[8]

Attendants at the Tunnel Hill field hospital "bathed the pale faces and bound up the ragged wounds" of the men. After a sleepless night, James Taylor was given coffee and two oranges and boarded on a train to a hospital in Chattanooga. Each day Taylor's arm continued to swell, and the pain worsened. On May 15, he was "packed" on the hospital train to Nashville and arrived the next morning at Hospital No. 19 at the Morris and Stratton Building on Market Street.[9]

The attack at Buzzard's Roost Gap successfully diverted attention away from McPherson's passage through the undefended Snake Creek Gap. However, McPherson balked at making a full-scale attack at Resaca when the Confederates put up a strong resistance, despite their inferior forces (four thousand Rebels compared to McPherson's twenty-five thousand). Maj. Gen. David S. Stanley "was profuse in his praise of the Ninety-Sixth for the resolute manner" in which they advanced into a "strongly defended position at Buzzard Roost Gap."[10] The regiment's new colors were already being covered in glory.

Five days after Buzzard's Roost Gap, the 96th was engaged at Resaca, the first major engagement of the Atlanta Campaign, in a reserve position. Companies A and B were again sent out front as skirmishers to search for the enemy and "occupy his attention." Late in the afternoon on May 14, the 96th saw Confederate general Carter L. Stevenson's division forming into line, and then Confederate lieutenant general John Bell Hood's troops approached in two lines. The Union skirmishers fell back to rejoin the regiment and report what they had seen. The 96th heard rifle fire as the Rebel battle line assaulted Whitaker's brigade on the right. The men could not see the enemy, but they could hear the peculiar Rebel yell, which grew more exultant.[11]

The men were kneeling or lying prostrate on the ground ready for what was to come. Colonel Champion called out, "Steady, men! Hold your fire until I give the word!" When the bushes directly in front of the regiment started to shake and weave, the men's thoughts returned to recent battles and the losses they had seen, but they held to their training and waited for the colonel's command: "Fire!" And in an instant a terrible volley crashed into the thicket as the Rebels emerged. The regiment's fire hit its mark and "a great winrow of dead" fell before them like a long row of cut grain left to dry in a field.[12]

Halfway through reloading their muskets they realized that the assault to their front had been stopped, but the Rebel infantry was advancing and rushing past both flanks. "A wicked fire was poured lengthwise of the line." Colonel Champion gave the order to retreat and rally at the breastworks, but amid the pounding noise of battle and enemy fire he could not be heard. Each veteran soldier's survival instincts told him to move to the rear, but it turned into a rout, a disorderly retreat that scattered the regiment. For the first and last time in its service, the regiment was in utter confusion.[13]

Fortunately for the 96th, they entered a ravine with a growth of pine and brush. While the bushes slowed their hurried retreat, it provided some cover. A majority of the men, including James Murrie, followed the ravine, which led them to the left of Capt. Peter Simonson's 5th Indiana Battery. On either side of the battery, officers of every rank were shouting orders to form some semblance of a line. There was no time for men to find their regimental flags before the Confederates emerged from the timber.[14]

While a retreat can reflect poorly on a command, the 96th's retrograde movement saved them from capture. The regiment was then able to fight from the position of the battery and in the breastworks. A portion of the 96th's men moved with Major General Hooker's XX Corps, which had come on the double quick to reinforce them, halting only when the enemy fled in a panic into the forest. The 96th's strays were called to rejoin the rest of the regiment at the breastworks where their officers, the colors, and many of their comrades awaited them.[15]

On May 15, the heaviest day of fighting at Resaca, the 96th was held in reserve and halted at the right of the Dalton and Resaca road. Partridge wrote that they were not in a position to fight, but enemy musket balls came "pattering down to the Regiment's position . . . pelting the ground, striking logs and trees." Not long into the battle, the men watched as stretcher-bearers returned from the front with "ghastly loads." While such gruesome results were often hidden in the midst of battle by the enveloping smoke of cannon fire and muskets, the men had full view of the white canvas stretchers stained by the crimson blood of the fallen.[16]

At midafternoon, Lieutenant Earle and a detail from the regiment were sent to the right to build breastworks on a high ridge. The rest of the regiment joined them at dusk. Meanwhile, Sherman's forces crossed the Oostanaula River using pontoon bridges and advanced on the Confederates' railroad supply line. Confederate general Johnston was forced to withdraw from Resaca. By now, the men of the 96th were habituated to the hard knocks of military life. Even so, they were severely tried by the Atlanta Campaign.[17]

The day after the battle, members of the regiment searched the immediate area for any trace of missing comrades. The bodies of some of the dead were found, and a few Rebels who had been left on picket were taken prisoner. From the Rebels it was learned that Deloss Rose of Company G and William Lewin and Orange Ayers of Company C had been captured unharmed.[18] James Murrie was now the only member of the Stateline Road group still with the regiment.

In the coming days, Union morale soared as Confederate general Johnston's "pattern of retreating in order to avoid battle" enabled Sherman's men to cover a good deal of distance. On May 20, with the enemy's retreat, Sherman gave his troops a well-deserved rest of three days. "I am pretty well worn," Orson Young wrote to his parents. "So are all of us. But as long as we are crushing rebellion we will bear it all as well as we can. God helping us." Previous to the Atlanta Campaign, most of the men had experienced fights only at "infrequent intervals," allowing for time in camp to rest, write letters and look after themselves. Now they were engaged in what seemed a "continuous battle." Whether the unit was engaged with the enemy or assailed by random skirmish fire, the sounds and perils of combat were nearly constant.[19]

First on the men's list for their break was to bathe and thoroughly wash their clothes. Since doing laundry was considered "women's work," some units maintained a company washer, but soldiers had to pay for that service. A well-maintained uniform protected against the elements and promoted good health. Out of necessity, the men washed their clothes when the opportunity arose. A number of the men visited the deserted town of Cassville, Georgia. Of particular interest was the library of the Cassville Female Seminary, one of the most renowned female seminaries in the state. Although the librarian and all the students were absent (not to mention most of the townspeople), the soldiers were overjoyed to find the large collection of books intact. Men like Orson Young, who bemoaned "the loss of schooling" as the "greatest sacrifice" for military service, delighted in the chance to indulge their minds.[20]

After their rest, the men stuffed their knapsacks, haversacks, and supply wagons with twenty days' rations in anticipation of operating away from their railroad lifeline. On May 25 at New Hope Church, the 96th Illinois was hurried forward as part of the reinforcements for Hooker's XX Corps, which had engaged the enemy. Despite an initial rapid advance, the sky darkened at sundown and it began to rain, slowing the march of the reserve troops. The rugged terrain and dense woods compounded the situation, making it difficult to determine the enemy's position. The regiment was "shifted around from place to place" until nine o'clock. They were too late to aid Hooker's command, which took heavy losses.[21]

On May 27 at the Battle of Picket's Mill near Dallas, Georgia, the 96th Illinois took its place in the front line and used a partial line of breastworks for cover. Despite this cover, James Murrie was shot in the left foot and lost a toe, disabling him for several months. He was initially treated in the field hospital by the assistant surgeon, Dr. Moses Evans.[22]

The fighting continued over the next few days. While under fire the men in the main line worked to enforce the trench. This position was on the brow of a hill, and the men endured shelling at that elevation, but none of the shells burst at the exact point of the earthworks. Orson Young wrote to his parents that rain had filled the pits, "[s]o we had to bail out with our cups. The Rebels pits were 200 yards from ours, and while we were bailing, they would shoot at us for amusement." When the Rebels would bail, the Federals returned the favor. "When we would be tired of shooting at each other, we would stop and talk to each other a while to vary the amusement." The Federals suffered extreme physical hardships from the rain, continuous fire from the enemy, the stench of death, and shortage of food. As Kathryn Shively Meier said, "Soldiering was a miserable business," and none more miserable than during this week of the Atlanta Campaign.[23]

The same day that James Murrie was wounded, James Taylor's condition worsened at the Nashville hospital. It had been eighteen days since he was shot at Rocky Face Ridge. On May 27, the wound began to bleed and his arm was amputated. Taylor later noted in his diary, "I suffered no pain," indicating that chloroform was used for the surgery. On June 4, Taylor's brother-in-law James Bater arrived from Millburn to care for him and ultimately take him home. Taylor did not think it necessary, but his sisters were still in shock from John's death and wanted to take every precaution. Bater remained at Taylor's bedside for ten days, but the doctor expected it would take several weeks before James could be released.[24]

In a letter from his sister Isabella Low, Taylor learned that Billy Lewin had "destroyed the rest of your private letters as you told him." Also in the letter was the delicate matter of their brother's remains and the family's continued struggle over John's loss. Isabella wrote that she understood that James wanted "to bring home John's remains. Do as you think best about it." By bringing his brother's body home for burial, James hoped to ease his family's grief and exert some control over what had happened, since he had been powerless to help John.[25]

"We all would have liked to have had him buried at Home if we could have had it done when he died," Isabella continued. "[B]ut it would be a means of renewing our sorrow so much that I shrink from the thought of it not so much on my own account as Mary [Bater] and James Low [Isabella's husband] would not give any thing to defray the expenses." The prospect of bringing their brother's remains home proved emotionally and financially difficult. "[A]s far as my own judgment dictates let him rest till the last trump shall sound, but counsel is not command. He was your Brother and you have a perfect right to do as you think best." Though the older sibling, Isabella deferred to her brother as the male head of the family. "When you come Mary wishes to have a funeral sermon preached any how."[26]

For James, the matter of bringing his brother's remains home would have to wait. His recovery had many complications. The amputation wound was not healing, and by late June it had developed an infection. He seemed to be on the same downward path his brother had taken seven months earlier. Remarkably, with continued wound care and a change in diet, James's health began to improve. On July 27, he was furloughed from the hospital.[27]

While Taylor had been struggling to regain his health, the 96th Illinois continued in Sherman's campaign to Atlanta. Captain Gillmore of Company G wrote a letter to the *Waukegan Gazette*: "The enemy . . . will soon have to retreat, as Gen. Sherman is able to flank them out of any position they can take here."[28]

In Union operations around Kennesaw Mountain near Marietta, Georgia, the 96th had several men killed, wounded, and captured. On June 19, Company C's William H. Ehlers was taken prisoner. Throughout the long day and into the evening of June 20, the Rebels repeatedly attacked, and casualties were frequent along the line. Colonel Champion was wounded in the face and taken back to the field hospital. Lt. Col. John C. Smith assumed command but was wounded while inspecting his front line when a bullet tore through his shoulder. He was carried to the rear. With Major Hicks absent due to exhaustion, the command fell to Capt. John Pollock of Company C. Captain Pollock worked with Captain Rowan of Company F to look over the line and determine the best position for the breastworks. The regimental pioneers were sent to work, but the enemy was preparing for their fifth charge of the day.[29]

The Rebels moved silently along the breastworks, overtaking the 35th Indiana and forcing them to abandon their works. An assault was planned for the 40th Ohio to regain the works, and the 96th was needed for support. Captain Pollock sent Companies B, G, and K under Captain Rowan. Before they were aware of it, they had reached the breastworks and were hit by Rebel fire. The regiment's history noted, "Several fell at the first volley, others ran back for shelter, but many remained, loading and firing as rapidly as possible, a few using the bayonet." Amid this fierce fire, the 40th Ohio came up and retook the works. The 96th's three companies rejoined the regiment, but they had sustained terrible losses, including Capt. Evangelist Gillmore of Company B who was hit three times, once in the head, and died five days later. Also among the wounded was stretcher-bearer George Smith of Company D, who was shot in the ankle, but remained on duty.[30]

The 96th was "in front of Kennesaw Mt." building fortifications, and they also participated with the brigade in pursuing the enemy. The regiment came under fire and sustained a high number of casualties during these first weeks of the campaign. By the end of June, the 96th Illinois's ranks had dwindled to about two hundred men.[31]

"A Fine View of Atlanta"

On July 5, the regiment reached the Chattahoochee River. Here the men were able to set up camp and indulge in bathing and washing their clothes. For a week they settled into a new routine with intervals of battery fire between the lines. During this encampment, George Smith wrote to his sister Susie about his "fine view of Atlanta." He made special note that "every thing being so quiate [*sic*] . . . it does really seem strange . . . after a long noisey dream." For Smith and his comrades, the reprieve from the constant noise and danger of enemy fire was a strange yet welcome relief.[32]

On July 17, Confederate president Jefferson Davis removed Gen. Joseph E. Johnston from command, noting Johnston's "constant withdrawals before Atlanta" amounting to a long and demoralizing retreat. In his place, Gen. John B. Hood was appointed commander of the Army of Tennessee.[33]

The 96th Illinois was at Peachtree Creek with Thomas's Army of the Cumberland. On July 20, the Confederates hoped to halt Thomas's advance southward to Atlanta (McPherson and Schofield were advancing their armies toward the city from the east). A delay in the Confederate attack allowed the 96th and other units to fortify their position on the south side of Peachtree Creek. According to the regiment's history, by this time in their military career, the men of the 96th had "acquired great proficiency in building breastworks." The fortified Union line and Union artillery batteries won the day.[34]

Two days later at the Battle of Atlanta, the 96th Illinois had "no active part." They "lay in line anxiously awaiting the outcome of the terrible struggle."

All were saddened to learn that Major General McPherson had been killed by Rebel skirmishers. Sherman described his close friend and leader of the Army of the Tennessee as "the impersonation of Knighthood."[35]

Outside Atlanta at the end of July, George Smith wrote home: "Imagine me last night just layed [*sic*] down for the night . . . looking at the star spangled cover of the house of nature & the flash of gun & shell along the line, like heat lightning along the horizon of a warm summers night with the exception of the heavy jarring report." Some of the Rebels' "monsters" exploded in the 96th's camp but caused no damage. The Federal batteries responded by shelling the city, and soon the evening sky was alight in a "bright blaze" from buildings burning in Atlanta.[36]

In a strange juxtaposition, the Ladies Aid Society at home was preparing a barrel of pickled cucumbers to send to the men to relieve their suffering. In a plea to the readers of the *Waukegan Gazette*, the society asked fellow citizens for cucumbers "for the use of our sick and wounded soldiers. . . . They will be precious to the soldier, though of so little account to us. Don't throw any more away. Let them be sent to the soldiers. The whiskey is ready to pickle the barrel, bought and paid for and waiting for the cucumbers."[37]

On August 25, the movement to the rear of Atlanta commenced. The 96th Illinois remained under the command of Maj. George Hicks, and along with the rest of Thomas's troops marched out and occupied Red Oak. While the 96th "engaged with enemy every day either skirmishing or fighting," other regiments destroyed rail lines. "The rails were torn up, heated, and twisted so that they were useless."[38]

Amid Sherman's troop movements south of Atlanta, the 96th was detailed to guard a wagon train on September 1. The Federals were concentrating at Jonesborough where they had encountered the majority of the Confederate Army. Late in the afternoon, the 96th was ordered to Jonesborough, "passing close up to the skirmishers before swinging into line-of-battle." The 96th was part of six infantry corps, coming under heavy fire in an exposed position as an overwhelming force of Federals attacked Confederate lieutenant general William J. Hardee's forces. At nightfall, Hardee's troops fell back to Lovejoy's Station.[39]

On the night of September 1–2, Hood realized he could no longer hold Atlanta and evacuated the city. The next day "found the army jubilant over the news . . . that Atlanta was occupied by Union troops, and there was lusty cheering all along the lines." George Smith wrote to his sister, "I suppose that before this you have heard of Sherman's great victory in Atlanta, which is another perfect Banker's trick on the Southern Confederacy which I think they will hardly be able to pay back very soon." The capture of Atlanta gave hope that the war would soon come to a close. Through the spring and summer of 1864, the armies' losses caused the morale of Northern civilians to drop and in turn boosted support for the Copperheads. The fall of Atlanta bolstered Northern morale and convinced many that "the Confederacy was doomed," ensuring Lincoln's reelection. In the 96th, a formal canvas of soldiers indicated their strong preference for Abraham Lincoln. Come November 8, in their exuberance for the Union, soldiers voted for Lincoln (three to one) and encouraged their families to do the same.[40]

Days later, on the second anniversary of the 96th Illinois's organization, the regiment was with the brigade in pursuit of the enemy. Within two or three miles, they were in sight of a long line of Rebel works near Lovejoy's Station. "One company after another was thrown upon the skirmish line, until nearly the entire Regiment was deployed." Under the direction of Major Hicks, the regiment was successfully propelled along in a bold charge, driving the enemy more than a mile into their skirmish pits. As more troops arrived in support, the 96th's skirmishers again advanced, taking possession of the pits.[41]

For four months they had been hard at work, and they were much relieved to have the Atlanta Campaign come to a close. The men were physically and mentally exhausted from "severe combat stress" and constant contact with the enemy. The 96th Illinois celebrated a much-needed rest and went into camp about two miles from Atlanta, "near the Augusta railroad, and pitching its tents near the graves of the brave men who fell with the gallant McPherson." During this period of rest, which included loading forage wagons and daily dress parades, James Murrie rejoined the regiment after recovering from his wound received at Dallas. Each day, a few men were given passes to visit Atlanta, and "in time all who cared to do so had made the circuit of the breastworks, and gone over the numerous and now historic battlefields about the town."[42]

When the 96th Illinois paraded through Atlanta, they unfurled their "battle torn standards to the breeze." Alex Thain described the boys as having "almost nothing to wear. At least every file had a pair of shoeless feet and as for dirt well we were all dirty." In the Atlanta Campaign, the Federal losses were more than three thousand officers and enlisted men killed, sixteen thousand wounded, and twenty-seven hundred captured.[43]

8. 🌼 Rally 'Round the Flag

The Franklin-Nashville Campaign
(September 18–December 27, 1864)

After abandoning Atlanta to the Federals, Confederate lieutenant general Hood took the remnants of his Army of Tennessee north, hoping to draw Sherman away from Atlanta and the heart of the Confederacy. The two armies had been butting heads for many months, but now Sherman turned his attention toward the Carolinas and his "March to the Sea." Historian Brooks D. Simpson explained that in preparing for his new campaign, Sherman chose the "best units under his command" for his fight through Georgia, trusting Maj. Gen. George H. Thomas "to defeat Hood. . . . [I]t would be no mean feat for Thomas to do [this] with inferior forces and reinforcements scattered all over the place." The 96th along with the IV Corps were separated from Sherman's command to join Thomas in Nashville to stop Hood's invasion. Sherman also detached Major General Schofield and his XXIII Corps to assist Thomas in defending the city.[1]

As the 96th marched north, they crossed the old battlefield at Chickamauga on October 29. A number of men who had fought there were still with the 96th, including Lt. Charles Earle, Sgt. Maj. Charles Partridge, Alex and Richard Thain, George Smith, and Orson Young. It was familiar, ghostly ground, but the march was too rapid and the men too fatigued to venture beyond their ranks to stop and reflect. As Partridge recalled, the men were unprepared to "go over that portion of the field where the Ninety-Sixth met its bloody baptism . . . and where its members were sleeping their last long sleep in unknown graves." There were still visible traces of the battle—shattered trees, burned fences, mounds beneath which the bodies of soldiers from both armies lay. For soldiers, there was no worse fate than having their remains left on the field for the enemy.[2]

On November 29, the IV Corps (Army of the Cumberland) under Maj. Gen. David S. Stanley escorted eight hundred wagons and forty artillery pieces. When Stanley learned that the Union garrison at Spring Hill was under attack, two IV Corps brigades were rushed up the turnpike. Confederate general Nathan Bedford Forrest's cavalry reached Spring Hill to find the IV Corps brigades waiting. The Rebel cavalry lacked the numbers to overcome the Federal infantry. As historian Derek W. Frisby noted, they "could only watch as the Union wagon train rumbled through Spring Hill."[3]

That night the Federals marched past the Confederates without notice. The 96th was within eight hundred yards of the enemy and spent an anxious night walking through a cornfield along the Columbia Pike. The road was so congested with ambulances, stragglers, artillery, and citizens that the 96th had to move into a farm field. While out to reconnoiter, Sgt. James Murrie and Corporal Swazey of Company C passed between the pickets of the enemy, nearly going to the Rebel campfires. Had this been most any other engagement in the war, Murrie and Swazey would have been fired upon or captured. According to Frisby, it was due to the "complacency and miscommunication in the Confederate high command [that] allowed Schofield's column to march past in the darkness without being challenged." Major General Stanley reported the remarkable circumstance of the Confederates allowing the Federal army "to pass them with impunity during the night."[4]

On November 30, the 96th passed through Franklin and bivouacked with other troops on a little hill near a cemetery close to the Harpeth River. On the north bank of the river stood Fort Granger, which the men had spent many hard days building in the spring of 1863. From the hill's vantage point, the 96th watched as the Second Battle of Franklin began. Hood's Army of Tennessee swept across the open field with a hundred battle flags waving to make a frontal assault on entrenched Federal forces. Partridge recalled that their view "was a grand one." The 96th sent out skirmishers, and "the bullets flew thick and fast." The regiment's movement was halted in reserve just behind the main line near Whitaker's second brigade. The firing continued after nightfall as the Rebels made a final assault, but the outcome of Hood's attack on Franklin was a devastated Army of Tennessee.[5]

The order was given at midnight for the Federals to withdraw to Nashville. The 96th with other troops of the First Division crossed the Harpeth River on the wagon bridge. Most of Schofield's XXIII Corps crossed on the railroad bridge. Before all the skirmishers were across, the Federals set fire to both bridges to prevent the enemy from following. Hundreds of Union wounded had to be left in town.[6]

The march from Franklin to Nashville tested the men both physically and mentally. Major General Stanley noted in his report, "Our men were more exhausted, physically, than I have ever seen on any other occasion." For a week the men were constantly on the road or building breastworks or skirmishing. Charles Partridge described the situation: "With us, both mind and body were kept at full stretch, and it was only by night marches and the constant use of entrenchments that we could hope to save ourselves." Historian James M. McPherson noted that the campaign of 1864 "caused the greatest toll of psychiatric as well as physical casualties" due to the armies' "daily contact for months on end," fighting and skirmishing. As Partridge recalled, all the men were "greatly in need of rest. But there was no alternative, and wearily the long column moved forward along the only pike leading northward." At one point, Captain Pollock of Company C and Captain Blowney of Company G were so desperate for just five minutes of rest that they sat on the ground while the column moved on. They fell asleep only to be shook awake by the rear guard and ordered to march on. Straggling was a method popularly used by soldiers to relieve the strain of fatigue and environmental hardships.[7]

Once the 96th Illinois and the rest of Thomas's army reached Nashville on December 1, they were issued clothing and given passes to visit the city. Nashville had been in Union hands since February 1862 and had become a critical supply depot for Northern forces. It was also the second most fortified city in the United States after Washington, D.C. When Major General Thomas's combined armies arrived outside the city, they expanded those fortifications. The experienced fortification builders of the 96th reinforced their lines, extended trenches, and stood picket duty. Hood's army had also reached Nashville and occupied hills across from the Federals. Due to the enemy's presence, there were occasions when the alarm sounded for the troops to fall into line.[8]

Although the city was protected by a force of nearly seventy thousand, Hood was determined to draw Thomas's forces out to attack him and take Nashville for the Confederacy. Lieutenant General Grant, who was at City Point, Virginia, overseeing Union military operations, was anxious for Thomas to attack Hood's diminished army. Brooks D. Simpson explained that Thomas had "gathered enough infantry to feel comfortable with taking the offensive," but he delayed action due to a lack in "sufficient cavalry to contend with Forrest."[9] An early winter ice storm was also a factor in Thomas's delay.

On December 15, with adequate reinforcements and better weather, reveille sounded at four o'clock in the morning. Before the first glimpse of dawn, Union forces were on the move—the Battle of Nashville had begun. The Federals attacked the Confederate right, while the actual main assault struck at fortifications on the Confederate left. There was fierce close-range combat, but the first day's assault had the 96th (as part of the IV Corps) on the second line. Meanwhile, the First Division marching between the Hillsboro and Granny White Pikes pressed the enemy back. The 96th followed, Partridge wrote, "sometimes under heavy fire from both musketry and artillery, but without an opportunity to take position in the front line or to return the fire." There were moments of long halts when the men of the regiment hugged the ground to avoid being hit.[10] That first night Hood's forces retreated two miles to the south.

On the morning of the second day of battle, the 96th advancing with the Second and Third Brigades near Franklin Pike swept forward for over a mile past farm buildings and fields. The enemy had begun firing on the Federals, and orders came to cross the open field and drive the Rebel skirmishers back. The men left the cover of the woods and rapidly advanced over a ploughed field without shelter and no support to the left. Enemy bullets hummed toward them. Occasionally, a man raised his musket and fired, but the majority moved forward silently with their Enfields on their right shoulders. John Washburn of Company B had a premonition that he would not survive the battle and gave his watch and pocketbook to a comrade to send to his wife. Seconds later, he was shot through the body and died.[11]

The 96th continued to be under severe fire and later stormed an entrenched Rebel battery before its occupants could reload their guns. Color guard Sgt. John Vincent of Company A, carrying the Stars and Stripes, "bravely mounted the works and ran along the parapet." The adjutant general of Illinois reported, "the Regiment behaved gallantly, carried the enemy's line near Franklin Pike, planted the first colors on his earthworks." Several men were wounded in the charge, including Henry H. Cutler of Company C, a former tentmate of Ed Murray, Loughlin Madden, Billy Lewin, and James Murrie, who received a mortal injury. Richard Thain included the news of Cutler's death in a letter to Susie Smith: "Poor Henery Cuttler of Co. C was killed. he received a Mortall wound on the 16 and died on the 17th. I belive Henery died happy. I was with him the night before he died." In a few lines, Thain expressed sadness over a comrade's death and the importance of dying well. By coming to his dying comrade's side to offer solace, Thain was acting as surrogate for the man's family. A "Good Death" reassured the living and gave the death meaning. For Cutler, it meant dying bravely and "happy" after taking part in a gallant charge in battle.[12]

That afternoon, Thomas attacked the three main Confederate positions. One by one, the Confederate lines of defense fell. Hood ordered the retreat, and the shattered Confederate Army escaped to the south. The Union's victory at Nashville ended the war in Tennessee, thereby enhancing Thomas's reputation.[13]

The next day the men of the 96th were on the road early with the IV Corps, chasing Hood and hoping to intercept remnants of his army at the Tennessee River. On December 23, between the Duck River and Lynnville, the Confederates halted and resisted the Union advance. The 96th and 115th Illinois were deployed, and after a brisk firefight they broke the enemy's line, in the process killing the Rebel captain and capturing five prisoners. It was here, the adjutant general reported, that "the Ninety-sixth exchanged the last infantry shots with the enemy."[14]

The 96th marched in a cold rain on Christmas day. The supply wagons were far behind, and there was very little left to forage in the countryside. That evening they went into camp several miles southwest of Pulaski, Tennessee, on a sloping hillside covered with stones. Alex Thain wrote to Susie Smith, "[A] rather sorry Christmas it was. We had marched away from the supply trains, our rations was out. . . . If I remember right my Christmas dinner was an ear of corn parched in a frying pan."[15]

Thain noted that the year closed in the pursuit of "Hood and his band of stragglers," ending with Hood's retreat across the Tennessee River on a pontoon bridge near Florence, Alabama. Major General Thomas's General Orders announced the end of the campaign: "Although short, has been brilliant in its achievements, and unsurpassed in its results by any other of this war, and is one of which all who participated therein may be justly proud."[16]

The year had been difficult for soldiers and civilians. Enthusiasm for the war had waned in the North due to military losses, but the triumph of the Atlanta Campaign had renewed hope and lifted Abraham Lincoln to victory in the November election. Susie Smith wrote to Richard Thain, "Our Boys in Blue grow hopefull as they see the bright glad sun of peace gleaming through the darkness of this terrible war." Thain replied that "the trembling hosts of barefooted southern hirelings flee before Thomases Noble Army. . . . Yes our cause is gaining ground I hope soon to see that sun of peace burst forth in its full brilliancy."[17]

1865

On New Year's Day, the cold and hungry soldiers huddled around campfires frying corn mush in bacon fat. For Alex Thain and his comrades, it was "not very sumptuous . . . but still very acceptable to a hungry man." The 96th had camped near Lexington, Alabama, and would be on the move again, anticipating a much-needed break in winter quarters. On January 3, the regiment crossed a newly constructed bridge over the Elk River and halted at Athens, Alabama. By nine o'clock on the morning of January 5, they marched through the village of Huntsville and camped about one mile outside of town. The men were quite taken by the village though the war had destroyed much of its beauty.[18]

A requisition was made for necessary items, including 150 pairs of shoes. The regimental history noted, "[T]he long march had worn out the shoes of the men." The troops set about laying out a camp and constructing cabins. Protection from winter's cold and snow inspired them to build elaborate quarters. Abandoned buildings were torn down and small groups of soldiers united to build a "shebang." Once the men were settled, dress parades and drills resumed. Captain Pollock returned from Pulaski, where he had remained due to illness, and took command of the regiment. Alex Thain described Pollock as a "very easy-going good hearted man but he possesses very little military genius or power of command so he takes no pride in putting us through a daly course of sprouts."[19]

The men went on foraging and scouting expeditions and occasionally encountered mounted Rebels. Otherwise, their days were occupied with reading, gathering wood for fires, attending church services in town, forming a glee club, and racing horses. Alex Thain visited slave quarters near Huntsville and met an "ancient African" whose mistress claimed was the "ripe age of a Century and a quarter." Thain implored, "God save me from such a cheerless old age. . . . After the poor slave has drudged out his years of usefullness and is no longer a source of profit to his master he is begrudged the miserable remains of his existance."[20]

Their stay in Huntsville was the longest in any one place for the 96th. In mid-March, it was determined that the IV Corps would move by rail to East Tennessee to be ready to march—if need be—to Richmond, Virginia, to defeat Confederate general Lee's army. The 96th abandoned its winter quarters, and the men were transported by freight cars to Strawberry Plains where they camped until March 25. From there, the men marched to Russellville, Tennessee, where they guarded a railroad bridge and pursued Rebel guerillas. On two occasions in early April, scouting parties of fifty to ninety men accompanied Capt. William O. Sizemore, a Rebel deserter turned Unionist. They pursued "Rebel bushwhackers" who were harassing loyal citizens and conscripting men into the Confederate Army. Though the soldiers were "inured to all the horrors of war," they drew the line when Sizemore brutally killed two Rebel prisoners after they had surrendered. The men of the 96th believed the "desperadoes" deserved punishment, but according to military law and not as it had been done. The incident stopped the regiment's further collaborations with Sizemore, whose lawless behavior went unpunished until he was shot dead in a revenge killing in 1867.[21]

On April 10, while encamped at Russellville, the men received news of the April 3 capture of Richmond, Virginia, and the surrender of General Lee and his army to Gen. Ulysses S. Grant at Appomattox Court House on Palm Sunday, April 9. Partridge recalled that the men were "wild with joy and daily shouted themselves hoarse." Historian Gary W. Gallagher noted that those who had labored and died to save the Union "believed victory over the slaveholders" strengthened the nation and prepared the country for its "continuing growth and vitality."[22]

Amid the revelry, James Murrie was suffering from a painful attack of rheumatism. When the regiment left Russellville, they left him behind. The regiment marched thirteen miles to rejoin Whitaker's brigade at Shields Mills in East Tennessee. To celebrate the Union's victory, Major General Stanley ordered the troops to mass "amid the rugged mountains" on April 14. A veteran band played, and addresses were given by Brig. Gen. Nathan Kimball, Lt. Col. George Hicks (96th Illinois), and the abolitionist Methodist chaplain William S. Crissey (115th Illinois). Thousands of voices joined together to sing the popular patriotic song, "Battle Cry of Freedom."[23]

The war was won! The sounds of music and shouts of happiness could be heard through the night. For four days the men celebrated the fall of the Confederacy, unaware that at 10:15 p.m. Eastern Time on April 14, President Lincoln had been fatally shot at Ford's Theater by John Wilkes Booth.

Saturday, April 15, dawned cold and cloudy, but spirits were high. As supply teams arrived, an officer accompanying them rode ahead and reported in low tones the terrible news that had come across the wires from the nation's capital—"Lincoln is Assassinated!" The words spread quickly and a hush fell over the camps. Partridge revealed that "a great sorrow welled up in every heart. . . . The day before had seemed to these brave veterans the gladdest in all their lives; and now an unspeakable grief had blotted out their happiness and a gloom that seemed well-nigh impenetrable was upon them."[24]

Never before had an American president been assassinated—that alone was too much to bear—but to happen at the moment the nation's goal had been achieved was beyond comprehension. The men stood around campfires speaking in hushed tones or not at all. All were shocked by the jolt of sorrow after such joyous news of victory. The loss was personal for the soldiers. President Lincoln was a father figure who had stood at the nation's helm during the terrible war, only to be snuffed out at the moment of victory.[25]

Army chaplains gave sermons to remain "steadfast in one's faith," and the War Department issued General Orders No. 44, stating, "The nation mourns the untimely and violent death of the late President of the United States, Abraham Lincoln. . . . All officers . . . will wear the usual badge of mourning upon the left arm for thirty days."[26]

The men found solemn comfort in one another's presence and a sense of universal grief, which was echoed in newspaper headlines. The *Waukegan Weekly Gazette*'s read: "The Terrible Tragedy at Washington. President Lincoln Assassinated!" The paper went on to say, "No event has ever transpired in this country which cast so deep a gloom over it, or so moved the souls of the people with inexpressible anguish." The *Chicago Tribune*'s postscript at four o'clock a.m. read, "Terrible News. President Lincoln Assassinated at Ford's Theater. A Rebel Desperado Shoots Him Through the Head and Escapes."[27]

For some, Lincoln had been sacrificed as the war's last martyr. Scottish-born Alex Thain struggled with the emotions of the day: "We rejoiced without stint untill the sad news of Lincolns death changed our joy to mourning. There was something of anger mixed with sorrow—anger for his enemies and for those who might rejoice over the sad event . . . Yes even here in the army many such men were found but they were at once placed under arrest and treated with due severity."[28]

"Revenge!" was the word that brought relief. Historian Martha Hodes explained that Union soldiers fantasized about meeting the Confederates on the battlefield to "brutally [attack] their already vanquished enemies." Orson Young wrote, "A man in our brigade said he was glad that the President was killed. Gen Kimball ordered his head shaved and had him drummed the length of the division to the tune of the rogues march."[29]

On the home front, the perception of "universal mourning" was shattered when "nativism joined racism in slicing through the wished-for communal grieving." Hodes noted that across the nation incidents of racism toward African American mourners and soldiers and nativist outbursts against Irish, Scots, Germans, Jews, and Roman Catholics reminded many "that reconstruction would come hard to the postwar nation." In Waukegan, Horace Hinckley gave an "assassin sympathizer a good sound flogging" after the man said it was "a damned small loss" that the president was murdered.[30]

The president's funeral was held in Washington, D.C., on April 19. His remains were escorted from the White House down Pennsylvania Avenue in a procession lined with thousands of mourners to the Capitol Rotunda, where he lay in state in an open coffin. On April 21, the president's funeral train set out for his hometown of Springfield, Illinois, retracing the route he had traveled to Washington as president-elect in 1861. The train's route and schedule were widely published, and wherever the train went, whether stopping in a large city such as Philadelphia or passing through the countryside, mourners gathered to watch. Even in the darkness of night, people gathered by lantern light and bonfires to watch the funeral train as it carried their late president to his final resting place.[31]

On May 1, the train arrived in Chicago. Among the 125,000 mourners to view Lincoln's body was Leonard Doolittle of Company C, 96th Illinois. Doolittle's right leg had been shot below the knee at Chickamauga, and he was subsequently a prisoner for ten days with Edward Murray. His wound was such that an amputation was discussed, but Doolittle pleaded with the Union surgeons to reassess his leg, and they agreed the limb could be saved. He was sent to the U.S. Government Hospital at Camp Douglas to recuperate but was never again able to serve.[32]

Drew Gilpin Faust noted that the funeral observations "acknowledged and intensified" the connection between the late president and the American people. Illinoisans felt a special connection to the man they had first known as a lawyer, senator, and friend. On the day of the train's arrival in Chicago, Leonard Doolittle left the hospital to go "down to the city" where the viewing was to take place at the Cook County Courthouse.[33]

At about 11 o'clock on the morning of May 1, the train pulled into the city, stopping on a trestle built a short distance into Lake Michigan. The funeral train's bell tolled to notify citizens of its arrival. The streets were muddy from a morning rain, but nothing could deter the mourners, who poured out of their residences and businesses eager to participate in the funeral's rituals. Doolittle was overwhelmed by the sight. "I think that I never saw as many men women and children at one time in my life. In fact I know I never saw half as many at one time before as I saw today." Like the others, Doolittle struggled to find meaning in the assassination and wished to bid his president goodbye. Abraham Lincoln, who had figured so prominently in their lives over the last four years, was gone, but there was still a chance to see the man who had guided them to victory. Lincoln's face was the only one that Doolittle and the mass of mourners wished to gaze upon to find meaning and closure.[34]

Leaning on crutches, Leonard Doolittle stood in line for hours, shuffling along with thousands of mourners into the Cook County Courthouse. At last they came into a dimly lighted room where the president lay in state amid patriotic decorations. Those who anticipated a moment to look upon the martyred president's face and pray for his eternal soul were disappointed. In order to allow the great multitude to view the remains, each person was permitted only a second or two, giving them barely a glimpse. Perhaps that was a blessing. As Martha Hodes noted, by the time the president's body had reached Chicago, his "face had darkened nearly beyond repair." The art of embalming had yet to be perfected, and even with an attendant powdering the face, mourners expressed surprise that Lincoln did not look "as they fancied great men did."[35]

As one of the seven thousand people per hour that viewed Lincoln's remains in Chicago, Leonard Doolittle hopefully found the closure he sought. For Doolittle, as for many soldiers, the president's was the final death of the war, representing each soldier's death and all soldiers' deaths.[36] Amid the long shadow cast by the president's assassination was the fact that the war was over and won. Now the men began to contemplate their journey home to resume their civilian lives.

9. ❖ Heroes of the Army of Liberty

With the nation still in its early days of grief, the men of the 96th Illinois were anticipating their last days as soldiers. On April 17, Lt. Gen. Ulysses S. Grant sent a communication to Maj. Gen. George H. Thomas stating, "The freedom of Virginia from occupation by an armed enemy renders the occupation of East Tennessee in large force longer unnecessary. You may commence the withdrawal of the Fourth Corps to Nashville immediately."[1]

As rapidly as trains could be secured, the regiments started for Nashville to rendezvous with the IV Corps. The 96th Illinois reached the city on the evening of April 22. The next morning, they marched five miles out and settled at Camp Harker, which had been named for Brig. Gen. Charles Harker who fell in the charge at Kennesaw Mountain. Though situated in a "delightful spot," the soldiers' hearts were set on mustering out and going home. Rumors abounded that the 96th would be sent with the IV Corps to Texas or possibly to Atlanta or Montgomery. There were still large Confederate forces operating in North Carolina, Alabama, Mississippi, and Louisiana, but ultimately the Army of the Cumberland would not be called to assist in their pursuit.[2]

With the war nearing a close, drilling ceased, roll calls were infrequent, guard duty was light, and dress parades were held in pleasant weather. Even with their days as soldiers numbered, the men demanded that cleanliness be maintained, and crowds of them bathed daily in the Cumberland River. George Smith, ever the humorist, referred to Camp Harker as "Camp Suspence." Since "having finished the job for which we en listed, the time now drags more heavily upon us. . . . Souldiering with us went up the spout the moment that Rebelion fell."[3]

On May 4, there was a grand review of the IV Corps. Charles Partridge described "a brilliant galaxy of distinguished army officers," led by Major General Thomas, who rode the lines, and each regiment presented arms as they passed. Though the men were cheerful, "feeling that it was, in all probability, their last review," it also meant they would soon be saying goodbye to their comrades.[4]

On the evening of May 17, the 96th Illinois with the enlisted men of the First Division "organized a grand torch-light procession and marched to Corps Headquarters." Partridge explained the intent was to "testify the good-will of the enlisted men toward their commanders" with a hope that they would receive official word "as to the plans and prospects for the future." Brigadier General Stanley and Maj. Gen. Nathan Kimball made speeches to the five thousand men in line.[5]

On June 1, division commander Major General Kimball addressed a "Congratulatory Order" to (brevetted) Col. John C. Smith, commanding the 96th Illinois, stating, "Your deeds will live forever." Kimball paraphrased President Lincoln's second inaugural address: "Return to your homes with enmity toward none and charity for all." Military commanders, preachers, and the like turned to the late president's words "malice toward none" and "charity for all" to diffuse the anger so many felt for his loss and to encourage mercy and forgiveness.[6]

The first of June was designated by President Andrew Johnson as a national day of fasting and prayer in honor of Abraham Lincoln. At home in Millburn, Susie Smith attended a service at the Congregational church and noted in her diary: "This is the day set apart . . . on account of the loss of our late President Abraham Lincoln, who was murdered by the blood thirsty assassin J.W. Booth." While some Northerners perceived the day as a holiday, the abolitionist congregation in Millburn turned to the challenges ahead for the nation and hopes for African American suffrage and citizenship.[7]

The following week, the 96th was notified that the original group of enlistees would be mustered out. Other enlisted men whose three-year service did not expire prior to October 1, 1865, were to be assigned to the 21st Illinois Infantry—General Grant's first regiment.[8]

Once the rolls were completed for each company and each man signed his name, the 96th Illinois was declared mustered out on Saturday, June 10, 1865. Of the band of five men from the Stateline Road in Newport Township, only James Murrie had made it to the mustering out. Murrie was also one of twenty-seven men (out of ninety-three) who had enlisted with Company C in September 1862 and remained for its entire term of service.[9]

On June 11, the regiment was ordered to Camp Douglas in Chicago for final pay and discharge. James Murrie formed in line with the regiment, who together gave "hearty cheers for the Union and the flag" as the band played "Get Out of the Wilderness." If only his comrades Ed Murray, Billy Lewin, Loughlin Madden, and John Taylor had made it to the moment with him.

The remnants of the 96th marched toward Nashville to catch their train to "God's country," all the while singing and shouting. Though many were genuinely overjoyed to be on their way home, some hid concerns for how they would readapt to civilian life and live each day without their comrades by their side.[10]

The men rode in freight cars overnight to Louisville, Kentucky. With such a large number of troops going north, rail transportation became congested and delayed. At Louisville, a railroad official informed the 96th's Colonel Smith that Chicago-bound trains were several hours behind schedule and suggested he and his men walk four miles to New Albany, Indiana, where passenger cars would be waiting. The day was "excessively hot," but the men voted unanimously to make the march. At New Albany they found a freight train recently unloaded of cattle and ice. The colonel demanded the passenger train as promised, but in vain. Railroad officials assured them that if they took the freight, passenger cars would be available in Bloomington, Indiana. The veterans felt it "an outrage for the railroad officials to attempt to ship men in the damp, seatless cars." With thoughts only of getting home, the men shoveled out the sawdust, waste, and melted ice and crowded into the smelly cars. George Smith wrote, "Tumbling onto freight cars . . . rather disheartend us."[11]

They reached Bloomington about midnight, and Colonel Smith quickly became convinced that they would not be given passenger cars "unless he compelled it." The colonel placed himself at a switch blocked by the freight on which they had come from New Albany, and stood his ground to prevent the freight from moving until his demands were met. Over the course of a few hours, the colonel and the railroad officials threatened one another until the railroad was compelled to surrender. His men thought very highly of him for "standing up for their rights."[12]

Only a couple hundred miles remained of their journey, and spirits were high as they headed closer to home and farther from the battlefields. The boys had traveled into the heart of peril, and victoriously restoring the Union and abolishing slavery. Partridge wondered, "[A]t what frightful cost had that change been brought about!" They were uncertain if the war's achievements would hold and what life would be like after three years away from home. Historian Mark L. Bradley noted that much was left unresolved, including the "civil, political, and economic status [of freed blacks] in the postwar South."[13]

Chicago was sleeping at one o'clock in the morning on June 14 when they arrived on the Michigan Central Railroad at the Union Depot. Three years earlier, they had stood on this very spot, nearly one thousand strong, now the men of the 96th Illinois stepped off the train with little more than four hundred in their midst. Partridge described the scene: "Then the uniforms were new and clean; now they were travel-stained and battle-grimed. Then the faces were mainly young and fair; now all were bronzed, and many prematurely old." Colonel Smith commanded: "Fall in, boys!" "Stack arms!" "Rest at will!" After a moment's confusion, the men recognized their commander's good humor. A few headed out to find rooms at nearby hotels while most, including George Smith, spread out blankets to sleep on the depot platform, weary from the long ride.[14]

The next morning, they were provided breakfast by the Great Northwestern Sanitary Fair. The men were well acquainted with the U.S. Sanitary Commission, which the fair was organized to support. During the war, the commission had sent agents to inspect military camps and hospitals, lobby for better conditions, and distribute extra rations. While it continued to raise funds for convalescing soldiers, it collaborated with the Young Men's Christian Association in finding employment for returning veterans.[15]

The 96th Illinois was treated by Chicagoans as if they were "sons and brothers." They paraded on Michigan Avenue in the drenching rain, their hearts swelling with pride as they marched into the Sanitary Fair's Union Hall to resounding applause and a band playing "When Johnny Comes Marching Home." The 96th's Lt. Col. George Hicks voiced the regiment's "heartfelt thanks . . . for their expressions of respect and love to the men." The band played "Red, White and Blue," which was followed by three cheers for the 96th Illinois, three for Chicago, and three for the ladies. The excitement at this welcome and the impressive exhibitions at the fair filled them with great hope for the future, but for some it was merely a delay in getting home.[16]

After dinner at the Soldiers' Rest, news came that their former commander William T. Sherman was in Chicago. The regiment formed on Michigan Avenue and marched up Lake Street to the Tremont House "for the purpose of serenading" the general. The men faced the hotel's north balcony and the band played a patriotic tune. Sherman appeared on the balcony to the cheering soldiers and welcomed them home "to your old Illinois." With "no more 'rebs' to shoot and no more 'rebs' to shoot us," the general wished the men peaceful lives on their farms and in their former employment.[17]

The men were proud of their service and grateful for these parting words, but some wondered how they would manage their homecoming. They were no longer wide-eyed farmers learning to march in line but seasoned soldiers. They would have no bugle call or drumbeat to tell them when their day began and ended. The regimental history stated, "They were to be thrown out into the great busy world; to grapple with its work, each in his own way."[18]

The paymasters had yet to pay off the 96th, and while the men waited, they were quartered in barracks at Camp Douglas. During this time, the Lake County men were allowed to visit their homes. George Smith delayed going home because he only had "twenty five cents to save me," which was not enough for train fare. "Our things were all in a heep at the depot and some of those hotheads, would have lost every thing if someone hadnt stayed to take care of them. so I saw that they got to camp all safe." Smith was conscientious and aware of the surge in crime as thieves and tricksters preyed upon discharged soldiers, especially at railroad stations. Pickpockets and thugs knew that soldiers had their discharge pay, and crime had been on the rise in Chicago for months as troops returned from the war.[19]

Word spread quickly of the 96th Illinois's arrival in Chicago. In Millburn, Susie Smith waited with nervous excitement for the return of her brother and the other boys. At the Grub School where she taught, she stood at the window looking down the road for any sign of the men. After a rainy morning on June 15, she got word that the Thain brothers were in the neighborhood. During the past year, she and Richard Thain had kept a lively correspondence, and though she had known him before the war, she now had more personal feelings for him. The schoolgirls shared her excitement about the "soldier boys" coming home. Susie recalled that they crowned her head with "oak leaves and roses, so, as they say, that their teacher may look pretty, if she should have company this afternoon." When Richard came to the school that afternoon, Susie was in "such a tremble of excitement" that she "could hardly speak to him." Richard made quite an impression in his Union blues.[20]

Four days later, Susie was having tea at a friend's house when "a load of soldiers came up in full force" in a horse-drawn wagon. Among the men was her "own dear Brother," and she rushed out to embrace him. Together they headed north to their family home, stopping twice at local residences to take cover from rain showers. Susie wrote, "It was the most beautiful shower that I ever saw. . . . [E]very drop of rain seemed changed to one of gold, and the trees and shrubs sparkled in the yellow light beautiful as a dream, pretty soon a bright rain bow arched over the Eastern sky. A good omen."[21]

Two days later, George walked Susie to her school but found the schoolhouse empty. The children had been told Miss Smith would not be teaching because her brother was home from the war. George and Susie spent the day together, and that evening their friends, Richard and Alex Thain, stayed all night. "Sang, talked, and had a good time generaly. Indeed I write it as the happiest day of my life. So what do I care whether 'school keeps or not.'"[22]

Though home looked much the same, his sister and the townsfolk had also been changed by the war. To support the Union and the soldier boys, Susie Smith participated in aid society donations and became a contributor and "editress" of the *Millburn Union Casket*, a pro-Union literary newsletter. Her coeditor was John Bonner, whose brother William was still missing following the Battle of Chickamauga. In February 1865, Susie wrote in the newsletter, "We know that Millburn is not the same place to us it was one year ago. . . . [T]he people have awakened up to duty, and are busy and active in good. . . . [T]he Aid keeps nimble fingers at work preparing comforts for our brave and noble soldiers."[23]

This support from his family and community sustained George Smith and the Millburn boys throughout the war and eased their transition coming home. Without their neighbors' "awakened up to duty," the morale of the boys in the 96th would have plummeted. That connection over so great a distance was possible due to remarkably fast mail service. The Union army understood the importance of letters from home and did everything in its power to ensure efficient delivery. Susie's letters had an effect on all who received them. As Richard Thain wrote, "Dear Friend you have no idea how much good your letters do me." In return, the soldiers' letters, especially those from her brother, kept Susie's spirits up, even during 1864 when morale overall was flagging on the Northern home front.[24]

While at home on leave, George Smith was quick to lend a hand on the family farm, spending part of a day shearing sheep with his father. On a rainy Sunday, George went to services at the Millburn Congregational Church with his family. Susie wrote, "O. how thankful we are to greet them once in the places which they have kept vacant so long." The next morning, with their furlough at an end, the Millburn soldiers were taken to Waukegan to catch the train to Chicago.[25]

On June 28, the regiment was paid and disbanded. The men from Lake and Jo Daviess Counties, who had joined to form the 96th Illinois Volunteer Infantry, were now faced with their inevitable separation. The adjutant general of Illinois estimated that the 96th had marched or traveled by rail or steamer over five thousand miles in the service of the United States. As reported, this "careful estimate of the distances traveled" spanned their departure from Camp Fuller, Rockford, Illinois, on October 8, 1862, to their return home at Camp Douglas, Chicago, on June 14, 1865. That journey had been undertaken by men, both native and foreign born, from two distinct geographic areas of Illinois, and yet they had bonded and supported one another through the trials of life as soldiers fighting to save the Union. In the process of serving together, these men had the unique opportunity to experience the nation's ethnic diversity and find commonality in a shared cause.[26]

The war united Northerners in a patriotic fervor to preserve the Union, whether Republicans or Democrats, native or foreign born. The vast majority of immigrant men, such as Edward Murray and his companions, enlisted in non-ethnic regiments. The popularity of these units, historian William L. Burton explained, "affirms the position that most ethnics consciously sought assimilation." However, ethnic tensions still arose. For Germans, language and cultural differences fueled prejudice against them, and their sense of ethnic identity increased out of a fear it could be lost. The Irish, according to historian Susannah J. Ural, faced a "perceived disloyalty" in part for their opposition to Lincoln's Emancipation Proclamation. Despite the challenges, many Irish and Germans bonded with their native-born comrades and came through the war with a stronger connection to their adopted country. Irishman Edward Malone, who immigrated in 1849, enlisted in the 96th Illinois's Company G and was promoted to sergeant. The regimental history heralded him as "conspicuous for his courage" and for uplifting "the drooping spirits of the men" with his wit and humor. German-born Frederick G. Worth enlisted just five years after his arrival in the United States and marched side by side with the men of the 96th "in nearly every skirmish and battle." His bond with his comrades continued throughout the remainder of his life as a member of the local Grand Army of the Republic post.[27]

The men's esprit de corps forged them into a family, and many endured a bitter parting with tears and quivering lips. The 96th's history noted the men's brave "cheers for each other,–with good-byes and God-bless-yous," before they went their separate ways. Their service together ended, but the shared hardships they had endured "were too strong to untie them."[28]

Welcome to the Heroes

The four Lake County companies were paid first, allowing them to take a special train to Waukegan to attend a reception on the afternoon of June 28. A telegram was sent to confirm their departure on the Chicago and North Western. Though many men had returned home in the preceding days, this celebration marked their official welcome. At 3:40 p.m., the locomotive's whistle was heard as the train came into Waukegan. "Here they come!" thousands of citizens exclaimed as they lined the bluff to watch the arrival of approximately 120 men who had survived battle, death, and disease.[29]

Bells rang in the city as women waved white handkerchiefs and men removed their hats in respect. The veterans leapt onto the station's platform, and as Partridge remembered, "their valiant hands were grasped with an earnestness that spoke louder than words."[30] The men were very much changed by war—their faces drawn and thin, their bodies wrecked from wounds and illness, and some were missing limbs. Some family members did not even recognize their loved ones, for they had been so transformed in body and spirit, but all were greeted as heroes with flowers and praise.

A band led the grand procession, followed by the reception committee, the soldiers, and the citizens. They proceeded from the depot up the bluff, where two lines of young women showered the men with summer flowers. Then they walked alongside the soldiers as they marched past the courthouse square, ending in front of Dickinson Hall. A stand was placed in front of the hall for attorney Clark W. Upton to make the reception speech. He bid welcome to the "Soldiers of the glorious old Ninety-Sixth Regiment Illinois Volunteers, heroes of the Army of Liberty," and declared, "You so nobly helped secure . . . freedom of all men, black as well as white." It had been five years, though it seemed a lifetime since the late President Lincoln had stood in that very hall. It was fitting to pay tribute to the veterans and their fallen comrades in the place where Lincoln had declared that "civilization had pronounced human slavery wrong." Here were the men who had put down slavery and rebellion to save the Union.[31]

The speech continued with special focus on the brave lives lost. "Those martyred heroes still live, though their bones may rest in unknown graves . . . their heroic achievements and brilliant deeds shall live embalmed in story and in song." Among Company C's fallen were John Taylor, Loughlin Madden Jr., William Bonner Jr., Squire Inman, Henry Cutler, and Orange Ayers. For the returning soldiers, the absence of these men was keenly felt, especially when, as historian Brian Matthew Jordan explained, they "reaped the laurels for battles won with the blood of their dead comrades." The war had taken thousands of men from their families in death and changed the survivors forever. Celebrating the return of the veterans—the living—stirred memories of the dead. As Drew Gilpin Faust noted, honoring those lost "became inseparable from respecting the living."[32]

On behalf of the regiment, Lt. Col. George Hicks recounted the valiant acts of the 96th and how they "took the field knowing what was before them."

After his remarks, the soldiers were ushered into the hall to enjoy a feast prepared by the women of Waukegan. Cigars were provided, and Henry Blodgett regaled the regiment's "glorious record." Blodgett had won the soldiers' deep regard for his efforts to bring them aid and support. He made special mention of the women who "worked so incessantly" for the soldiers' welfare. When the volunteers went off to war, women were also filled with patriotism, and they found ways to support the soldiers. Nancy Dixon Murray, Susie Smith, Mary Bater, Hannah Clarke, and others aided the troops by making quilts for army hospitals; sending care packages filled with apples, crocks of butter, and hand-knitted socks; collecting monetary donations; and writing letters to keep up the men's spirits. The soldiers gave "three rousing cheers" for their unwavering support.[33]

Patriotic citizens acknowledged the soldiers' service through homecoming celebrations, but communities and the federal government were not prepared emotionally or structurally to alleviate the challenges that awaited the men. People were desperate for a return to normalcy, but the support that had comforted soldiers through long years of war was needed more than ever as veterans struggled to find their place in the world again. The harsh reality of returning to civilian life played out differently for each man and depended on many factors. Ed Murray, Billy Lewin, James Murrie, and James Taylor faced physical and emotional challenges, but they were aided in their transition to postwar life by family and an unbreakable bond with comrades.[34]

Regimental affiliation was particularly important as they navigated their return home. When they happened upon one another at fairs or church picnics they were immediately drawn together, their esprit de corps as strong as if they had never mustered out. They were ever united in shared experiences of hardship and loss, as well as victory, and the knowledge that they were stronger together. But their hard-won Union triumph was being undermined by President Andrew Johnson's pardons of rebel leaders. The lack of justice emboldened the South to slip back into its antebellum ways and place harsh restrictions on freedmen. In response, the veterans united in advocating for the civil, economic, and political rights of those freed.[35]

The homecoming festivities continued on the Fourth of July, when citizens and veterans attended a picnic at Druce Lake. The *Waukegan Gazette* announced, "Citizens of the county—and especially the soldiers—are invited to be there." Susie Smith and her family set out for the celebration at eight o'clock in the morning with her brother and four other soldiers. She wrote that each had "baskets of goodies . . . laden with beautiful flowers." They stopped in Millburn where the boys took down a large American flag "to carry with us, and purchased a goodly supply of candy."[36]

The euphoria of the war's end and the men's return kept the little group talking, laughing, and joking as they traveled by wagon. "O, so joyfuly. O, so thankfully," as Susie recalled. "By our sides sat those brave hero boys who, one year ago, were engaged amid the din and cloud of battle fighting for their much loved country. God had spared them and now they [are] at home once more."[37]

In a hickory grove on the banks of the glacial lake, the group met James Taylor, who had recently returned from Philadelphia where he had been fitted with an artificial arm. Though the loss of a limb hindered many veterans from earning a living, an ambitious Taylor had attended Bryant and Stratton Commercial College while waiting for the arm to be finished. On his return to Illinois, he became a lawyer.[38] This picnic was the first opportunity he had to meet many of his comrades since being wounded at the Battle of Rocky Face Ridge.

Susie Smith was so moved by James Taylor's presence that she made special mention of him in her diary: "One poor fellow, who had loved a much loved brother in the strife for Freedom, and whose own right arm had been lifted up, for this our own proud land, wears now the nerveless arm that tells no pulses, feels no pain." As she stood before Taylor with his "nerveless arm," the war's brutality became much more real. She reflected on that moment in her diary: "That stiff gloved hand that never is uncovered, does it not tell a history? Does it not bid us think, and all the more respect the hero man who wears it? Till we almost come to bless the very arm that fills the place of that he gave to make us free?"[39]

Only a fraction of these "empty sleeves" as the amputees came to be called, wore artificial limbs. Many could not afford them or found them uncomfortable. Some soldiers chose not to have prosthetics, and as Brian Matthew Jordan explained, they believed their empty sleeves were "living monuments of the late cruel and bloody Rebellion." Susie Smith saw and understood this valuable lesson, but not all civilians were comfortable with the reminder when all they wanted was to put the war and its divisiveness behind them.[40]

The *Chicago Tribune* promoted the levy of a tax for state military asylums, "to provide for the comfort of the disabled soldier." The editorial noted that "every loyal and generous heart" was looking for a way to show "gratitude to the maimed warrior," touching on the problem for how to appropriately express appreciation beyond parades and welcome speeches. "He who has left his leg or arm on the battlefield as his offering to Union . . . can never be regarded as an object of charity." The sense that these wounds were a sacrifice made at the altar of war was a common theme. Susie Smith illustrated this in her comment regarding James Taylor's arm having been "lifted up" for the sake of the Nation.[41]

While James Taylor was able to go to school even as he struggled to regain his health and make his way in the world, many limbless veterans had difficulty supporting themselves and their families. Taylor's comrade from the 96th Illinois, John H. Cruver, had his right arm amputated and, like many disabled veterans, was unable to work. However, he was inspired to enter a left-hand penmanship competition sponsored by William Oland Bourne, the editor of the *Soldiers' Friend*. Bourne's "appeals for left-handed manuscripts appeared in newspapers across the country." On September 18, 1865, Cruver wrote from his home in Gilmer, Lake County, Illinois, "I have determined to make an effort although my wound has been so painful and trouble some." Cruver had his arm "shattered at the elbow" at Chickamauga. He endured three operations, which ultimately removed the "entire elbow joint . . . and five inches of the bone from the elbow up." Part of Cruver's motivation for entering the competition was "to offer a specimen for the premiums." The possibility of being one of ten entries awarded $50 by an esteemed panel of judges, which included Gen. Ulysses S. Grant, was great impetus to participate.[42]

The twenty-three-year-old's recounting of his "experience as a soldier in Co. 'B'" read like a rough draft of the regimental history. "The boys stood up well and amid the thickest of the fight not one man flinched from his duty." It was so important to expound on his unit's brave and manly record at Chickamauga that Cruver struggled through pain to write a four-page manuscript. "It was at this battle that I happened to be so unfortunate as to be severely wounded through my right elbow joint, which renders the arm useless and very painful. The wound is still unhealed and much swollen. Since that unhappy event I have been in hospitals much of the time." Although Cruver did not win the prize money, his essay was among the several hundred submitted and exhibited at Seaton Hall in Washington, D.C., in May 1866. The proceeds from the public exhibition benefitted disabled veterans in military hospitals around Washington.[43]

Death and suffering had become the soldiers' ultimate sacrifice, but the overwhelming number of dead became a tragedy too great to bear. The nation became preoccupied by death, as songs and poetry that redefined death as eternal life became popular. In Christian faith or in a view that life is providential, many believed that God controlled all things. Historian Reid Mitchell explained that the believer merely had to persevere in "service to

God, family, and country." Soldiers, in particular, reflected on the meaning of ever-present death.[44]

Following Lincoln's assassination, Alex Thain remarked on the dependability of death in the army: "I know of no better place to disabuse one of the vague terrors surrounding death and the dead than the army. Death goes with on our campaigns and gives us many sad proofs of his power every day. He camps with us when the campaign is over . . . his sternness neither softened by poetical fancies nor increased by superstitious terrors." Thain's prose expressed his deep reflection on the meaning of death and his acceptance of it at his side. Death went with soldiers everywhere, keeping lost comrades close at heart. While friends and family struggled with loss and were made aware of the war's horrors through casualty lists in newspapers and Mathew Brady's photographs, they had not experienced battles and could only imagine the suffering. With the return of limbless veterans such as James Taylor, citizens were faced with the war's uncomfortable realities. Brian Matthew Jordan concluded that most wanted to deny the "lingering consequences of Civil War soldiering" and were "inept [at] recommending 'appropriate' expressions of sympathy and appreciation."[45]

Susie Smith was humbled that her brother had remained safe. "I look across to where my Brother sits, he who has fought amid the fiercest battles and has been where the whistling shell, and whispering balls, sang the dirges of his just fallen comrades, and still he came out safe: That noble Brother whom as I look up to I pray to God to make me worthy of and when I see his brow unmarked, his heart unscathed, shall I not think and praise my God that he has brought him safe through all the trials and dangers of the past few years."[46]

Over the coming months, Susie Smith and Richard Thain would spend a good deal of time in each other's company, and Susie began to fall in love with Richard. But Thain had ambitions in Chicago, and he spent less and less time in Millburn. Susie was heartbroken. On New Year's Day, 1867, she wrote in her diary, "I did hope to see Richard to day and I know he would have come if it had been possible but I was so grieved over it . . . I did cry." Eventually, Susie accepted that their lives were on different paths. Someone closer to home began to win her heart—another veteran of the 96th, David J. Minto, who was a farmer and schoolteacher. On May 20, 1869, Susie and David were married. The following spring, Susie's brother George married Susanna G. White.[47]

On August 2, 1865, James Taylor and his sister Mary Bater visited the home of Rev. William B. Dodge. Though he had retired from the pulpit, the reverend's good counsel was still sought by the community. James was living in Waukegan and practicing law, but his roots were in Millburn where he, Mary, and their brother John had started their life in Illinois. Thoughts of their dear brother brought James and Mary to the Dodge home. Over a cup of tea, they discussed the funeral sermon they wished to have preached for John at the Millburn Congregational Church. In the midst of their visit, Susie Smith and Mary Hastings dropped in. Susie recalled that they had a "very pleasant time" together.[48]

Circumstances of the war had made it impossible to properly grieve for John. James had been denied a place at his deathbed, and John's burial, hundreds of miles from home in Nashville, made it difficult for his family to accept the loss. The war was over, but it still held claim on their lives. The Taylors had the small consolation of knowing where their brother's remains were laid to rest, but many families endured one of the war's remaining horrors: the great number of dead still unidentified and unburied. Many men had been buried without proper identification on the battlefields where they had fallen, at hospitals, or in prisons, and in shallow graves or trenches. The government initiated the Federal Reburial Program, but its task was uncommonly challenging. When the reinterment program concluded in 1871, the remains of approximately three hundred thousand Union soldiers and officers had been located and reburied. About 42 percent of Union dead remained unidentified.[49] Regrettably, the South would be excluded from the program, as politicians decided to leave the reburial of the Southern dead to the former Confederacy.

Among the beneficiaries of the program were John Y. Taylor and Loughlin Madden Jr. After Taylor's death at Army Hospital No. 12 in Nashville, his body was respectfully prepared for burial by members of the Sanitary Commission or the Christian Commission. His body was placed in a coffin, given a religious service (including the firing of arms by a military escort), and buried by a local undertaker hired by the Federal Army. A headboard with Taylor's identification was placed at the grave in the Due West City Cemetery. With the high number of Federal hospitals established in Nashville, the available land in the cemetery was used quickly, and it became necessary to purchase adjacent acreage that became known as U.S. Burial Grounds Due West City Cemetery and U.S. Burial Grounds Southwest City Cemetery.[50]

By mid-1866, there was growing advocacy in the North for the government to care for the dead. Conscription legislation of 1863 had mandated that citizens fight in the nation's defense. Drew Gilpin Faust explained that citizenship was defined as "a contract in which the state and the individual both assumed certain rights and duties, for which either could be called to account." These principles motivated relief organizer Clara Barton and others to hold the government responsible for identifying and burying the dead. The reburial of the North's fallen soldiers became the work of the Quartermaster Corps, the U.S. Army, and the federal government.[51]

National cemeteries became the first form of memorializing for the grieving nation. In July 1866, the sixty-four-acre Nashville National Cemetery was established. Major General Thomas selected the site and declared that "no one could come to Nashville from the north and not be reminded of the sacrifices that had been made for the preservation of the Union." The reburial of 16,485 Federal soldiers (including John Taylor), moved from original burial sites at the city cemeteries and at battlefields in Tennessee and Kentucky, and into the new cemetery between October 1867 and January 1868.[52]

John's siblings were unable to overcome the cost and emotional strain of bringing his body home for burial, but the Nashville National Cemetery was an honorable tribute for a Scottish lad who wanted "to be respected and acknowledged" as a good American citizen. These mass cemeteries were unlike any graveyard Americans had seen before, with thousands of graves of the Civil War dead laid out in ranks like soldiers on a battlefield. It impressed the reality of the war on all who saw it.[53]

Shortly after the Andersonville prison camp was liberated in May 1865, efforts began to identify and commemorate the Union soldiers who died there, including Loughlin Madden Jr. In spring 1865, to bypass the federal bureaucracy, Clara Barton reached out to soldiers and families of the missing and founded the Office of Correspondence with the Friends of the Missing Men of the United States Army. Dorence Atwater, a former prisoner at Andersonville, heard of Barton's efforts and convinced her that it was possible to identify the graves at Andersonville. During his imprisonment, he had worked in the hospital and secretly kept a copy of the hospital's register. Barton agreed to collaborate with him and won the support of the secretary of war, who ordered an expedition to accomplish the task. In late July, the group arrived at Andersonville under the command of Capt. James M. Moore, assistant quartermaster, and included Barton and Atwater, along with dozens of workmen. Atwater's death records and the captured hospital records (which in some cases were insufficient) were used to confirm where the soldiers were buried and who they were.[54]

Unlike those at Nashville, the soldiers at Andersonville were not reinterred but left as they had been placed at the time of their burials, in trenches without coffins, side by side. Barton wrote, "It seems that the dead had been buried by Union prisoners, paroled from the stockade and hospital for that purpose. Successive trenches, capable of containing from 100 to 150 bodies each, thickly set with little posts or boards, with numbers in regular order carved upon them, told to the astonished and tear-dimmed eye the sad story of the buried treasures." The laborers placed "a more substantial, uniform and comely tablet," marking the name, company, regiment, and death date of "the soldier who slept beneath." In addition to the grave markers, the grounds were enclosed, "appropriate mottoes" placed at the gates and along the walkways, and a flagstaff located at the center of the cemetery.[55]

Alexander R. Thain, Company D. *Partridge,* History of the Ninety-Sixth Regiment.

Richard S. Thain, Company D. *Partridge,* History of the Ninety-Sixth Regiment.

Orson V. Young, Company D. *Partridge,* History of the Ninety-Sixth Regiment.

David J. Minto, Company C. *Bess Bower Dunn Museum of Lake County, Lake County Forest Preserves.*

Charles A. Partridge, who served in Company C with the 96th Illinois and became the regiment's historian. *Al Westerman.*

Map Showing the Lines of March (South of the Ohio River) of the Ninety-Sixth Regiment Illinois Volunteers. Partridge, History of the Ninety-Sixth Regiment.

William "Dr. Billy" Lewin with his medical bag, Russell, Illinois, circa 1905. *Margie Queen.*

Edward Murray and Nancy Dixon Murray with their daughter Emma Jane Murray Simmons and grandchild Leland W. Simmons, circa 1892. Leland Simmons donated to the museum the portrait that inspired this book. *Bess Bower Dunn Museum of Lake County, Lake County Forest Preserves.*

Soldiers and Sailors Monument, Waukegan, Illinois: "In Memory of Our Heroic Dead, 1861–1865." *Al Westerman.*

Lake County Civil War veterans in front of Soldiers and Sailors Monument, August 29, 1899. A bearded Edward Murray is pictured in the front row, standing third from right. *Bess Bower Dunn Museum of Lake County, Lake County Forest Preserves.*

10. ❧ Lest We Forget

Within three months of his discharge, Edward Murray knew that he would need assistance in order to provide for his family, as his disability did not allow him "to pursue any occupation." On November 16, 1864, Murray appeared before the county clerk to make a claim for pension. Accompanying him to testify to his identity and disability were his brother-in-law John Murrie and his neighbor James Oliver.[1]

The handwritten claim detailed war injuries sustained at the Battle of Chickamauga, where a bullet from an enemy's musket "pass[ed] into him between his shoulders and . . . down into his right side where the bullet is now lodged." The subsequent paralysis of the "lower part of his body and his legs" made him "unfit for active labor." Murray suffered from "parts of his person being benumbed and at times uncontrollable."[2]

Murray was faced with one of the most daunting hurdles of any veteran's postwar life—securing a pension claim. Veterans viewed pensions as a "sacred debt" that the public and the U.S. government owed them for their service. The process of obtaining a pension, or an increase in one, was cumbersome and intrusive, requiring the veteran to swallow his pride by asking for aid and enduring a physical examination to prove disability. The regimental history described Ed Murray as "a mere wreck of the strong man who entered the service in 1862." He and Nancy had seven children aged three to ten years old and another baby on the way, and Ed could not afford to waste a minute in self-pity.[3]

Murray's claim was approved for a pension of eight dollars per month backdated to his discharge on August 19, 1864. The pension was provided even if Murray earned a living by means other than manual labor, which he did in part by serving as township treasurer. During the months he had been away, Nancy looked after their children and supported her husband through letters, and she had worked as a correspondent for the Northwestern Sanitary Commission. Nancy now turned her attention to Ed's physical and emotional care. His disability was apparent to all who met him, but he did not allow his loss of strength and mobility limit his life. He expanded his farm's acreage, became a stock raiser, served in public office, was active in his church, and remained close to his war comrades. Like many veterans, Ed Murray had a personal battle to fight each and every day. It was the memory of lying helpless on the battlefield and not knowing if he would see his loved ones again that would "never be erased as long as life lasts." That moment followed him on his return to civilian life, haunting him all his days.[4]

The war's collateral damage struck another member of the Murray clan: Ed's niece, Nancy "Nannie" Murrie. While others saw their loved ones return from the war, Nannie never had the chance to embrace her soldier boy again. She struggled to overcome the loss of her fiancé John Taylor. Ed Murray had been so startled by her reaction to Taylor's death that he noted it in his memoirs. John had been part of Ed's small band of comrades and was forever bonded with him in the commemorative portrait taken at Camp Fuller. Though nearly fourteen years separated them in age, Ed had connected with John through their shared Scottish heritage and that entertaining afternoon he spent giving John fiddle lessons. Ed felt guilt in Taylor's loss, but he understood that in the chaos of the charge on Horseshoe Ridge there was little any man could do to help another, and he also took solace in the fact that his own brother had cared for the lad at the hospital in Nashville. His struggle was one many veterans faced: a life straddling the past and the present, the living and the dead.[5]

In early 1866, less than a year after the war's end, the *Waukegan Gazette* reported that life in Newport Township was returning to normal. "The monotony of the long winter evenings is varied by spelling schools, singing schools and lyceums, and many of our returned soldiers are taking active parts in these institutions; and many are striving to make up for the intellectual losses they have sustained during the fiery ordeal through which they have passed."[6]

The article emphasized a reintegration of soldiers to their old lives and a sense of looking forward. Indeed, Northern civilians were eager to forget the war and its consequences and focus on the nation's future of prosperity and unity. Many veterans were still quite young and sought to continue their education, marry, and start families, or explore new ventures such as raising sheep or moving to the West. Individual struggles such as Ed Murray's did not make it into the newspapers.[7]

On March 5, 1867, at thirty-eight years old, Murray went before the county clerk seeking an increase in his "Invalid Pension." The previous year, Congress had raised total disability pension rates from eight to twenty dollars per month. His petition stated, "Said wound wholly incapacitates . . . has nearly paralyzed both his legs, the left leg he has no feeling and has frequent bleeding at the lungs and at times requires the personal aid of another person."[8] Nearly four years since being wounded at Chickamauga, his struggle continued.

James Murrie

James Murrie returned to Newport Township with sergeant stripes on his sleeve and the accolades of a grateful country. His family embraced him and thanked God for his safe return. When James Murrie, Billy Lewin, and Ed Murray met after the war, they spoke of their experiences, battles, camp life, and fallen comrades—John Taylor and Loughlin Madden. It was difficult to understand why some men survived and others did not, creating a sense of guilt and regret among the survivors of their small band.[9]

At twenty-three years old, Murrie was the only member of the Stateline Road group to complete his full term of service and make it to the mustering out. During his enlistment, he suffered from digestive illnesses and rheumatism, and he was shot in the left foot at the Battle of Picket's Mill near Dallas, Georgia. These wartime ailments and injuries were not sufficiently bothersome to motivate him to apply for a disability pension.[10]

He returned to working his father's farm, and within a year he took over the operation. With the new responsibility came a readiness for the next chapter in his life. On October 3, 1866, James married Mary Jane Dixon. The bride was the younger sister of Ed Murray's wife, Nancy.[11]

In 1873, James's father sold the family farm to the Chicago, Milwaukee, and St. Paul Railroad. The coming of the railroad brought about the development of the town of Russell along Stateline Road. James and Mary purchased land in Millburn, where James continued farming, and James became a member of the local Masonic Lodge. He also served as a justice of the peace and joined the Lake County Soldiers and Sailors Association.[12]

By the age of thirty-nine, Murrie was "partially" disabled. In October 1881, he went to Waukegan to apply for a pension. Murrie stated that he was unable to subsist by manual labor due to his war injuries. As with all pension claims, Murrie's military service records were checked. In 1885, his former company captain, John K. Pollock, submitted an affidavit to verify his claims. Pollock stated that, prior to the war, Murrie had been a "sound hearty man" but had been "attacked with Rheumatism" on at least one occasion during his military service and was unable to march with the regiment. With Murrie's claims validated, he received a pension of up to twelve dollars per month.[13]

On November 3, 1893, at fifty years old, James Murrie became a naturalized citizen. A year later, Murrie was elected to a four-year term as county treasurer. After the election, James and Mary moved to Waukegan, where he served his term and became a member of that city's Grand Army of the Republic Post 374. He also served as a justice of the peace and earned a living providing real estate loans, selling insurance, and making collections.[14]

William B. Lewin

Shortly after his honorable discharge on May 24, 1865, in Springfield, Illinois, Billy Lewin arrived by train at the Waukegan depot and made his way home for good. In the following months, his health and physical appearance improved, but he remained partially debilitated for the rest of his life. Undoubtedly, he struggled from the horrors he had experienced at Andersonville and Florence Prisons. The dread of hunger and memories of the misery he endured clung to him and former inmates. More than any other group of soldiers, the survivors of Rebel prisons endured a lifetime of psychological trauma. Brian Matthew Jordan noted that "the trials of captivity, the humiliation of starvation, and the omnipresence of death . . . indelibly marked Union ex-prisoners of war."[15]

For the nation the war was over, but for veterans the consequences of war remained unresolved. Just as Lewin was returning to a life in his family's home, the hospital records from Andersonville became public. In early May 1865, the *Chicago Tribune* published "The Martyrs of Andersonville," a listing of the prison's daily deaths as numbers without names, emphasizing the powerful anonymity of the multitude of Civil War dead. The *Tribune* noted, "Three-fourths of these boys were deliberately murdered by starvation." The next month, the *Waukegan Gazette* printed the names of "Lake County Soldiers Starved at Andersonville." Painful memories reemerged as Lewin read the names of men with whom he had served, including German comrades Charles Sturm and Hugo Rodenberger, Scotsman William McCreadie, and the bright-eyed Irish lad Loughlin Madden Jr. With so many lost to save the Union, Lewin was troubled that President Johnson's lenient Reconstruction policies toward the South were undermining all he and his comrades had endured.[16]

Veterans instinctively turned to one another, and when one of their war heroes, Maj. Gen. John A. Logan, spoke in Waukegan on August 29, 1866, thousands of veterans, including David Minto, turned out to see him. Returning to Illinois after the war, Logan traveled the state speaking mainly about a Copperhead threat and issues pertaining to Reconstruction and the defeated South's unwillingness to compromise. Logan declared, "Let every survivor of the war remember the graves of the heroes[,] . . . saying, 'Sustain the cause of the Union and don't let the traitors who killed me get possession of the country.' If you can forget this you are no soldiers, you have lost your manhood." David Minto gave monthly donations to "Freedmen" to advance the war's unfinished business.[17]

In November 1866, Billy Lewin assisted his father in moving the family from their homestead to a nearby eighty-acre farm. There, Lewin worked as a farmer and stock raiser. By the end of the decade he began providing veterinary services, eventually getting licensed by the Board of Livestock Commissioners of Illinois.[18]

On January 4, 1871, Billy married Susan P. Heath in the presence of twenty witnesses. The couple settled in the old Lewin homestead along the banks of the Des Plaines River where they welcomed two children, Harriet and Roy. Billy continued to take on more responsibilities, and in 1881 he was elected as Newport Township supervisor, which gave him a seat on the county board of supervisors. In 1888 the county board elected him its chairman.[19]

Lewin made his first claim for a pension on May 31, 1886. He went before the county clerk accompanied by his friend and comrade James Murrie. Lewin stated that he was "partially disabled" from the "gun shot wound on the Head also on the back of shoulder" received at the Battle of Chickamauga. His service records noted his status as a prisoner of war, but his injury at Chickamauga had been characterized simply as "wounded shoulder slightly." The adjutant general's office could find "no further evidence of disability," which delayed the approval for Lewin's claim.[20]

While Edward, James, and William individually set about reclaiming their lives, they also turned to one another for support, as well as to memorialize their dead comrades and war record. On November 9, 1865, the Lake County Soldiers Monument Association was organized at Waukegan with John G. Ragan as its president. Ragan's patriotism and active role in encouraging enlistment and aiding the war effort through the Sanitary Commission garnered him a membership in the Soldiers and Sailors Association of Lake County—the only civilian given the honor.[21]

The monument association's stated purpose was to "construct a monument to the memory of Lake County's soldier dead—embracing all soldiers from Lake County who have fallen in battle, or died in the service, or from the effects thereof, during the late war." Support for the monument faced an uphill climb during the economically difficult postwar years. The project's best ally was a veteran of the 37th Illinois, Brig. Gen. Eugene B. Payne, who was serving in the Illinois State Legislature. By 1868, Payne passed a bill empowering Lake County to appropriate public funds for the construction of a war memorial. Unfortunately, the Lake County board lacked the will to issue the bonds, which disappointed the veterans, who felt a sense of duty to remember their fallen comrades. It was also difficult to fund the memorial while so many soldiers had returned home debilitated and in desperate need of assistance. The living expenses and medical needs of veterans had to take precedent over honoring dead comrades.[22]

The men of the 96th Illinois held their first reunion on September 28 and 29, 1875, in Waukegan. The veterans of Lake and Jo Daviess Counties met one another with handshakes and great emotion at the depot. The men formed ranks and marched to the former Dickinson Hall where they were greeted by one of their strongest war allies, Henry W. Blodgett. After enjoying a banquet prepared by local women, toasts were made long into the night.[23]

On November 25, 1878, the 96th's veterans enjoyed their first reunion with their commander, (brevetted) Brig. Gen. John C. Smith. The invitation for the "Informal Social Gathering" at Smith's home in Chicago marked the fifteenth anniversary of the Battles of Lookout Mountain and Missionary Ridge. "The Battle Above the Clouds" stood out to the men for its rugged landscape, and as Alexander Thain poetically wrote, it was "[a]s steep as a roof, mist-drenched, cloud-high." The *Chicago Tribune* covered the reunion, noting that with Hooker's division of the Federal Army, the 96th had "stormed the defenses of Lookout Mountain, and, after a hot contest, planted the Stars and Stripes on the battlements of this Confederate stronghold." It was the victory they had desperately needed after Chickamauga, and the raising of the flag on Lookout Mountain was one of the most vivid memories of the war.[24]

Forty-five men attended, including John K. Pollock, Addison Partridge, Charles Partridge, John H. Cruver, James Murrie, David Minto, Andrew T. White, and George E. Smith Jr. Their commander at Lookout Mountain, Col. Thomas E. Champion, was memorialized, having died in 1873 while serving as mayor of Knoxville, Tennessee.[25]

Annual reunions became a powerful tool in affirming the events of the war and providing veterans with an official podium to share their experiences. Men gave speeches, and some, such as Edward Murray and Charles A. Partridge, had their reminiscences published. The veterans were not merely speaking to their comrades but also to the broader community. Though some

Lake Countians were disinclined to look back at the terrible war years, many hundreds, even thousands, attended the reunions to hear firsthand accounts of the war's triumphs and tragedies. Historian John R. Neff explained that these gatherings amplified veterans' memories and "ennobled northern deaths and inhibited reconciliation" with the South. Though large pockets of the North's population put the war behind them for more than a decade, not all veterans had been inactive. In Lake County, the first informal gathering of soldiers took place on July 4, 1865, at Druce Lake, and later that same year the Lake County Soldiers Monument Association was formed.[26]

The Soldiers and Sailors Association of Lake County met annually beginning in 1878 and officially recorded its name in 1881. In attendance at the August 31, 1881, meeting and paying their fifty-cent membership dues were Edward Murray and James Murrie. The substance of the reunions generally included speeches, patriotic songs, and, in 1902, the viewing of glass slides of Civil War battlefields shown on a stereopticon projector.[27]

At the September 1892 "annual camp fire," association president Henry S. Vail, veteran of the 38th Wisconsin Infantry, recognized that while reunions allowed the men to "swap yarns, talk over old times," between the reunions there was "opportunity for valuable and patriotic service." As part of this "patriotic service," the association advocated for "Raising flags" over schoolhouses. Their initial efforts "received much attention" and were endorsed by the superintendent of schools and teachers. Today, the American flag is ubiquitous at schools across the nation, but in 1892 it took the concerted effort of Civil War veterans to raise the flag. These activities gave the men a unified purpose in the postwar years.[28]

Grand Army of the Republic

In addition to the Soldiers and Sailors Association, men joined local Grand Army of the Republic posts. The GAR was formed in 1866 in Decatur, Illinois, in part to assist fellow disabled veterans in need. The first Lake County GAR chapter was established on November 17, 1883, in Wauconda Post 368. More followed: Waukegan Post 374 (January 3, 1884), Antioch Post 487 (October 1884), Lake Forest Post 676 (July 13, 1889), and Rockefeller/ Libertyville Post 742 (March 9, 1892). Additionally, since the village of Barrington straddles both Lake and Cook Counties, Post 275 (June 12, 1883), located there, served GAR members from each. The GAR brought men together through shared war experiences, and each post had a "relief fund" to assist comrades in need. Brian Matthew Jordan noted that it became "one of the most significant social-welfare organizations of the nineteenth century." Through its national reach, the GAR also advocated for veterans' benefits, the establishment of Memorial Day as a national holiday, and the election of Republican presidents.[29]

The veterans had been strong as brothers-in-arms, and now as citizens they united as the Grand Army of the Republic. Membership in the GAR, which peaked in 1890 at 490,000, gave the men a voice on the nation's stage. Through their emotional narratives, the veterans kept the history of the war alive and relevant. In 1884, William Lewin became a charter member of Waukegan Post 374. Two years later, he stood before its members and shared his experiences from the time of his capture at the Battle of Resaca through his imprisonment and parole. As a living witness to the horrors of Andersonville and Florence Prisons, Lewin felt a deep motivation to share his story. True to his generous spirit, he expressed "a debt of gratitude to all of my army comrades, for I feel that through them my life was saved, and I shall always have a warm place for them in my heart."[30]

Lewin turned to his GAR comrades for brotherhood and compassion. He spent years wrestling with the horrors that were imprinted on his memories. Some wounded veterans and former prisoners of war hoped to achieve understanding for what they had gone through by sharing their personal war stories with a wider public audience. "Corporal Lewin's Narrative," read at the GAR post, was printed in its entirety in the 96th's regimental history. Lewin also wrote poetry to express his patriotism and war experiences:

> *We meet not now to mourn the past,*
> *Or grieve because our years are few,*
> *We will rejoice while life shall last,*
> *Because we are the Boys in Blue.*
> *'Tis more than forty years ago*
> *Since we, a strong and sturdy band,*
> *Went marching forth to meet the foe,*
> *To guard the flag and save the Land.*[31]

About 1880, a "revival" of interest in the war prompted a promulgation of Civil War literature, including regimental histories and the popular series of articles in *Century Magazine* that were later published in a four-volume set titled *Battles and Leaders of the Civil War*. The publication of the 96th

Illinois's regimental history in 1887 followed this trend, and was possibly the most significant and impactful accomplishment of its veterans. For years, the men had spoken about the need for a written history, but the financial burden seemed too great. At last, the Historical Society of the Ninety-Sixth Regiment Illinois Volunteers was formed under the laws of the State of Illinois. Charles A. Partridge was chosen as editor due to his service with the regiment and his fifteen-year stint as editor of the *Waukegan Gazette*.[32]

The decision was made to tell the story of the regiment and not simply the personal achievements of a few men. The 938-page volume, including battle maps and photos of many of the enlisted men and officers, was one of the finest regimental histories ever compiled. The history was written with an eye to setting the record straight and glorifying the service of its members. The history represented how these men saw themselves after two decades of reflection. Lt. Charles W. Earle wrote, "Cherishing the memory of every comrade, whether living or dead; proud of the fact that it was our privilege to be associated with them in the days when they were making a record of which any soldier might be justly proud."[33]

In that handsome volume, the veterans could be satisfied that they had established the regiment's war service for perpetuity. Their war story could be disseminated far beyond the meeting hall and reunion campfires to be shared with future generations. One of the grandest gatherings of the "old boys" of the 96th Illinois was held in Chicago on July 20, 1893, at the home of Brig. Gen. John C. Smith and the "mother of the regiment," Mrs. Charlotte Smith. The reunion coincided with the World's Columbian Exposition. Many veterans had attended the World's Fair on May 30 for the GAR reunion, which was also attended by several thousand Confederate veterans.[34]

Among the Smiths' 200 guests about 125 were veterans, including Edward Murray, William Lewin, and James Murrie, as well as the man who had enlisted them, John K. Pollock. Also in attendance were Charles Partridge and Richard Thain. Ed Murray was one of the few who brought his "best girl," his wife of forty years, Nancy Dixon Murray. The reception booklet noted the "spirit of patriotism" that "flamed in the hearts of the grizzled veterans."[35]

Among the war relics displayed in the general's home were the war-torn battle flags of the 96th Illinois. The regimental flag was a sacred trophy for the veterans, validating their service and the peril they had faced and conquered. Many such relics were collected by veterans and their families as tangible souvenirs of the war. For Edward Murray, a battle relic remained with him each and every day—the minié ball that had lodged near his spine.[36]

The nostalgic evening began with a roll call of those "present for duty." Throughout the evening the orchestra played old favorites, including "The Flowers of Edinburgh," which pleased Scotsmen Ed Murray and James Murrie. The reunion's guest of honor, (brevetted) Col. George Hicks, had rallied the men for the second charge on Horseshoe Ridge at Chickamauga after Lt. Colonel Clarke was fatally wounded. Hicks reminded his comrades that every one of them was responsible for the progress that had made America one of the "great nations of the earth," and it was because of them that the nation was not divided. He credited the victory they won as the reason the "marvel of the century," the World's Fair, was possible. Had the "soldiers of the Union faltered and failed," Chicago would not have prospered and become the "admiration of the world." Gary W. Gallagher wrote that these men held to a vision that their nation was "built on free labor, economic opportunity, and a broad political franchise they considered unique in the world," and that America was "stronger in the absence of slavery." The men with immigrant roots knew well the burning desire for equal opportunity against class privilege and hereditary rule. As Gallagher explained, having fought to save the Union, they had "kept a democratic beacon shining in a world dominated by aristocrats and monarchs."[37]

Chickamauga Revisited

In 1895, the battlefields of Chickamauga-Chattanooga became the first national military park. The U.S. Congress authorized the secretary of war to acquire seventy-six hundred acres for the purpose of "preserving and suitably marking for historical and professional military study the fields of some of the most remarkable maneuvers and most brilliant fighting in the war of the rebellion." Brian Matthew Jordan found that veterans saw themselves as "custodians of their battlefields" who collected relics as physical and very personal reminders of their war experience. They also marked those battlefields with monuments.[38] The veterans of the 96th Illinois looked forward to commemorating their fight at Chickamauga, but again they encountered strife there.

Components of the military park commission included placing regimental monuments to memorialize the battle and having the park function as a training ground for young military officers. To this end, each regiment was allowed to place a memorial where it had done its best fighting, and all the regiments had to agree with its placement. This process brought back rumors that had blindsided the 96th Illinois following the battle; rumors that claimed the 96th had made a hasty retreat and left the field after the first charge. Nothing could have been further from the truth. The placement for the 96th's monument should have marked their charge along the spur, but their advance under the command of Lt. Col. Isaac Clarke took them so far ahead of the other units that no one had witnessed it.[39]

After the battle, the rumors had angered and perplexed the men. Capt. Evangelist J. Gilmore of Company B wrote to his wife that "it was awful to see the boys falling about us." He added his fears that "some will try to make out that we tried to get out of it." Orson Young proudly expressed the 96th's heroism: "We went forward in the [face] of an awful fire from the batteries and musketry. We went on till we were directly under the cannon mouth. . . . We lay down and loaded and fired and gave them the best we had while the grape and shell and rifles of the rebels tore great holes in our ranks." In his published report, Major General Granger included a "long list of officers conspicuous for their bravery," including Captain Hicks of Company A and other field officers of the 96th.[40]

In the end, the 96th Illinois's granite block monument was placed on the right flank by Battery M, 1st Illinois Light Artillery, located along the hiking trail at Snodgrass Hill. Brig. Gen. John C. Smith and various soldiers of the 96th protested the placement of the marker without satisfaction. One man wrote, "Allow me to say that no man in our regiment was ever where the 96th Regt. Ill. Vol. Monument is, during the war."[41] This disappointment was further impetus for its veterans to share their accomplishments in as many public forums as possible. No matter the inaccurate placement of that monument, they knew their brave record.

A Monument of Their Own

Amid the struggle to place a monument at Chickamauga, the men of the 96th Illinois were close to a victory at home—the dedication of the Soldiers and Sailors Monument at the county seat in Waukegan. In conjunction with the resurgence of interest in the war, which sparked an avalanche of publications, there was also an epidemic of monument building in the late 1880s and early 1890s. During the immediate postwar era, the prospect of raising funds for expensive monuments was daunting. The monuments were no less expensive at the end of the century, suggesting an initial reluctance by civilians and government officials to honor Union soldiers' sacrifices.[42]

In 1868, Lake County had been authorized by the state to issue bonds for the memorial, but officials there had lacked the conviction to do so. In 1891, with veterans serving in public office and the public experiencing a national "revival" of interest in the war, the board agreed to issue and appropriate $2,000 toward the total cost. This significant monetary commitment was added to contributions from private citizens, schoolchildren, and the Women's Relief Corps (auxiliary to the GAR), bringing civilians and veterans together to honor the county's war record. Enough funds were secured for the project to proceed in building a monument at a total cost of nearly $5,500.[43]

Support for the veterans was at a peak. In 1898, an estimated three thousand veterans, their families, and patriotic locals attended a reunion in Grayslake. The *Lake County Independent* reported, "It was the greatest crowd in the history of the association and more old soldiers were present than ever before." The following year, the Soldiers and Sailors Association decided to hold the reunion in the "court house yard" to coincide with the monument dedication.[44]

On August 4, 1899, the monument's twelve-ton granite pillar arrived from Barre, Vermont, on the Elgin, Joliet, and Eastern Railroad. It took over a dozen horses to pull the pillar up the bluff from the depot. Like countless monuments being erected across the nation in public squares, graveyards, and battlefields, this one was topped by a bronze statue of a common soldier, a color bearer. The soldier represented all men who had fought and died, native and foreign born alike. Four bronze panels by artist Edith F. Sherman, depicting infantry, artillery, cavalry, and navy were affixed to the sides of the pillar.[45]

Special trains brought thousands of visitors to Waukegan for the dedication on August 29. The city was festooned with flags and bunting, and businesses closed for the afternoon. Twelve hundred soldiers from the U.S. Army post at Fort Sheridan joined hundreds of veterans wearing faded Union uniforms. The *Chicago Daily Tribune* reported that "[t]he army of 1899 shared in the honors accorded the army of 1861," and spectators threw flowers before them as they paraded through town. Among the veterans were Edward Murray (riding in a wagon), James Murrie, and Alexander Thain.[46]

As a link between the past, present, and future, seven-year old Blanche Alexander, the granddaughter of veteran John H. Maynard, was given the privilege of pulling the cord to release the flag covering the monument. The crowd of twelve thousand cheered, church bells rang, and a twenty-one gun salute sounded from the USS *Michigan* anchored offshore.[47]

The Lake County monument, with its inscription "In Memory of Our Heroic Dead 1861–1865," and the observance of Memorial Day (begun in 1868) spoke to the ongoing value of the sacrifices that had been made to save the Union. The day after the unveiling, the veterans met to share stories of camp life and campaigns, basking in the presence of their comrades. Brian Matthew Jordan described these men as living "somewhere between the past and the present, between the dead and the living, between innocence and guilt."[48]

For their part, the citizens of Lake County felt that they had sufficiently honored the veterans and their fallen comrades, but they could never fully understand them. The rituals, reunions, and constant reminiscing were beyond civilian comprehension. And when the nation tried to put the Civil War to rest—forgive and forget—veterans were provoked into waving the "bloody shirt" as the defenders of the Union.[49]

In 1912, a massive granite and bronze Illinois monument was placed in Section F at Andersonville, commemorating the state's 889 known dead. The monument consisted of a large figure of Columbia, with a young boy "Youth" and young girl "Maiden" standing with her. At the sides of the monument were placed the figures of two veterans in somber contemplation, reflecting on memories of the war. Fittingly, the figure of Columbia pointed with outstretched hand to the heroes resting in their graves. Drew Gilpin Faust explained that the ordered rows of "humble identical markers" held a powerful significance. At Andersonville and other national cemeteries, the thousands upon thousands of Civil War dead would forever testify to the "unfathomable cost of the war."[50]

The Final Camping Ground

In 1887, Ed and Nancy Murray left the sprawling farmstead on Stateline Road in Newport Township they had built shortly after their marriage, the place Edward had lived since 1841. The Murrays retained ownership of their farm, but settled into a modest house in Waukegan.[51]

At nine o'clock on the evening of November 28, 1900, Edward Murray died at home after being bedridden for two weeks, as his condition from his war wounds had worsened. His death occurred on the eve of Thanksgiving, a holiday he had unforgettably commemorated on his return home from the war on November 26, 1863.[52]

The camp life that veterans' often reminisced about was a factor in their poor health. The constant exposure to the elements and disease from unsanitary camps caused their bodies to atrophy. In addition to exposure, the wounds Murray had suffered at Chickamauga were ultimately his demise. The

Waukegan Daily Sun announced Murray's death was the result of a Civil War bullet wound rather than his "advanced" age. It was also believed that a tumor had grown around the bullet, which had remained lodged near his spine since 1863, putting a tremendous strain on his body and causing heart failure.[53]

His funeral was held on Saturday, December 1, at ten o'clock in the morning at the family's home, then a service was held at eleven o'clock at the Baptist church. There was a great outpouring of respect, with many citizens and Civil War comrades attending the funeral, along with over one hundred family members.[54]

The intended interment at Mount Rest Cemetery near the Murrays' old homestead was postponed due to the winter season's bad roads. It was decided to temporarily place Murray's remains in the vault at Oakwood Cemetery in Waukegan. The pallbearers of Sgt. Edward Murray's coffin were Maj. John K. Pollock, Capt. George H. Bartlett (Company B), Pvt. Henry Bater (Company C), and James Malone. The GAR post's members attended the religious and cemetery services to "pay our last tribute of respect to this dead soldier," then laid evergreen wreaths and flowers on his coffin.[55]

After her husband's death, Nancy was faced with her grief and a severe loss of income. She and Edward had been living off his disability pension of thirty dollars per month and income from their farm. Within three weeks of her husband's death, Nancy went to the courthouse to apply for her widow's pension and to present her husband's last will and testament. Though Edward had written his will in June 1896, he had not filed it with the court. The probate court accepted the will, but the battle for her widow's pension had just begun.[56]

For over a year Nancy waited for a decision, but to her dismay the pension claim was denied. Her husband's comrade Sgt. Maj. Charles A. Partridge came to her aid. As the GAR's assistant adjutant general of the Department of Illinois, Partridge wrote to the commissioner of pensions, laying out a sad and very real tale of hardship: "Mrs. Murray is sick and in bed. The little home, where they had lived for many years was mortgaged and she surrendered her equity in it because she could not keep up the payments from the little income she has from the farm." Partridge added that Edward Murray had been a "patriotic, upright Christian gentleman" and that "his widow is a most estimable lady." Thanks to Partridge's intervention, Nancy Murray was awarded a widow's pension of twelve dollars per month.[57]

Nancy Dixon Murray died on January 30, 1916, following a brief illness. She and Edward were interred at Mount Rest. The local paper reported Nancy's passing and described both her and Edward as "pioneers," and Nancy one of the "best known and most beloved residents of the county." Her status as a Civil War widow was not mentioned. With her husband gone and the nation on the verge of a world war, the Civil War and what it had meant to Nancy and her family was too distant for modern sentiments.[58]

In 1894, William Lewin moved his family from the old homestead into a new home in Russell. Five years later, Lewin applied for an increase in his invalid pension. At fifty-six years old, he declared that he was "unable to earn a support by manual labor by reason of Severe Stomach trouble, Rheumatism, General Debility, terrible Headaches, Gun Shot wound of head." James Murrie testified to Lewin's disability, stating that in late November 1863, at camp in Nickajack Cove, Georgia, he saw Lewin convalescing from a "gun shot wound on the head and deep furrow down his back." Murrie noted that Lewin suffered from "dull heavy pains in his head" and that after the war had "been a frequent sufferer with his head and other causes resulting from exposure while a prisoner."[59]

By 1900, Lewin's full-time occupation was as a veterinary surgeon. Affectionately called "Dr. Billy" and known for his kind heart and generosity, Lewin's veterinary practice spanned northeastern Lake County, Illinois, and Kenosha County, Wisconsin. He had a great love of horses and would sit up all night with a sick horse, and then waive the fee if the family could not afford to pay him. Though he had given up farming, veterinary work was also physically and mentally challenging. When he again filed a claim for invalid pension in April 1902, more details of his war injuries and health were revealed: "I received Gun Shot wound of head. Fracture of skull causing chronic head ache and disease of stomach. On which I now claim pension. . . . Wound causes impaired or deranged mental powers."[60]

Although trained and licensed as a veterinarian, Lewin also acted as a "family doctor." He professed knowledge of human medicine from a "medical course" taken in his youth, but local physicians protested his lack of a medical degree. His personal reputation in the community put him in good standing as a professional, whether for humans or animals. On three occasions, medically trained physicians took him to court for prescribing to human patients, and each time the jury would acquit him of any violation of the law.[61]

On April 1, 1907, Lewin's wife Susan died at their home after suffering for two years with tuberculosis. The date also happened to be Lewin's birthday. For a man who did so much to help his neighbors, it was profoundly heartbreaking for William to watch his wife of thirty-six years succumb to a disease that he had been studying in cattle for years. At the time, tuberculosis was incurable, and the common course of treatment was fresh air and a good diet. Susan's death and the grief that followed exacerbated his own poor health and stirred memories of war comrades he had tried to save.[62]

The war was never far from Lewin's thoughts as he continued to battle for a livable pension and his health continued to decline. In 1911 he suffered a stroke, and remained in critical condition for several days. Two years later, he again took action to increase his pension. For proof of his age, he appeared before a notary public carrying the "bible of his father's family" with his birth recorded "in his father's hand."[63]

As a man of medicine, Lewin appeared to have known that his days were numbered. On the afternoon of January 10, 1914, he spoke to a neighboring widow and gave her four envelopes for her children. In each envelope was a dollar bill from his monthly twenty-four-dollar pension. The *Waukegan Daily Sun* reported, "He said no more for he choked and shed tears." That evening, Lewin waited at home for his neighbor to take him by buggy to a meeting of the Russell Camp's Modern Woodmen of America. As he got up from his chair, he took a step and fell to the floor, dying instantly from a brain aneurysm. His death was linked to an automobile ride he had taken a few days earlier. The *Daily Sun* concluded that the "ride of several miles and the unaccustomed jarring is believed to have had a bad effect upon him for he was not quite himself after that," and he suffered a series of "hemorrhages."[64]

Lewin's death was a shock to the community that loved and trusted him. News of his passing spread quickly through word of mouth and local newspapers. He was buried at Mount Rest Cemetery. For a proud and aging Civil War veteran and former prisoner of war, Old Glory represented unity, liberty, and freedom. In a poem he coauthored with his sister-in-law, Lewin put those feelings into words and revealed that he was personally affronted by his neighbors' lack of respect for the American flag.

"Honor the Flag"

Over our schools it is floating
And over our homes so free
But the Fourth of July I saw it
In a place it never should be.
I walked the streets of our village
The sight has caused me to grieve,
I took my camera with me
For I thought no one could believe.

The saloon had been decorated
Look at the picture, I beg,
The flag that our forefathers died for,
Floats over each empty keg.
Its sacred folds have enshrouded
Many a heroes' last sleep;
It was wrapped around an old beer barrel,
A sight to make angels weep.[65]

William Lewin had followed the American flag into battle. For him as a young immigrant, it was a potent symbol to rally around as he fought for his adopted homeland. To see that symbol disrespected and its value neglected caused this Union veteran to "grieve."[66]

From the mid-1890s, James Murrie and his wife Mary lived in Waukegan, a short distance from Ed and Nancy Murray. Murrie was active in veterans' associations, consistently attending meetings and annual reunions from 1878 to 1921. By March 1921, his advanced years were evident by his shaky signature in the local GAR post's attendance ledger. The last meeting he attended was on August 13, 1921. He was one of only seven comrades signing the "rolls."[67]

After his retirement, Murrie continued as a justice of the peace until ill health forced him to resign. At his last claim for pension in 1918, he attested to suffering from "varicose veins of both legs and rheumatism and resulting heart disease." He died on November 19, 1921. The headline of his obituary read, "Jas. Murrie, Civil War Veteran, Dies at Home." The month before he had suffered "a severe fall." Murrie was known to friends and family as a man of gentle nature who said the blessing at every meal. He enjoyed singing Scottish songs and regaling stories of the beautiful countryside of Fife, Scotland, where he spent the first ten years of his life.[68]

Murrie's obituary distinguished him as "one of the few remaining Civil War veterans." He was also the last of the small band of men who had marched off to war fifty-nine years earlier. A graveside ceremony was conducted by the Grand Army of the Republic. James Murrie was buried at Mount Rest Cemetery where comrades Edward Murray and William Lewin also laid in their final camping ground.[69]

The day after her husband's burial and in the grip of sorrow, Mary Jane Dixon Murrie applied for a widow's pension. The seventy-eight-year-old presented herself to the circuit court clerk dressed all in black. She received a widow's pension of thirty dollars per month for the rest of her life. In 1928, she died from "complications of old age."[70]

As the county's veterans died, their service was once again commemorated. Funerals were conducted by the local GAR, obituaries were filled with details of their military and public service, and their gravestones marked them forever as soldiers. In 1939, Athlyn Deshais of the *Waukegan Daily Sun* wrote, "They are gone now those gallant soldiers who marched and fought beneath the banner on which was inscribed the magic figures, 96."[71]

Edward Murray, Loughlin Madden Jr., James Murrie, William Lewin, and John Taylor settled on the frontier, farmed the good earth of northeastern Illinois, and built a community around them. When war came, their reasons for enlisting included a commitment to defending their adopted homeland and a desire to be good Americans. The challenges and unfamiliar ways of army life bonded them and created an esprit de corps that went beyond their small group to include the entire regiment.

They gave every ounce of themselves in the defense of the nation. Cpl. John Y. Taylor (1842–63), injured at Chickamauga, lost his right arm and ultimately his life; Pvt. Loughlin Madden Jr. (1842–64), taken prisoner on Missionary Ridge, lost his life to starvation and the inhuman conditions at Andersonville Prison; Cpl. William B. Lewin (1843–1914), injured at Chickamauga and taken prisoner at Resaca, lost his health to scurvy at Andersonville and Florence Prisons and suffered from debilitating headaches; Sgt. James B. Murrie (1842–1921), affected by the unsanitary conditions of camp life, suffered from illness and rheumatism and was wounded in the Atlanta Campaign; and Sgt. Edward Murray (1828–1900), shot three times at Chickamauga and left paralyzed on the field of battle, suffered from crippling wounds for the rest of his life.

Edward, Loughlin, James, William, and John, a small band of immigrant farmers, proudly enlisted together and represented their community. In the process of becoming soldiers, they integrated with their regiment and earned the right to be called Americans. Ed, Billy, and James survived to return to their families and farming and became pillars of public service and good citizenship. Each struggled with emotional and physical disability, and each reunited with war comrades to support and aid one another while advocating for veterans' benefits, taking steps to ensure that their sacrifices—and especially those of their fallen comrades—would be remembered.

In his twilight years, Billy Lewin turned to poetry as a way to reflect:

Comrades our march is almost done
The final Camping Ground is near
Low in the west we see the sun,
It tells us night will soon be here.
And when our lives have passed away,
And we have sought our last repose,
We shall not sleep like common clay,
Forgotten when the grave shall close.[72]

Through reunions, the publication of the regimental history, and the dedication of monuments at Waukegan and Chickamauga, the veterans of the 96th Illinois set out to preserve their legacy and honor fallen comrades. Indeed, the historical volume and monuments still exist, but the contribution of these immigrant soldiers has not been fully realized. The postwar reconciliation between the North and South and the historical emphasis on the "brother's war" and battles in the Eastern Theater have overlooked the importance and legacy of the Western Theater and its Union soldiers.[73]

Thousands of immigrants and sons of immigrants (about 43 percent of all Union forces) willingly fought and died to save the Union, giving the North a decisive advantage. Their service was essential to the Union's ultimate victory.[74] Ed Murray and his comrades came to the United States to find opportunity and liberty. They were friends, neighbors, and townsmen who had worked on each other's farms and gathered at the same Union meetings. Murray was the first to sign the regimental rolls, setting an example for the others to follow. He was the group's linchpin and the most respected among them in their community.

In the autumn of 1862, these men took a commemorative portrait at Camp Fuller to mark their personal bonds and service as American soldiers. Their patriotic enthusiasm and pride in their new Union-blue uniforms was evident in their bright eyes and straight posture. For these foreign-born men, it was much more than America's war. It was a war to uphold their dreams of an America that stood for opportunity, freedom, equality, and self-rule. With the coming of war, they feared the nation—not yet a century old—was imperiled and their hopes for the future in doubt.

It was a critical time for the nation and for these immigrants, who had grown to manhood believing in the dream of America. They had come from countries ruled by aristocracy and privilege and understood what could be lost. When Abraham Lincoln referred to America as "the last best hope of earth" for popular government to succeed, these men had as much to lose or gain in the war as their native-born comrades, and in some ways they better understood what was at stake. They struck at the heart of the Confederacy in the Western Theater with pickaxe, shovel, and rifle, fortifying Union lines and fighting, as one of their comrades' described, "till half their men were slain" at Chickamauga. Their tireless and gallant fight to preserve the Union earned them the right to be called Americans.[75]

John and Loughlin died for that cause, and Ed, Billy, and James struggled for the rest of their lives with disability and haunted memories. As Mark Twain wrote in *The Gilded Age*, the Civil War "uprooted institutions that were centuries old, changed the politics of a people, and wrought so profoundly upon the entire national character that the influence cannot be measured short of two or three generations."[76]

Far removed from that generation, a single photographic portrait of five immigrant Union soldiers unlocked the story of their motivations to fight for the Union and illuminated the sacrifices they made. The *Waukegan Gazette* editor's words resonate just as strongly today as they did when the men of the 96th Illinois marched off to war: "Let not those who have volunteered be forgotten."[77] With their stories told, the spirits of Ed Murray, Loughlin Madden Jr., James Murrie, Billy Lewin, and John Taylor—our Boys in Blue—once again return home to greet us with a salute.

Appendix

Notes

Bibliography

Index

Appendix: Company C Roster

Company C's roster at enlistment in September 1862 with highest rank achieved as listed in Partridge, History of the Ninety-Sixth Regiment Illinois Volunteer Infantry. *Key: D, discharged; DD, died of disease; DR, dropped from rolls, Rockford; K, killed, mortally wounded; m.o., mustered-out with regt.; O, deserted; P, prisoner; PK, died as prisoner of war; T, transferred to another unit; W, wounded.*

CAPTAIN
John K. Pollock—W, m.o.

FIRST LIEUTENANTS
Charles W. Earle—W, P, m.o.   William M. Loughlin—T
Addison B. Partridge—D

2ND LIEUTENANT
Charles A. Partridge—W, m.o.

FIRST SERGEANTS
Lewis H. Bryant—W, m.o.   Samuel B. Payne—K
Ellis L. Schooley—D

SERGEANTS
Harvillah Cooley—D   Edward Murray—W, P, D
Martin Efinger—W, m.o.   James B. Murrie—W, m.o.
Harrison Huntington—PK   Joseph B. Porter—D
James McCredie—W, m.o.   James M. Taylor—W, D
Andrew T. White—D

CORPORALS
George N. Ayers—D   Norris Hamilton—K
John W. Bailey—W, m.o.   James Kearney—P, D
Henry P. Barnum—W, P, D   William B. Lewin—W, P, D
Edwin A. Bartles—DD   Oscar Rector—W, m.o.

Samuel Clark—m.o.
Henry H. Cutler—W, P, K
George C. Dodge—W, P, D
George L. Stewart—D
John J. Swazy—m.o.
John Y. Taylor—K
Christian Weistoff—P, m.o.

MUSICIAN
Julius Schwarm—D

PRIVATES

Amelius Ames—m.o.
Willard Ames—D
Orange M. Ayers—PK
Henry Bater—W, D
John Bensinger—PK
John W. Besley—m.o.
Timothy W. Bliss—m.o.
William Bonner—K
Hiram Clark—m.o.
Samuel Clements—DD
Caleb E. Colgrove—DD
Ira Cribb—W, m.o.
William Diver—W, D
Samuel W. Dodge—T
Leonard S. Doolittle—W, D
John H. Ehlers—K
William H. Ehlers—W, P, D
John Fidler—K
Timothy Finley—D
Charles Fordham—O
Henry C. Green—PK
Columbus Haycock—O
Orrin Howe—W, P, D
Hamden Huntington—DD
Squire W. Inman—W, PK
George Johnson—T
Henry F. Jones—m.o.
Reuben C. Jones—DD
Henry Kern—W, D
Joshua King—DR

Loughlin Madden—PK
Watson Markley—m.o.
James McBride—T
William McClellan—PK
William McCreadie—PK
Frank Milheiser—W, m.o.
David J. Minto—D
William Morley—T
Marshall Newton—O
Henry C. Payne—W, PK
Charles Phillips—T
William F. Rider—D
Hugo Rodenberger—PK
Charles Sammons—m.o.
Jerry Savage—T
Joseph Savage—P, D
Henry Schnell—DD
Joseph Schweri—P, m.o.
John Shatswell—D, T
Benjamin Shumerski—DR
Jonathan Smith—m.o.
Henry Sneesby—W, m.o.
Charles Sturm—PK
Henry H. Swan—DD
Michael Umbdenstock—W, D
William G. Walmsley—O
Chase E. Webb—m.o.
Nelson C. West—D
Charles W. White—m.o
Joseph C. Whitney—m.o.

Notes

AGO   Adjutant General's Office

ALPL   Abraham Lincoln Presidential Library, Springfield, IL

BBDM   Bess Bower Dunn Museum of Lake County, Lake County Forest Preserves

CHM   Chicago History Museum

CWM   Civil War Museum, Kenosha, Wisconsin

GAR   Grand Army of the Republic

HMCA   Historic Millburn Community Association

IL AGR   Illinois Adjutant General Report

ISA   Illinois State Archives, Springfield, IL

LCIC   Lake County (IL) Clerk

LCIGS   Lake County (IL) Genealogical Society

LCIRD   Lake County (IL) Recorder of Deeds

LOC   Library of Congress

NARA   National Archives and Records Administration

NPS   National Park Service

NRS   National Records of Scotland

OR   *The War of the Rebellion: A Compilation of the Official Records of the Union and Confederate Armies*

RG   Record Group

TSLA   Tennessee State Library and Archives

WHS   Waukegan Historical Society

Introduction

1. Murray, *Soldier's Reminiscences*, 3.
2. IL AGR.
3. BBDM.
4. Doyle, *Cause of All Nations*, 170; Doyle, "Civil War Was Won"; Burton, *Melting Pot Soldiers*, 231.
5. Keating, "Immigrants," 10; Brown, "Microhistory," 10–11, 19; Lepore, "Historians," 133, 141; Kisantal, Review of *What Is Microhistory?* Recent books by historians Lesley J. Gordon, Susannah Ural Bruce, and Mark A. Snell are

evidence of a continuing trend of the microhistorical approach to examine and find new meaning in the lives of common soldiers, immigrants, and Civil War battles.

6. Johnson, *Liberty Party*; Gallagher, *Union War*, 35; Halsey, *History of Lake County*, 122.

7. Partridge, *History of the Ninety-Sixth*, 27; Griffith, *Battle Tactics*, 44, 51.

8. Partridge, *History of the Ninety-Sixth*, 28; Author's calculations utilizing Partridge's *History of the Ninety-Sixth*; Burton, *Melting Pot Soldiers*, 228.

9. *Portrait and Biographical Album*, 379; John Taylor to Isabella Low, May 23, 1863, ALPL; Burton, *Melting Pot Soldiers*, 9; Ural, *Civil War Citizens*, 4; *OR*, 857–58; Partridge, *History of the Ninety-Sixth*, 176, 735; Powell, "Chickamauga: Barren Victory," 215.

10. Phillips, "Battling Stereotypes."

11. Murray, *Soldier's Reminiscences*; Ural, *Civil War Citizens*, 114; Partridge, *History of the Ninety-Sixth*, 60, 101.

12. Weber, *Copperheads*, 2, 69, 71, 83; Neely, *Union Divided*, 40, 42–43, 46; Girardi, "I Am for the President's Proclamation," 410; Partridge, *History of the Ninety-Sixth*, 101–3; Kolakowski, *Stones River*, 98–99.

1. Far from My Native Land

1. Photo tintype, BBDM.

2. Dunkelman, *Brothers*, 9, 19; Partridge, *History of the Ninety-Sixth*, 36; Murray, *Soldier's Reminiscences*, 4; Humphreys, *Marrow*, 20; Photo tintype, BBDM.

3. *Portrait and Biographical Album*, 378; Irish-Genealogy-Toolkit.com.

4. *Portrait and Biographical Album*, 378; Haines, *Past and Present*, 419.

5. *Portrait and Biographical Album*, 378; Murray, *Soldier's Reminiscences*, 3; Unadilla Valley Historical Society, *Historical Sketches*.

6. 1840 and 1850 U.S. Census, Ancestry.com; Murray, *Soldier's Reminiscences*, 3.

7. Clifton, *Prairie People*, 238.

8. Murray, *Soldier's Reminiscences*, 3; Labadie et al., "History and Development." There was also a transatlantic ship named SS *Great Western*; "Buffalo to Chicago Line," *Southport Telegraph*, May 4, 1841, 4; Palmer, *Early Days in Detroit*; Goodspeed, *History of Cook County*; "Emigration," *Southport Telegraph*, June 1, 1841, 2.

9. *Portrait and Biographical Album*, 378; LCIRD; Murray, *Soldier's Reminiscences*, 3.

10. 1840 U.S. Census; Halsey, *History of Lake County*, 75; *Journal of a Pioneer*, BBDM.

11. *Illinois, Public Land Purchase Records, 1813–1909*, Ancestry.com; LCIGS, *Illinois Marriages 1839 to 1859*; *Kenosha City Directory, 1858*; *Portrait and Biographical Album*, 378; Mullin, "Tuberculosis"; Meier, *Nature's Civil War*, 13, 18; Zion Genealogical Society, "Newport Mt. Rest Cemetery," 15.

12. LCIRD; *Portrait and Biographical Album*, 379, 402; RG 15, NARA.

13. *Portrait and Biographical Album*, 379; Burton, *Melting Pot Soldiers*, xiv.

14. Johnson, *Liberty Party*; B. F. Shepard, "Tells of First 4th Celebration Here 74 Years Ago," uncredited news clipping, n.d., ca. 1918; Halsey, *History of Lake County*, 75, 87.

15. 1840 U.S. Census; Dillon, "Antislavery Movement"; Schools Collection, BBDM; LCIRD; LCIC; Meier, *Nature's Civil War*, 17; "History of Lake County," *Waukegan Daily Sun*, July 6, 1928; ISA.

16. McManus, *Political Abolitionism*, 5; Gates, *Lincoln*, 69; LCIGS, *1838–1888 Report*.

17. Halsey, *History of Lake County*, 93, 131.

18. Johnson, *Liberty Party*; Halsey, *History of Lake County*, 110–11, 131; Cole, Collections, 14:864; Meites, "1847 Illinois Constitutional Convention"; Guasco, *Confronting Slavery*, 113.

19. Meites, "1847 Illinois Constitutional Convention"; Office of Illinois Secretary of State, "100 Most Valuable Documents."

20. Dillon, "Antislavery Movement," 163, 155; Girardi, "I Am for the President's Proclamation," 396; Heinzel, "To Protect the Rights," 391.

21. *Portrait and Biographical Album*, 378; Putnam, *Baptists and Slavery*, 31; Gallagher, *Union War*, 2; Jeansonne, "Southern Baptist Attitudes."

22. Halsey, *History of Lake County*, 122–23, 138; *Portrait and Biographical Album*, 379.

23. "Another Letter from Waukegan," *Chicago Daily Tribune*, September 9, 1854; Partridge, *History of Lake County*, 645.

24. *Portrait and Biographical Album*, 378–79; Heinzel, "To Protect the Rights"; Meites, "1847 Illinois Constitutional Convention."

25. Irish Immigrants, New York Port Arrival Records, 1846–1851, Ancestry.com; National Museum Liverpool, "Liverpool and Emigration."

26. Ó Danachair, "Cottier and Landlord," 154–65; New York, Passenger Lists, 1820–1957, Ancestry.com; Miller, *Emigrants and Exiles*, 292; Keating, "Immigrants."

27. Miller, *Emigrants and Exiles*, 280, 298; Doyle, *Cause of All Nations*, 8.

28. New York, Passenger Lists, Ancestry.com; National Museum Liverpool, "Liverpool and Emigration"; Uzelac, "G. P. Griffith."

29. 1855 Wisconsin Census, Ancestry.com; 1861 Map of Lake County; 1860 U.S. Census; Bruce, *Harp*, 15–16.

30. Bruce, *Harp*, 15–16; McManus, *Political Abolitionism*, 101; "Doing It Up Brown," *Chicago Daily Tribune*, February 26, 1855.

31. Bruce, *Harp*, 18; McManus, *Political Abolitionism*, 100; Miller, *Emigrants and Exiles*, 297; "To the Point," reprinted from the *Christian Advocate* by the *Waukegan Gazette*, January 27, 1855.

32. Devitt, *Centenary Program*; *Portrait and Biographical Album*, 378; LCIGS, *Illinois Marriages 1860 to 1880*; 1860 U.S. Census; Miller, *Emigrants and Exiles*, 332, 298, 318, 329; Bruce, *Harp*, 52, 13.

33. *Portrait and Biographical Album*, 753.

34. Ibid., 753; 1841, 1851 Scotland Census, NRS.

35. *Portrait and Biographical Album*, 395, 753; LCIRD; "History of Newport: Russell School," 1918, BBDM; Corris, *Russell Illinois*, 10; Corris, *Russell Illinois*; Barnard, "Excerpts from Barnard-Walldan."

36. *Portrait and Biographical Album*, 396, 754; Haynes, *Disciples of Christ*, 246, 247, 656; Lawson, *History of Warren Township*, 50. John Taylor to Isabella Low, May 27, 1861, ALPL; "Republican Meeting in Newport," *Waukegan Gazette*, September 9, 1860.

37. Massachusetts, Passenger and Crew Lists, 1820–1963, Ancestry.com; 1851 England Census, Ancestry.com; LCIRD.

38. Schools Collection, BBDM.

39. Methodist Churches, *Historical Centennial*; Halsey, *History of Lake County*, 692; Margie Queen, interview by author.

40. Painter, "Pro-Slavery Argument"; Halsey, *History of Lake County*, 693; Buckley, *History of Methodism*; "Dr. W. B. Lewin Dead," *Southport Telegraph*, January 15, 1914; Meier, *Nature's Civil War*, 17, 22.

41. *Portrait and Biographical Record of Christian County*, 309–10; "Isabella Lawrence," Bodie.ca, Bodie-Antle Family & Ancestors.

42. Bennett, *Post Office*; 1855 Land Valuation, Scotland, NRS; 1841, 1851 Scotland Census, NRS.

43. There is conflicting documentation for the Taylors' year of immigration (1853 or 1854); *Portrait and Biographical Record of Christian County*, 309–10; Campey, *Fast Sailing*, 111–12; Dobson, *Ships from Scotland*; Waukegan's population was approximately thirty-two hundred.

44. "Isabella Taylor Low," HMCA, Inc., accessed May 1, 2018, http://www. historicmillburn.org/Families/l_jlow.htm; Millburn Congregational Church, *First Hundred Years*, 9.

45. Millburn Congregational Church, *First Hundred Years*, 10; Halsey, *History of Lake County*, 110; "Dr. R. L. Cooper," *Freeman's Advocate*, July 1, 1854, transcription online, HMCA, Inc., accessed May 1, 2018, http://www.historicmillburn.org/Clippings/c1854_07.htm.
46. *Portrait and Biographical Record of Christian County*; Lawson, *History of Warren Township*; 1860 U.S. Census; Westerman, *History of Waukegan Township*, 49–50; LCIRD.
47. Turner, *Underground Railroad*, 223; "Minister Pays Tribute to His Flock," Rev. Melvin I. Frank, *Waukegan Post*, August 15, 1940.
48. Taylor Diary, 1859–1860, ALPL; "Our Nation's Birthday," *Chicago Press and Tribune*, July 6, 1860; Currey, "Mr. Lincoln's Visit."
49. Taylor Diary, 1859–1860, ALPL; John Taylor to David Minto, December 28, 1860, BBDM.
50. Doyle, *Cause of All Nations*, 8.
51. William Wilson to Thomas Wilson, September 8, 1851, CHM.
52. 1860 U.S. Census.

2. May God Save the Union

1. Currey, "Mr. Lincoln's Visit"; "Lincoln in Waukegan," *Chicago Press and Tribune*, April 2, 1860.
2. Currey, "Mr. Lincoln's Visit."
3. Lincoln's candidacy for president was announced at the State Republican Convention in Decatur, Illinois, on May 9–10, 1860 (The Historical Marker Database); "Millburn Wide-Awakes," *Waukegan Weekly Gazette*, October 13, 1860; "The Libertyville Wide Awakes," *Chicago Tribune*, October 4, 1860; Grinspan, "'Young Men for War'"; "Grand Republican Mass Meeting, at Waukegan, on Friday, Sept. 7, 1860," *Waukegan Gazette*, n.d., 1860; Partridge, *History of Lake County*, 646; *Portrait and Biographical Album*, 379.
4. Bruce, *Harp*, 42; Halsey, *History of Lake County*, 144; Samito, *Becoming American*, 26.
5. "How to Settle It," *Chicago Tribune*, January 15, 1861.
6. Duerkes, "I for One Am Ready"; Doyle, "Civil War Was Won."
7. John Taylor to David Minto, May 20, 1861, BBDM; Halsey, *History of Lake County*, 631.
8. Burton, *Melting Pot Soldiers*, 35; "To Arms!" *Kenosha Times*, April 18, 1861.
9. Partridge, *History of Lake County*, 646; Partridge, "Lake County War History," 461.

10. Currey, "Mr. Lincoln's Visit"; Haines, *Past and Present*, 461; Wilder, *Thirty Seventh Illinois*, 28–29; E. B. Payne Civil War Letters, Lake Forest College Archives.

11. Edward Hearns, letter to the editor, *Waukegan Gazette*, April 27, 1861.

12. Burton, "Illinois Ethnics"; Haines, *Past and Present*, 462; "Another Meeting in Newport," *Waukegan Gazette*, May 11, 1861.

13. "Union Meeting in Newport," *Waukegan Gazette*, May 4, 1861; John Taylor to David Minto, May 20, 1861, BBDM.

14. "Waukegan Volunteers," *Waukegan Gazette*, April 27, 1861.

15. Neely, *Union Divided*, 12; Eddy, *Patriotism of Illinois*, 80–81; 1860 U.S. Census.

16. Mark Daley, "A Card to the Citizens of Millburn," *Waukegan Gazette*, May 4, 1861; Gallagher, *Union War*, 2.

17. Bruce, *Harp*, 24–25; Welch, "America's Civil War"; Doyle, *Cause of All Nations*, 173–74.

18. Bruce, *Harp*, 4, 52; 1860 U.S. Census; Welch, "America's Civil War"; Miller, *Emigrants and Exiles*, 332–33; ISA; 1860 U.S. Census Mortality Schedules; Doyle, *Cause of All Nations*, 174.

19. John Taylor to David Minto, April 12, 1861, BBDM.

20. Partridge, "Lake County War History"; ISA; Andrew White to David Minto, July 1, 1861, BBDM.

21. *Biddlecome School History*, BBDM; John Taylor to James Taylor, December 22, 1861, ALPL; *Lake County Citizen*, March 10, 1859; Ural, *Civil War Citizens*, 4.

22. Bowery "Civil War," 29.

23. Griffith, *Battle Tactics*, 44; Groom, "Why Shiloh Matters"; "Chicago Sanitary Commission," *Waukegan Gazette*, April 12, 1862; "Soldiers Aid Society," *Waukegan Gazette*, August 30, 1862.

24. Manning, *What This Cruel War Was Over*, 83; Gallagher, "Civil War Watershed," 13; Halsey, *History of Lake County*, 150.

25. Doyle, *Cause of All Nations*, 185, 211, 216; Gallagher, *Union War*, 90.

26. Duerkes, "I for One Am Ready," 313; Partridge, *History of the Ninety-Sixth*, 28.

27. "What Lake County Is Doing," *Waukegan Gazette*, August 2, 1862.

28. Partridge, *History of the Ninety-Sixth*, 705; Partridge, "Lake County War History"; "Now is the last chance to VOLUNTEER!" *Waukegan Gazette*, August 16, 1862.

29. Partridge, *History of the Ninety-Sixth*, 25, 730, 738; Haines, *Past and Present*, 356; Soldiers' Record, William Lewin, BBDM; William Minto to David Minto and Chase Webb, October 9, 1862, BBDM.

30. Murray, *Soldier's Reminiscences*, 3.
31. James Taylor to Isabella Low, May 23–24, 1863, ALPL; *Portrait and Biographical Record of Christian County*; John Taylor to Isabella Low, May 23, 1863, ALPL; Duerkes, "I for One Am Ready," 319, 327.
32. IL AGR, 5:444; ISA, "Loewin [*sic*], William B."; Doyle, *Cause of All Nations*, 160; Duerkes, "I for One Am Ready," 324; *Portrait and Biographical Album*, 396.
33. Ural, *Civil War Citizens*, 5; Samito, *Becoming American*, 29; Keating, "Immigrants"; Doyle, *Cause of All Nations*, 174–76.
34. Duerkes, "I for One Am Ready," 317.
35. Charles Partridge to H. Clay Evans, January 15, 1902, BBDM; Millie Ramsay, conversation with author, August 2012; Duerkes, "I for One Am Ready," 314; American flag, BBDM.
36. "Lake County and the War," *Waukegan Gazette*, August 16, 1862.
37. Partridge, *History of the Ninety-Sixth*, 25, 753, 730.
38. Murray, *Soldier's Reminiscences*, 4; Faust, *This Republic*, 7; Keating, "Immigrants."
39. Duerkes, "I for One Am Ready," 321; Hicks, *Personal Recollections*; Mitchell, *Vacant Chair*, 12.
40. Dunkelman, *Brothers*, 19.
41. IL AGR, 5:437–60; ISA, "96 IL US INF"; Partridge, *History of the Ninety-Sixth*, 739–752.
42. Burton, "Illinois Ethnics"; Duerkes, "I for One Am Ready," 324.
43. Murray, *Soldier's Reminiscences*, 4; Taylor Diary, July 4, 1860, ALPL.
44. Partridge, *History of the Ninety-Sixth*, 731; Meier, *Nature's Civil War*, 102.
45. Partridge, *History of the Ninety-Sixth*, 731–32.
46. Ibid., 732.
47. Partridge, *History of Lake County*, 644.
48. David Minto's Bible, BBDM; Jane Minto to David Minto, August 10, 1862, BBDM; George Smith to Susie Smith, August 30, 1863, BBDM.
49. 1880 U.S. Census; Murray, *Soldier's Reminiscences*, 4.
50. Partridge, *History of the Ninety-Sixth*, 29.
51. James Taylor to Sister, September 6, 1862, ALPL; Dunkelman, *Brothers*, 19; Partridge, *History of the Ninety-Sixth*, 30.
52. Partridge, *History of the Ninety-Sixth*, 28–30; Dunkelman, *Brothers*, 6, 16.
53. Meier, *Nature's Civil War*, 150.
54. Partridge, *History of the Ninety-Sixth*, 32, 733; McNamara, "Why Were Flags."
55. Murray, *Soldier's Reminiscences*, 4.

56. Ibid., 5; Partridge, *History of the Ninety-Sixth*, 35–36.

57. Herdegen, *Iron Brigade*, 95; Evangelist J. Gillmore to Elizabeth Gillmore, September 23, 1862, CWM; Girardi, "Illinois' First Response," 171.

58. Partridge, *History of the Ninety-Sixth*, 35–38; Loughlin Madden Jr. to Christopher Madden, October 10, 1862, BBDM; Duerkes, "I for One Am Ready," 326; Doyle, *Cause of All Nations*, 165.

59. Murray, *Soldier's Reminiscences*, 5; Dunkelman, *Brothers*, 24–25.

60. Dunkelman, *Brothers*, 44.

61. Photo tintype, BBDM.

62. Loughlin Madden Jr., photo tintype, BBDM; Bruce, *Harp*, 4.

63. Doyle, *Cause of All Nations*, 216, 211.

64. Ibid., 185; Gallagher, *Union War*, 51, 76; Partridge, *History of the Ninety-Sixth*, 37; "The Views of the Army," *Chicago Tribune*, September 25, 1862.

65. Murray, *Soldier's Reminiscences*, 5–6.

66. Ibid., 6; "Ninety-Sixth Illinois Regiment," *Chicago Tribune*, October 9, 1862, 4; Griffith, *Battle Tactics*, 44.

67. Murray, *Soldier's Reminiscences*, 6.

3. A Cheer for the West

1. Partridge, *History of the Ninety-Sixth*, 41.

2. "Ninety-Sixth Illinois Regiment," *Chicago Tribune*, October 9, 1862; Partridge, *History of the Ninety-Sixth*, 41; Murray, *Soldier's Reminiscences*, 6.

3. Murray, *Soldier's Reminiscences*, 6; IL AGR, 5:461.

4. Murray, *Soldier's Reminiscences*, 6–7; Harrison, "Civil War in Kentucky"; McPherson, *For Cause*, 118.

5. Partridge, *History of the Ninety-Sixth*, 43, 45; Meier, *Nature's Civil War*, 2.

6. Murray, *Soldier's Reminiscences*, 7.

7. James Taylor to Isabella Low, October 18, 1862, ALPL.

8. Partridge, *History of the Ninety-Sixth*, 44, 747; Loughlin Madden Jr. to Christopher Madden, October 10, 1862, BBDM; James Taylor to Isabella Low, October 18, 1862, ALPL.

9. Ural, *Civil War Citizens*, 11; Reinhart, *Two Germans*, xxxvii, 167; Engle "Yankee Dutchmen," 19, 27.

10. IL AGR, 5:461; Partridge, *History of the Ninety-Sixth*, 48.

11. Murray, *Soldier's Reminiscences*, 8.

12. James Taylor to Isabella Low, October 18, 1862, ALPL; Partridge, *History of the Ninety-Sixth*, 49.

13. Sarah White to David Minto, October 23, 1862, BBDM; Meier, *Nature's Civil War*, 120.

14. Partridge, *History of the Ninety-Sixth*, 51.
15. IL AGR, 5:461; Ibid., 58; Meier, *Nature's Civil War*, 35, 112; Rutkow, *Bleeding*, 9; Murray, *Soldier's Reminiscences*, 13–14.
16. Partridge, *History of the Ninety-Sixth*, 59.
17. Ibid., 59–60; McPherson, *For Cause*, 119; Hahn, *Freedom*, 251; Teters, *Practical Liberators*, 2, 8; *OR*, 2nd ser., 1:778.
18. Hahn, *Freedom*, 252–53; Teters, *Practical Liberators*, 3–5, 36; Doyle, *Cause of All Nations*, 185; Partridge, *History of the Ninety-Sixth*, 60.
19. Teters, *Practical Liberators*, 94; *Portrait and Biographical Album*, 511; Partridge, *History of the Ninety-Sixth*, 60–62, 739.
20. Partridge, *History of the Ninety-Sixth*, 62; "November and December 1862," Company C, 96th Illinois Volunteer Infantry, AGO, RG 94, NARA.
21. Murray, *Soldier's Reminiscences*, 9; Partridge, *History of the Ninety-Sixth*, 82; Teters, *Practical Liberators*, 74; Blockson, *The Underground Railroad*, 267.
22. Murray, *Soldier's Reminiscences*, 9; Partridge, *History of the Ninety-Sixth*, 60; Hahn, *Freedom*, 254; "92nd Illinois Infantry," Illinois in the Civil War; Teters, *Practical Liberators*, 60, 65; "From the 96th Regiment," *Waukegan Gazette*, December 13, 1862.
23. Murray, *Soldier's Reminiscences*, 9; Herdegen, *Iron Brigade*, 156; Hahn, *Freedom*, 252–53; Gallagher, *Union War*, 80; Manning, *What This Cruel War Was Over*, 13–14.
24. Partridge, *History of the Ninety-Sixth*, 6; George Smith to Susie Smith, November 4, 1862, BBDM; Griffith, *Battle Tactics*, 110–11.
25. Partridge, *History of the Ninety-Sixth*, 67, 734; Griffith, *Battle Tactics*, 44–45.
26. Partridge, *History of the Ninety-Sixth*, 70; Taylor Brothers to Sister, December 4, 1862, ALPL; Meier, *Nature's Civil War*, 1, 35.
27. Partridge, *History of the Ninety-Sixth*, 70; Bradley, *Tullahoma*, 10.
28. John Taylor to Sister, December 4, 1862, ALPL; "November and December 1862," Company C, 96th Illinois, AGO, RG 94, NARA.
29. Partridge, *History of the Ninety-Sixth*, 62, 751, 72; Meier, *Nature's Civil War*, 3, 9, 15, 22.
30. George Smith to Susie Smith, February 23, 1863, BBDM; Meier, *Nature's Civil War*, 7, 72–73; Rutkow, *Bleeding*, 9.
31. Meier, *Nature's Civil War*, 109; John Taylor to Isabella Low, May 23 1863, ALPL.
32. Partridge, *History of the Ninety-Sixth*, 74.
33. George Smith to Susie Smith, January 25, 1863, BBDM; Partridge, *History of the Ninety-Sixth*, 76–77.

34. Sidlo, "Civil War Roads"; Partridge, *History of the Ninety-Sixth*, 77; "November and December 1862," Company C, 96th Illinois, AGO, RG 94, NARA.
35. IL AGR, 5:461; "November and December 1862," Company C, 96th Illinois, AGO, RG 94, NARA; Meier, *Nature's Civil War*, 149.
36. Gallagher, *Union War*, 75–76; Ural, *Civil War Citizens*, 114.
37. Partridge, *History of the Ninety-Sixth*, 101; IL AGR vol. 5; Orson Young to Parents, February 23, 1863, BBDM; Girardi, "I Am for the President's Proclamation," 404; Bradley, *Tullahoma*, 2–3; Gallagher, *Union War*, 51, 76; Ural, *Civil War Citizens*, 114; Klement, *Lincoln's Critics*, 107–8; Teters, *Practical Liberators*, 65–67.
38. Weber, *Copperheads*, 71; Neely, *Union Divided*, 40, 43, 46; Girardi, "I Am for the President's Proclamation," 410.
39. Partridge, *History of the Ninety-Sixth*, 101–3; Kolakowski, *Stones River*, 98–99; Weber, *Copperheads*, 2, 69, 83.
40. Neely, *Union Divided*, 43; Partridge, *History of the Ninety-Sixth*, 102; "From General Baird's Division," *Richmond (IN) Weekly Palladium*, March 27, 1863; McPherson, *For Cause*, 124.
41. Klement, *Lincoln's Critics*, 8, 154, 156.
42. George Dodge to David Minto, May 26, 1863, BBDM; Orson Young to parents, February 23, 1863, BBDM; Gallagher, *Union War*, 2; Girardi, "I Am for the President's Proclamation," 407, 417–18; Manning, *What This Cruel War Was Over*, 83.
43. Partridge, *History of the Ninety-Sixth*, 38.
44. James Taylor to Sister, January 20, 1863, ALPL.
45. "Company Muster Roll," Lewin, January and February 1863, RG 94, NARA; Meier, *Nature's Civil War*, 59; Partridge, *History of the Ninety-Sixth*, 760, 61–62, 90.
46. Murray, *Soldier's Reminiscences*, 11–12; Partridge, *History of the Ninety-Sixth*, 96–97; Jannet Minto to David Minto, April 3, 1863, BBDM.
47. David Minto Diary, March 25, 1863, BBDM; George Smith to Susie Smith, April 17, 1863, BBDM; Partridge, *History of the Ninety-Sixth*, 96; Meier, *Nature's Civil War*, 6; Teters, *Practical Liberators*, 95, 97.
48. Meier, *Nature's Civil War*, 7; Humphreys, *Marrow*, 7, 24; George Smith to Susie Smith, February 23, 1863, BBDM.
49. Kolakowski, *Stones River*, 98, 102–3.
50. John Taylor to Isabella Low, May 23, 1863, ALPL; John Taylor to Mary Bater, May 22, 1863, ALPL.
51. Partridge, *History of the Ninety-Sixth*, 107, 109–12; "March and April 1863," Company D, 96th Illinois, AGO, RG 94, NARA.

52. Partridge, *History of the Ninety-Sixth*, 113; Meier, *Nature's Civil War*, 64; George Smith to Susie Smith, April 17, 1863, BBDM.

53. Meier, *Nature's Civil War*, 6, 96, 120.

54. Griffith, *Battle Tactics*, 41; Partridge, *History of the Ninety-Sixth*, 739, 626.

55. Partridge, *History of the Ninety-Sixth*, 626; George Dodge to David Minto, April 17, 1863, BBDM; John Taylor to Isabella Low, April 13, 1863, ALPL.

56. Partridge, *History of the Ninety-Sixth*, 116; George Dodge to David Minto, April 17, 1863, BBDM; John Taylor to Isabella Low, April 13, 1863, ALPL; "March and April 1863," Company D, 96th Illinois, AGO, RG 94, NARA.

57. Partridge, *History of the Ninety-Sixth*, 118, 151; Dunkelman, *Brothers*, 25; John Taylor to Isabella Low, May 23, 1863, ALPL; Meier, *Nature's Civil War*, 102.

58. Partridge, *History of the Ninety-Sixth*, 128.

59. Ibid., 131–32; "May and June 1863," Company D, 96th Illinois, AGO, RG 94, NARA.

60. Johnson, *Battles and Leaders*, vol. 3, pt. 2, 635; Partridge, *History of the Ninety-Sixth*, 126; Kolakowski, *Stones River*, 106.

61. IL AGR, 5:462; Partridge, *History of the Ninety-Sixth*, 135–37; "May and June 1863," Company D, 96th Illinois, AGO, RG 94, NARA; Partridge, *History of the Ninety-Sixth*, 138–39; William Lewin to Sister, July 27, 1863, Queen Family Files.

62. Johnson, *Battles and Leaders*, vol. 3, pt. 2, 679; Bradley, *Tullahoma*, 92; Kolakowski, *Stones River*, 136.

63. Partridge, *History of the Ninety-Sixth*, 130–31, 145; A. J. McCreadie to David Minto, July 14, 1863, BBDM.

64. *OR*, 1st ser., vol. 23, pt. 2, 518.

65. George Smith to Susie Smith, July 11, 1863, BBDM.

66. Bradley, *Tullahoma*, 94, 141–42; Johnson, *Battles and Leaders*, vol. 3, p. 2, 635–36; Kolakowski, *Stones River*, 138.

67. "Report of the Soldiers Aid Society for May and June," *Waukegan Weekly Gazette*, July 4, 1863; "Call for Sanitary Supplies," *Waukegan Weekly Gazette*, June 6, 1863.

68. McPherson, *For Cause*, 124; "Enthusiastic Union Meeting at Libertyville," *Waukegan Weekly Gazette*, July 25, 1863.

69. Partridge, *History of the Ninety-Sixth*, 144; John Taylor to David Minto, August 30, 1863, BBDM; John Taylor to Mary Bater, May 9, 1863, ALPL; Meier, *Nature's Civil War*, 3, 45, 47.

70. Partridge, *History of the Ninety-Sixth*, 674–75; Meier, *Nature's Civil War*, 68, 22.

71. Meier, *Nature's Civil War*, 3, 151; John Taylor to Mary Bater, May 9, 1863, ALPL.
72. Meier, *Nature's Civil War*, 115; John Taylor to David Minto, August 30, 1863, BBDM; Schroeder-Lein, "'H.G.': A Medical History," 38; Taylor Diary, July 16–30, 1863, ALPL; George Smith to Susie Smith, August 30, 1863, BBDM.
73. Dunkelman, *Brothers*, 45; James Taylor to Isabella Low, August 23, 1863, ALPL.
74. "July and August 1863," Company C, 96th Illinois, AGO, RG 94, NARA; James Taylor to Isabella Low, August 23, 1863, ALPL.
75. John Taylor to David Minto, August 30, 1863, BBDM; McPherson, *For Cause*, 126.
76. John Taylor to David Minto, August 30, 1863, BBDM; McPherson, *For Cause*, 154, 160, 151; George Smith to Susie Smith, August 30, 1863, BBDM; John Taylor to Mary Bater, May 9, 1863, ALPL.
77. *OR*, 1st. ser., 30:852; James Taylor Diary, September 1–12, 1863, ALPL; John Taylor to Sister, September 18, 1863, ALPL.
78. Powell, "Battle of Chickamauga."
79. Partridge, *History of the Ninety-Sixth*, 156.
80. Schroeder-Lein, "'H.G.': A Medical History," 27, 30; Partridge, *History of the Ninety-Sixth*, 157.
81. Partridge, *History of the Ninety-Sixth*, 157; John Taylor to Sister, September 18, 1863, ALPL.
82. Partridge, *History of the Ninety-Sixth*, 151, 160; John Taylor to Sister, September 18, 1863, ALPL.

4. Brave Boys Are They

1. Partridge, *History of the Ninety-Sixth*, 161.
2. Ibid., 226; Johnson, *Battles and Leaders*, vol. 3, pt. 2, 680; Powell, "The Battle of Chickamauga."
3. Partridge, *History of the Ninety-Sixth*, 167; John Taylor to Sister, September 18, 1863, ALPL; Meier, *Nature's Civil War*, 112; Partridge, *Battle of Chickamauga*, 6.
4. John Taylor to Sister, September 18, 1863, ALPL.
5. Partridge, *History of the Ninety-Sixth*, 169, 170; Partridge, *Battle of Chickamauga*, 7, 9.
6. Murray, *Soldier's Reminiscences*, 24; Partridge, *History of the Ninety-Sixth*, 198.

7. "September 1863," 96th Illinois, AGO, RG 94, NARA; Partridge, *History of the Ninety-Sixth*, 170–71, 198.

8. Partridge, *History of the Ninety-Sixth*, 170–71, 198; Woodworth, *Six Armies*, 128; Partridge, *Battle of Chickamauga*, 8; McPherson, *For Cause*, 79.

9. *OR*, 1st ser., 30:861–62; Partridge, *History of the Ninety-Sixth*, 172–73, 175; Partridge, *Battle of Chickamauga*, 7–8; Hicks, *Personal Recollections*; McPherson, *For Cause*, 31.

10. Partridge to Charlotte Partridge, September 30, 1863, BBDM; Partridge, *History of the Ninety-Sixth*, 175; Partridge, *Battle of Chickamauga*, 8; *OR*, 1st ser., 30:57–58.

11. *OR*, 1st ser., 30:858; Partridge, *History of the Ninety-Sixth*, 176, 157; "James Murrie," "Sept & Oct 1863," 96th Illinois, AGO, RG 94, NARA; John Taylor to Isabella Low, September 1863, ALPL; Lewin, RG 15, NARA.

12. Partridge, *History of the Ninety-Sixth*, 228; Hicks, *Personal Recollections*; McPherson, *For Cause*, 31.

13. Partridge, *History of the Ninety-Sixth*, 229; Partridge, *Battle of Chickamauga*, 9.

14. Powell, "Battle of Chickamauga"; *OR*, 1st ser., vol. 30, pt. 1, 854.

15. *OR*, 1st ser., vol. 30, pt. 1, 860; Powell, *Glory or the Grave*, 462–63.

16. *OR*, 1st ser., vol. 30, pt. 1, 862; Partridge, *History of the Ninety-Sixth*, 229, 176, 178–79.

17. Murray, *Soldier's Reminiscences*, 26; Dunkelman, *Brothers*, 119–20.

18. Beach, *Fortieth Ohio*, 46; Hicks, *Personal Recollections*.

19. *OR*, 1st ser., vol. 30, pt. 1, 60.

20. Powell, "Battle of Chickamauga"; Johnson, *Battles and Leaders*, vol. 3, pt. 2, 667; Powell, *Glory or the Grave*, 198–99.

21. Powell, *Glory or the Grave*, 203.

22. Robertson et al., "Staff Ride," 54; ibid., 195, 226; Partridge, *History of the Ninety-Sixth*, 181, 179.

23. Partridge, *History of the Ninety-Sixth*, 181, 179, 183.

24. Hicks, *Personal Recollections*.

25. William W. Jellison, "Campaign of the 96th Illinois," April 12, 1864, Orson V. Young Collection, BBDM.

26. *OR*, 1st ser., vol. 30, pt. 1, 253, 862–63.

27. Griffith, *Battle Tactics*, 97; McPherson, *For Cause*, 38; Powell, *Glory or the Grave*, 484.

28. Johnson, *Battles and Leaders*, vol. 3, pt. 2, 667; Partridge, *History of the Ninety-Sixth*, 184, 186; Berg, "Battle of Chickamauga"; Partridge, *Battle of Chickamauga*; Powell, "Battles for Horseshoe Ridge."

29. Jellison, "Campaign of the 96th," Orson V. Young Collection, BBDM.

30. Powell, "Battles for Horseshoe Ridge"; Partridge, *History of the Ninety-Sixth*, 186.

31. *OR*, 1st ser., vol. 30, pt. 1, 863; Murray, *Soldier's Reminiscences*, 26; Steplyk, *Killing at Franklin*, 82.

32. *OR*, 1st ser., vol. 30, pt. 1, 865; Steplyk, *Killing at Franklin*, 97–98; Griffith, *Battle Tactics*, 112; Partridge to Charlotte Partridge, September 30, 1863, BBDM; Hicks, *Personal Recollections*; Faust, *This Republic*, 58.

33. Murray, *Soldier's Reminiscences*, 26; Griffith, *Battle Tactics*, 112.

34. Partridge, *History of the Ninety-Sixth*, 233; Griffith, *Battle Tactics*, 106; Faust, *This Republic*, 38.

35. Partridge, *History of the Ninety-Sixth*, 184–86.

36. Jellison, "Campaign of the 96th," Orson V. Young Collection, BBDM.

37. Partridge, *History of the Ninety-Sixth*, 217; *OR*, 1st ser., vol. 30, pt. 1, 863.

38. Partridge, *History of the Ninety-Sixth*, 234; Murray, *Soldier's Reminiscences*, 26–27; Steplyk, *Killing at Franklin*, 94.

39. Dunkelman, *Brothers*, 238; Herdegen, *Iron Brigade*, 299; Partridge, *History of the Ninety-Sixth*, 824.

40. *OR*, 1st ser., vol. 30, pt. 1, 865 (Report of Colonel Champion); Powell, *Glory or the Grave*, 499–500; Hicks, *Personal Recollections*; Partridge, *History of the Ninety-Sixth*, 824, 212.

41. *OR*, 1st ser., vol. 30, pt. 1, 858, 866; Partridge, *History of the Ninety-Sixth*, 186, 236.

42. *OR*, 1st ser., vol. 30, pt. 1, 865.

43. Partridge, *History of the Ninety-Sixth*, 235–36, 184–88.

44. Griffith, *Battle Tactics*, 58, 106–9; Partridge, *History of the Ninety-Sixth*, 239, 736.

45. Partridge, *History of the Ninety-Sixth*, 189; Woodworth, *Six Armies*, 130; Hicks, *Personal Recollections*.

46. Murray, *Soldier's Reminiscences*, 27.

47. Ibid., 27; Partridge, *History of the Ninety-Sixth*, 744.

48. Partridge, *History of the Ninety-Sixth*, 513.

49. Ibid., 515; Murray, *Soldier's Reminiscences*, 27.

50. Murray, *Soldier's Reminiscences*, 27; Griffith, *Battle Tactics*, 79.

51. Murray, *Soldier's Reminiscences*, 27; Partridge, *History of the Ninety-Sixth*, 524.

52. Murray, *Soldier's Reminiscences*, 28.

53. Ibid., 28; Steplyk, *Killing at Franklin*, 98.

54. Murray, *Soldier's Reminiscences*, 28.

55. Ibid., 28; Faust, *This Republic*, 9–10.

56. Partridge, *History of the Ninety-Sixth*, 239–40.

57. Ibid., 219.

58. Ibid., 193; Partridge to Charlotte Partridge, September 30, 1863.

59. Partridge, *History of the Ninety-Sixth*, 189–90, 193, 241, 735; Faust, *This Republic*, 55, 62; Powell, *Barren Victory*, 215; Steplyk, *Killing at Franklin*, 90.

60. Partridge, *History of the Ninety-Sixth*, 201; Steplyk, *Killing at Franklin*, 82, 93; Faust, *This Republic*, 32–34.

61. Partridge to Charlotte Partridge, September 30, 1863, BBDM; Steplyk, *Killing at Franklin*, 89.

62. Partridge, *History of the Ninety-Sixth*, 190; Faust, *This Republic*, xviii, 10; George Smith to Susie Smith, October 6, 1863, BBDM.

63. Partridge, *History of the Ninety-Sixth*, 192; Powell, *Barren Victory*, 207, 215. Powell notes in his calculations for Union losses the many variables for conflicting numbers. It depended on the type or severity of the casualties counted, as regimental and brigade reports often cited higher numbers than the official army returns. *OR*, 1st ser., vol. 30, pt. 1, 857–58; Faust, *This Republic*, 253–54.

64. "22nd Michigan Infantry," Southfield in the War (blog).

65. Hicks, *Personal Recollections*; McPherson, *For Cause*, 100.

66. John C. Smith to Charlotte Smith, September 20, 1863, Galena–Jo Daviess County Historical Society; McPherson, *For Cause*, 91.

67. Partridge, *History of the Ninety-Sixth*, 246, 736, 746; John Bonner, conversation with author, July 2014; Partridge to Father, September 25, 1863, BBDM.

68. Partridge, *History of the Ninety-Sixth*, 746; William Lewin to David Minto, December 11, 1863, BBDM; John Bonner, conversation with author, July 2014; Faust, *This Republic*, 170.

69. Taylor Diary, September 22, 1863, ALPL.

70. Powell, *Barren Victory*, 83–84.

71. Partridge, *History of the Ninety-Sixth*, 208, 188.

72. "The Great Battle," *Nashville Daily Union*, September 23, 1863, 2, Chronicling America: Historic American Newspapers, LOC, accessed January 29, 2016, https://chroniclingamerica.loc.gov/lccn/sn83025718/1863–09–23/ed-1/seq-2/.

73. Partridge, *History of the Ninety-Sixth*, 192.

74. *OR*, 1st ser., vol. 30, pt. 1, 60, 863, 865–66; Partridge, *History of the Ninety-Sixth*, 192, 199.

75. "The 96th Ill. Regiment," *Waukegan Gazette*, December 5, 1863; Partridge to Addison Partridge, September 25, 1863, BBDM.

76. "Flags for the 96th Regiment," *Waukegan Gazette*, November 14, 1863.

5. The Faded Coat of Blue

1. "The Late Battles in Northern Georgia," *Waukegan Weekly Gazette*, September 26, 1863; "Lieut. Col. Isaac Clarke," *Waukegan Weekly Gazette*, October 24, 1863.

2. Neely, *Union Divided*, 62–69; Gallagher, *Union War*, 130.

3. "Grand Soldiers' Aid Party," *Waukegan Gazette*, September 26, 1863; Meier, *Nature's Civil War*, 71–72; Humphreys, *Marrow*, 21.

4. Humphreys, *Marrow*, 7, 21–22.

5. Partridge, *History of the Ninety-Sixth*, 252–53; Henry W. Blodgett, "List of Casualties among the Lake County Soldiers in the 96th and 51st Illinois Regiments at the Battle of Chickamauga," *Waukegan Gazette*, October 3, 1863; "Nos. and Location of Hospitals in Nashville," *Nashville Daily Union*, January 16, 1863, Chronicling America: Historic American Newspapers, LOC, accessed January 29, 2016, http://chroniclingamerica.loc.gov/lccn /sn83025718/1863-01-16/ed-1/seq-1/. Lists nineteen Union Hospitals in Nashville.

6. "The Battle of Chickamauga: Particulars of Engagement," *Waukegan Weekly Gazette*, October 3, 1863.

7. "The 96th Illinois Regiment in the Fight," *Waukegan Weekly Gazette*, October 3, 1863; Dunkelman, *Brothers*, 133.

8. George Smith to Susie Smith, October 6, 1863, BBDM; Partridge, *History of the Ninety-Sixth*, 772.

9. *OR*, 1st ser., vol. 30, pt. 2.

10. Murray, *Soldier's Reminiscences*, 29.

11. Ibid.

12. Ibid., 29–30; Partridge, *History of the Ninety-Sixth*, 516; Meier, *Nature's Civil War*, 117.

13. Murray, *Soldier's Reminiscences*, 30; Rutkow, *Bleeding*, 46; Meier, *Nature's Civil War*, 92.

14. Murray, *Soldier's Reminiscences*, 30–31.

15. Ibid., 31; Partridge, *History of the Ninety-Sixth*, 736, 520.

16. Partridge, *History of the Ninety-Sixth*, 516; Faust, *This Republic*, 29; Murray, *Soldier's Reminiscences*, 31; Dunkelman, *Brothers*, 153.

17. Murray, *Soldier's Reminiscences*, 31.

18. Ibid.; Rubenstein, "Study of the Medical Support."

19. Murray, *Soldier's Reminiscences*, 32.
20. Ibid.
21. Charles Partridge to Addison Partridge, September 25, 1863, BBDM.
22. Murray, *Soldier's Reminiscences*, 32.
23. Ibid., 32–33.
24. Ibid., 33.
25. Taylor Diary, 1863, ALPL.
26. Partridge, *History of the Ninety-Sixth*, 188, 513, 735–36, 744; Robertson et al., "Staff Ride."
27. Humphreys, *Marrow*, 32; "Casualty Sheet," John Taylor, RG 94, NARA.
28. Partridge to Charlotte Partridge, September 30, 1863, BBDM; RG 15, NARA.
29. Partridge to Charlotte Partridge, September 30, 1863, BBDM; Woodward, *Medical and Surgical History*, 267; Partridge, *History of the Ninety-Sixth*, 242.
30. Partridge to Father, September 25, 1863, BBDM; Taylor Diary, 1863, ALPL; "Nos. and Location of Hospitals in Nashville," *Nashville Daily Union*, January 16, 1863, Chronicling America: Historic American Newspapers, LOC, accessed January 29, 2016, http://chroniclingamerica.loc.gov/lccn /sn83025718/1863–01–16/ed-1/seq-1/. Hospital No. 12 was located at the intersection of today's Broadway and Fourth Avenue; Rutkow, *Bleeding*, 103.
31. Meier, *Nature's Civil War*, 117; Schroeder-Lein, "'H.G.': A Medical History," 33.
32. Murray, *Soldier's Reminiscences*, 34; Humphreys, *Marrow*, 32.
33. "A Big Apple Bee," *Waukegan Gazette*, October 17, 1863; Partridge, *History of Lake County, Illinois*, 648.
34. Schroeder-Lein, "'H.G.': A Medical History," 32; James Taylor Diary, October 1863, ALPL; Humphreys, *Marrow*, 30, 31.
35. Schroeder-Lein, "'H.G.': A Medical History," 32; James Taylor Diary, October 1863, ALPL; King, "Civil War Medicine"; Humphreys, *Marrow*, 204; Rutkow, *Bleeding*, 174.
36. Schroeder-Lein, "'H.G.': A Medical History," 32; Partridge, *History of the Ninety-Sixth*, 744.
37. Schroeder-Lein, "'H.G.': A Medical History," 32; Murray, *Soldier's Reminiscences*, 34; Dunkelman, *Brothers*, 115.
38. Murray, *Soldier's Reminiscences*, 34–35.
39. Hunter and Chamberlin, *Sketches of War History*, 5:291; Rutkow, *Bleeding*, 111.
40. Taylor Diary, November 4, 1863, ALPL; James Taylor to James and Mary Bater, November 5, 1863, ALPL.

41. Taylor Diary, 1863, ALPL; William Lewin to Sister, Nov 15, 1863, Queen Family Files.

42. Murray, *Soldier's Reminiscences*, 35; Humphreys, *Marrow*, 32; Rutkow, *Bleeding*, 45; Meier, *Nature's Civil War*, 68; Plaisance and Schelver, "Federal Military Hospitals."

43. Humphreys, *Marrow*, 31.

44. Murray, *Soldier's Reminiscences*, 35.

45. Ibid.

46. Ibid.; *Kenosha, Wisconsin City Map*, 1857.

47. Murray, *Soldier's Reminiscences*, 35-36.

48. Ibid., 36.

49. William Lewin to David Minto, December 11, 1863, BBDM.

50. Murray, *Soldier's Reminiscences*, 36.

51. Ibid.; "Edward Murray," RG 94, NARA.

52. Murray, *Soldier's Reminiscences*, 36; Faust, *This Republic*, 267.

53. Murray, *Soldier's Reminiscences*, 36.

54. Ibid., 37–38.

55. "Edward Murray," RG 94, NARA; Plaisance and Schelver, "Federal Military Hospitals."

56. Murray, *Soldier's Reminiscences*, 39; Meier, *Nature's Civil War*, 71.

57. Murray, *Soldier's Reminiscences*, 40; "Quincy National Cemetery, Quincy, Illinois," NPS, accessed February 23, 2020, nps.gov; "Edward Murray," RG 94, NARA; King, "Civil War Medicine."

58. Murray, *Soldier's Reminiscences*, 41; Orr, "Shot in the Lung"; ISA; "Edward Murray," RG 94, NARA; "Murray," RG 15, NARA; Thompson, "From Chancellorsville to Gettysburg."

59. Murray, *Soldier's Reminiscences*, 41; "Discharge," Edward Murray, RG 94, NARA; Westerman, *History of Waukegan*, 102.

60. Orson Young to Parents, October 10, 1863, BBDM.

61. Partridge, *History of the Ninety-Sixth*, 243.

62. Evans, *96th Illinois Volunteer Infantry*, 57.

63. Partridge, *History of the Ninety-Sixth*, 524–25, 589–91, 191; Beach, *Fortieth Ohio*, 133.

64. "September 1863," 96th Illinois, AGO, RG 94, NARA; Partridge, *History of the Ninety-Sixth*, 525, 534, 592.

65. Partridge, *History of the Ninety-Sixth*, 592–93, 534, 527; *Portrait and Biographical Album*, 713; "Crew & Pemberton's Warehouse," Civil War Richmond, last modified 2015, https://www.civilwarrichmond.com/prisons/crew-pemberton-s-warehouse.

66. Sanders, *While in the Hands*, 76, 79.

67. Ibid., 145, 161.

68. Ibid., 162, 164, 183, 186.

69. Ibid., 188–89; "Memorandum from Prisoner of War Records," Loughlin Madden, RG 94, NARA; Partridge, *History of the Ninety-Sixth*, 532, 526, 745.

70. Sanders, *While in the Hands*, 189–90; NPS, "Danville National Cemetery, Danville, Virginia"; Partridge, *History of the Ninety-Sixth*, 532.

71. Sanders, *While in the Hands*, 190; Partridge, *History of the Ninety-Sixth*, 532; Loughlin Madden, RG 94, NARA.

72. Partridge, *History of the Ninety-Sixth*, 527; Sanders, *While in the Hands*, 191.

73. Sanders, *While in the Hands*, 196, 198, 202–3.

74. Ibid., 198, 204–5, 212–13, 223; Partridge, *History of the Ninety-Sixth*, 533.

75. "Determining the Facts, Reading 1: Andersonville Prison," NPS, accessed February 23, 2020, http://www.nps.gov/nr/twhp/wwwlps/lessons/11andersonville /11facts1.htm; Sanders, *While in the Hands*, 206.

76. "Personal War Sketch of William B. Lewin," WHS.

77. Partridge, *History of the Ninety-Sixth*, 559–60.

78. Ibid., 551, 560–61.

79. Sanders, *While in the Hands*, 222; Partridge, *History of the Ninety-Sixth*, 561–62, 553.

80. Meier, *Nature's Civil War*, 93; Partridge, *History of the Ninety-Sixth*, 563, 553.

81. Sanders, *While in the Hands*, 251.

82. Partridge, *History of the Ninety-Sixth*, 553.

83. Ibid., 553; Sanders, *While in the Hands*, 234; Miller, *Emigrants and Exiles*, 300.

84. Partridge, *History of the Ninety-Sixth*, 527; Loughlin Madden, cause of death "Diarrhea," RG 94, NARA; "U.S., Registers of Deaths of Volunteers, 1861–1865," Ancestry.com.

85. Partridge, *History of the Ninety-Sixth*, 553, 565; Sanders, *While in the Hands*, 252–53.

86. Partridge, *History of the Ninety-Sixth*, 566, 548.

87. Partridge, *History of the Ninety-Sixth*, 548, 556, 566; Fonvielle, *Wilmington*, 446; Sanders, *While in the Hands*, 253.

88. Partridge, *History of the Ninety-Sixth*, 558; Fonvielle, *Wilmington*, 421, 446.

89. Partridge, *History of the Ninety-Sixth*, 556, 567; Fonvielle, *Wilmington*, 421.

90. Partridge, *History of the Ninety-Sixth* 567; Fonvielle, *Wilmington*, 446–47.

91. Fonvielle, *Wilmington*, 22, 435–36.

92. Fonvielle, *Wilmington*, 447; Partridge, *History of the Ninety-Sixth*, 567.

93. Partridge, *History of the Ninety-Sixth*, 558; Fonvielle, *Wilmington*, 448.

94. Partridge, *History of the Ninety-Sixth*, 539, 567; Lewin, RG 94, NARA.

95. Jordan, *Marching*, 137–38; Meier, *Nature's Civil War*, 22.

96. Lewin, RG 15, NARA; Jordan, *Marching*, 129–30.

97. Lewin, RG 15, NARA.

6. Tenting on the Old Camp Ground

1. Woodworth, *Six Armies*, 129–30, 132.

2. Partridge, *History of the Ninety-Sixth*, 249; Woodworth, *Six Armies*, 134.

3. Johnson, *Battles and Leaders*; Company C, "September and October 1863," AGO, RG 94, NARA; Partridge, *History of the Ninety-Sixth*, 214.

4. Partridge, *History of the Ninety-Sixth*, 196–97, 739; Schroeder-Lein, "'H.G.': A Medical History," 30–31; Lewin, RG 15, NARA.

5. Woodworth, *Six Armies*, 134; Meier, *Nature's Civil War*, 2.

6. Woodworth, *Six Armies*, 134; Cubbison, "'That Awful Storm,'" 268.

7. Partridge, *History of the Ninety-Sixth*, 252; Johnson, *Battles and Leaders*, vol. 3, pt. 2, 683; Beach, *Fortieth Ohio*, 51.

8. Lewin, RG 15, NARA; William Lewin to Sister, November 15, 1863, Queen Family Files; Partridge, *History of the Ninety-Sixth*, 253–54; Woodworth, *Six Armies*, 142.

9. Johnson, *Battles and Leaders*, 687; Partridge, *History of the Ninety-Sixth*, 256; National Register Nomination, "Battles for Chattanooga."

10. Cubbison, "'That Awful Storm,'" 270; Partridge, *History of the Ninety-Sixth*, 250, 262.

11. Evans, *96th Illinois*, 67; Partridge, *History of the Ninety-Sixth*, 250–51; Cubbison, "'That Awful Storm,'" 270, 281.

12. Woodworth, *Six Armies*, 146; Partridge, *History of the Ninety-Sixth*, 256; IL AGR.

13. Woodworth, *Six Armies*, 152; Johnson, *Battles and Leaders*, 684.

14. Woodworth, *Six Armies*, 152; Partridge, *History of the Ninety-Sixth*, 257.

15. Johnson, *Battles and Leaders*, 685; Cubbison, "'That Awful Storm,'" 274; Evans, *96th Illinois*, 69; Woodworth, *Six Armies*, 146; Partridge, *History of the Ninety-Sixth*, 257–58.

16. Partridge, *History of the Ninety-Sixth*, 259; Woodworth, *Six Armies*, 162; Beach, *Fortieth Ohio*, 44.

17. Johnson, *Battles and Leaders*, 678; Cubbison, "'That Awful Storm,'" 278.

18. Cubbison, "'That Awful Storm,'" 276–77; Partridge, *History of the Ninety-Sixth*, 259–60, 157; IL AGR.

19. Taylor Diary, 1863, ALPL; George Smith to Susie Smith, November 19, 1863, BBDM; Partridge, *History of the Ninety-Sixth*, 262.

20. Taylor Diary, 1863, ALPL; Partridge, *History of the Ninety-Sixth*, 262; Beach, *Fortieth Ohio*, 52; *Portrait and Biographical Album*, 396.

21. Partridge, *History of the Ninety-Sixth*, 263; Beach, *Fortieth Ohio*, 52–53; Evans, *96th Illinois*, 72; Woodworth, *Six Armies*, 172.

22. Johnson, *Battles and Leaders*, 721.

23. Woodworth, *Six Armies*, 180–81.

24. Ibid., 185; Johnson, *Battles and Leaders*, 722.

25. Partridge, *History of the Ninety-Sixth*, 262–63.

26. Ibid., 644.

27. Ibid., 264.

28. Ibid., 265.

29. Johnson, *Battles and Leaders*, 702.

30. Partridge, *History of the Ninety-Sixth*, 265–67.

31. Ibid., 267–68; Woodworth, *Six Armies*, 187.

32. Partridge, *History of the Ninety-Sixth*, 270, 711; Beach, *Fortieth Ohio*, 55.

33. Partridge, *History of the Ninety-Sixth*, 271; Beach, *Fortieth Ohio*, 55–56; Woodworth, *Six Armies*, 188–89.

34. Johnson, *Battles and Leaders*, 704.

35. Partridge, *History of the Ninety-Sixth*, 269, 271–72; Beach, *Fortieth Ohio*, 56; Griffith, *Battle Tactics*, 122.

36. "November 1863," Company B, C, and D, 96th Illinois, AGO, RG94, NARA.

37. William Lewin to David Minto, December 11, 1863, BBDM.

38. Partridge, *History of the Ninety-Sixth*, 271.

39. Ibid., 275.

40. Ibid., 275–76; Woodworth, *Six Armies*, 191.

41. Partridge, *History of the Ninety-Sixth*, 647.

42. Ibid., 279; Cubbison, "Tactical Genius," 286.

43. Partridge, *History of the Ninety-Sixth*, 281; Woodworth, *Six Armies*, 213.

44. Partridge, *History of the Ninety-Sixth*, 281.

45. Taylor Diary, December 3, 1863, ALPL; James Taylor to Isabella Low, December 7, 1863, ALPL.

46. James Taylor to Isabella Low, October 18, 1862, ALPL; Taylor Diary, 1863, ALPL. Partridge, *History of the Ninety-Sixth*, 737; John Taylor, RG 94, NARA.

47. James Taylor to Isabella Low, December 7, 1863, ALPL.

48. Faust, *This Republic*, 144, 176.

49. Jane Taylor to James Taylor, January 12, 1864, ALPL.

50. Richard Thain to Isabella Low, February 15, 1864, ALPL; Faust, *This Republic*, 26, 144–45.

51. Meier, *Nature's Civil War*, 22; Humphreys, *Marrow*, 7, 14–15; Partridge, *History of the Ninety-Sixth*, 282.

52. Meier, *Nature's Civil War*, 14; Humphreys, *Marrow*, 14; Partridge, *History of the Ninety-Sixth*, 282; Mitchell, *Vacant Chair*, 74; Wolf, "General John Corson Smith," 281–84.

53. Meier, *Nature's Civil War*, 14; Humphreys, *Marrow*, 14; Wolf, "General John Corson Smith," 282; Mitchell, *Vacant Chair*, 74; Partridge, *History of the Ninety-Sixth*, 283; Gannon, "She Is a Member," 185, 191.

54. Partridge, *History of the Ninety-Sixth*, 283; Dunkelman, *Brothers*, 6, 16.

55. Taylor Diary, January 1864, ALPL; "The U.S. Sanitary Commission, The Soldiers' Home," *Nashville Daily Union*, September 23, 1863, Chronicling America: Historic American Newspapers, LOC, accessed January 29, 2016, http://chroniclingamerica.loc.gov/lccn/sn83025718/1863–09–23/ed-1/seq-1/; Taylor Diary, January 27, 1864, ALPL; Plaisance and Schelver, "Federal Military Hospitals."

56. Partridge, *History of the Ninety-Sixth*, 284–85.

57. Partridge, *History of the Ninety-Sixth*, 290–91; "February 1864," 96th Illinois, AGO, RG 94, NARA.

58. Partridge, *History of the Ninety-Sixth*, 239, 663, 774; Sanders, *While in the Hands*, 203.

7. Bonny Boys in Blue

1. George Smith to Susie Smith, June 16, 1864, BBDM; McPherson, *For Cause*, 168, 174.

2. McCarley, *Atlanta and Savannah*, 7; McMurry, *Road Past*, 2.

3. "May 1864," 96th Illinois, AGO, RG 94, NARA; Partridge, *History of the Ninety-Sixth*, 303, 737; McMurry, *Road Past*, 34.

4. "May 1864," 96th Illinois, AGO, RG 94, NARA; Partridge, *History of the Ninety-Sixth*, 850, 242–43, 308.

5. "May 1864," 96th Illinois, AGO, RG 94, NARA; Partridge, *History of the Ninety-Sixth*, 307.

6. "May 1864," 96th Illinois, AGO, RG 94, NARA; Partridge, *History of the Ninety-Sixth*, 309.

7. Partridge, *History of the Ninety-Sixth*, 310.

8. James M. Taylor, RG 94, NARA; Calvin, *History of Christian County*, 122; Taylor Diary, 1864, ALPL; "May 1864," 96th Illinois, AGO, RG 94, NARA; Partridge, *History of the Ninety-Sixth*, 310, 772.

9. Partridge, *History of the Ninety-Sixth*, 310; Taylor Diary, 1864, ALPL; *Nashville Daily Union*, January 16, 1863, Chronicling America: Historic American Newspapers, LOC, accessed January 29, 2016, http://chroniclingamerica.loc.gov/lccn/sn83025718/1863–01–16/ed-1/seq-1/.

10. McMurry, *Road Past*, 8; Partridge, *History of the Ninety-Sixth*, 311.

11. Partridge, *History of the Ninety-Sixth*, 320; Griffith, *Battle Tactics*, 155; McMurray, *Road Past*, 13.

12. Partridge, *History of the Ninety-Sixth*, 320.

13. Ibid., 321; "May 1864," 96th Illinois, AGO, RG 94, NARA.

14. Partridge, *History of the Ninety-Sixth*, 321–22.

15. Ibid., 326, 323.

16. Ibid., 327; Griffith, *Battle Tactics*, 150.

17. Partridge, *History of the Ninety-Sixth*, 328; McMurry, *Road Past*, 34.

18. Partridge, *History of the Ninety-Sixth*, 559.

19. Ibid., 340–41; McCarley, *Atlanta and Savannah*, 20–21; Orson Young to Parents, May 20, 1864, BBDM; McMurry, *Road Past*, 35; McPherson, *For Cause*, 165.

20. Partridge, *History of the Ninety-Sixth*, 340–41; Meier, *Nature's Civil War*, 102; Hébert, "Bitter Trial"; Orson Young to Parents, January 22, 1865, BBDM.

21. McCarley, *Atlanta and Savannah*, 20–21; Partridge, *History of the Ninety-Sixth*, 345.

22. Partridge, *History of the Ninety-Sixth*, 346, 674–75; "Personal War Sketch of James Murrie," WHS; James Murrie, RG 15 and RG 94, NARA.

23. Partridge, *History of the Ninety-Sixth*, 347; Orson Young to Parents, June 6, 1864, BBDM; McMurry, *Road Past*, 21; Meier, *Nature's Civil War*, 15.

24. Taylor Diary, May and June 1864, ALPL; Humphreys, *Marrow*, 30; James M. Taylor, pension certificate, ALPL; Schroeder-Lein, "'H.G.': A Medical History," 36.

25. Isabella Low to James Taylor, June 21, 1864, ALPL; Faust, *This Republic*, 20; Faust "Civil War Soldier," 38.

26. Isabella Low to James Taylor, June 21, 1864, ALPL.

27. Schroeder-Lein, "'H.G.': A Medical History," 38.

28. "From the 96th Regiment," *Waukegan Gazette*, June 25, 1864.

29. Partridge, *History of the Ninety-Sixth*, 359; "June 1864," 96th Illinois, AGO, RG 94, NARA.

30. Partridge, *History of the Ninety-Sixth*, 363–364; "June 1864," 96th Illinois, AGO, RG 94, NARA.

31. Partridge, *History of the Ninety-Sixth*, 373; "July and August 1864," AGO, RG 94, NARA.

32. Partridge, *History of the Ninety-Sixth*, 374; George Smith to Susie Smith, July 7, 1864, BBDM.

33. Partridge, *History of the Ninety-Sixth*, 387; McMurry, *Road Past*, 32–33; Bailey, "Other Side."

34. Partridge, *History of the Ninety-Sixth*, 387; McMurry, *Road Past*, 44.

35. McMurry, *Road Past*, 52; Partridge, *History of the Ninety-Sixth*, 382–384.

36. George Smith to Susie Smith, July 29, 1864, BBDM; Partridge, *History of the Ninety-Sixth*, 385–87.

37. "Cucumber Pickles for the Soldiers," *Waukegan Gazette*, August 20, 1864.

38. "July and August 1864," AGO, RG 94, NARA; Partridge, *History of the Ninety-Sixth*, 395; McMurry, *Road Past*, 54.

39. Partridge, *History of the Ninety-Sixth*, 387, 395; McMurry, *Road Past*, 54–55.

40. Partridge, *History of the Ninety-Sixth*, 396, 387; McMurry, *Road Past*, 57; George Smith to Susie Smith, September 11, 1864, BBDM; Weber, *Copperheads*, 135; Doyle, *Cause of All Nations*, 284.

41. Partridge, *History of the Ninety-Sixth*, 396.

42. Partridge, *History of the Ninety-Sixth*, 397–98, 400, 435; McPherson, *For Cause*, 165; *Portrait and Biographical Album*, 396.

43. Alex Thain to James Taylor, September 1864, ALPL; IL AGR, 469.

8. Rally 'Round the Flag

1. Simpson, "Failure to Communicate," 106–7; IL AGR, 463; Bailey, "Other Side of the Monument"; Frisby, *Campaigns in Mississippi*, 30–31.

2. Partridge, *History of the Ninety-Sixth*, 411; Faust, "Civil War Soldier."

3. Frisby, *Campaigns in Mississippi*, 38–39.

4. Partridge, *History of the Ninety-Sixth*, 421, 434; Frisby, *Campaigns in Mississippi*, 39; U.S. Congress, *Supplemental Report*, 398.

5. Partridge, *History of the Ninety-Sixth*, 424, 426–28; *Portrait and Biographical Album*, 396; Frisby, *Campaigns in Mississippi*, 46.

6. Partridge, *History of the Ninety-Sixth*, 428; Evans, *96th Illinois*, 134–35.

7. OR, 1st ser., vol. 45, pt. 2, 117; Partridge, *History of the Ninety-Sixth*, 430–31, 434; Meier, *Nature's Civil War*, 124–25; McPherson, *For Cause*, 165.

8. Partridge, *History of the Ninety-Sixth*, 435, 437; IL AGR.

9. Simpson, "Failure to Communicate," 108–9.

10. Partridge, *History of the Ninety-Sixth*, 439–40.

11. Ibid., 441–42; Faust, *This Republic*, 28–29.

12. IL AGR, 463; Partridge, *History of the Ninety-Sixth*, 445, 745; Richard Thain to Susie Smith, December 30, 1864, BBDM; Faust, *This Republic*, 25; Dunkelman, *Brothers*, 153.

13. Frisby, *Campaigns in Mississippi*, 63; Turner and Stabler, "No More Auction Block," 144.

14. Partridge, *History of the Ninety-Sixth*, 450, 452, 457–58; IL AGR, 464.

15. Partridge, *History of the Ninety-Sixth*, 453; Alexander Thain to Susie Smith, January 9, 1865, BBDM.

16. Alex Thain to Susie Smith, January 9, 1865, BBDM; Murray, "Preserving the Nashville Battlefield," 233; Partridge, *History of the Ninety-Sixth*, 455.

17. Richard Thain to Susie Smith, December 30, 1864, BBDM.

18. Alexander Thain to Susie Smith, January 9, 1865, BBDM; Partridge, *History of the Ninety-Sixth*, 457–58; "The 96th Ill. Regiment," *Waukegan Gazette*, January 21, 1865; IL AGR, 464.

19. Alexander Thain to Susie Smith, March 11, 1865, BBDM; Partridge, *History of the Ninety-Sixth*, 457–59. Meier, *Nature's Civil War*, 106.

20. Partridge, *History of the Ninety-Sixth*, 460–61; Alexander Thain to Susie Smith, March 11, 1865, BBDM.

21. Partridge, *History of the Ninety-Sixth*, 461, 464–66; Evans, *96th Illinois*, 148; Byrd, *Unionist in East Tennessee*; "Called Out and Killed: Another Victim of the Hawkins County Vendetta," *Columbia (TN) Herald and Mail*, June 3, 1870.

22. Partridge, *History of the Ninety-Sixth*, 467; Gallagher, *Union War*, 6.

23. Partridge, *History of the Ninety-Sixth*, 468; Murrie, RG 15, NARA.

24. Partridge, *History of the Ninety-Sixth*, 468–69.

25. Hodes, *Mourning*, 48, 62, 105.

26. *OR*, 1st ser., vol. 49, pt. 2, 48, 105.

27. Partridge, *History of the Ninety-Sixth*, 468–69; Hodes, *Mourning*, 115–16; "The Terrible Tragedy at Washington," *Waukegan Weekly Gazette*, April 22, 1865; "Postscript 4 o'clock a.m., Terrible News," *Chicago Tribune*, April 15, 1865.

28. Alex Thain to Susie Smith, April 25, 1865, BBDM.

29. Partridge, *History of the Ninety-Sixth*, 469; Hodes, *Mourning*, 121, 134; Orson Young to Parents, May 7, 1865, BBDM.

30. Halsey, *History of Lake County*, 157; Hodes, *Mourning*, 83, 162–63.

31. Hodes, *Mourning*, 143, 152.

32. Partridge, *History of the Ninety-Sixth*, 747; Humphreys, *Marrow*, 30.

33. Faust, *This Republic*, 156; Leonard Doolittle to David Minto, May 1, 1865, BBDM.

34. Hodes, *Mourning*, 149, 155–56; Leonard Doolittle to David Minto, May 1, 1865, BBDM.

35. Hodes, *Mourning*, 156.

36. Ibid., 157; Faust, *This Republic*, 156.

9. Heroes of the Army of Liberty

1. *OR*, 1st ser., vol. 49, pt. 2, 375.
2. Partridge, *History of the Ninety-Sixth*, 470–71.
3. Ibid., 473; George Smith to Susie Smith, May 15, 1865, BBDM.
4. Partridge, *History of the Ninety-Sixth*, 473–74; Jordan, *Marching*, 17.
5. Partridge, *History of the Ninety-Sixth*, 473–75.
6. IL AGR; Hodes, *Mourning*, 136.
7. Susannah D. Smith Diary (hereafter cited as Smith Diary), June 1, 1865, BBDM; Hodes, *Mourning*, 246.
8. IL AGR; Partridge, *History of the Ninety-Sixth*, 477.
9. Partridge, *History of the Ninety-Sixth*, 739–52.
10. Ibid., 477; IL AGR; Jordan, *Marching*, 22.
11. Jordan, *Marching*, 30; Partridge, *History of the Ninety-Sixth*, 477–78; George Smith to Susie Smith, June 18, 1865, BBDM.
12. Partridge, *History of the Ninety-Sixth*, 477–78.
13. Ibid., 479; Jordan, *Marching*, 71, 22; Bradley, *Civil War Ends*, 72.
14. Partridge, *History of the Ninety-Sixth*, 478–80; "Coming Home to Stay," *Chicago Tribune*, June 15, 1865, 4.
15. "Discharged Soldiers: Employment for the Veterans-Circular from the Young Men's Christian Association," *Chicago Tribune*, July 8, 1865; Jordan, *Marching*, 55.
16. Partridge, *History of the Ninety-Sixth*, 483; "The 96th Regiment," *Voice of the Fair*, June 15, 1865; IL AGR; Jordan, *Marching*, 19.
17. "Coming Home to Stay," *Chicago Tribune*, June 15, 1865, 4; Partridge, *History of the Ninety-Sixth*, 486.
18. Partridge, *History of the Ninety-Sixth*, 481; Jordan, *Marching*, 3.
19. George Smith to Susie Smith, June 18, 1865, BBDM; Jordan, *Marching*, 27–28; "The Garroters at Work: Four Citizens Garroted on the Public Streets," *Chicago Tribune*, April 11, 1865.
20. Smith Diary, June 15, 1865, BBDM.
21. Ibid., June 19, 1865.
22. Ibid.
23. *Millburn Union Casket*, February 2, 1865, BBDM.
24. McPherson, *For Cause*, 131–32, 162; Richard Thain to Susie Smith, January 17, 1865, BBDM.
25. Smith Diary, June 22–25, 1865, BBDM.
26. IL AGR; Ural, *Civil War Citizens*, 11.

27. Samito, *Becoming American*, 132, 173, 221; Engle, "Yankee Dutchmen," 42; Sheehan-Dean, *Long Civil War*, 115; Keating, *Immigrants*, 10; Ural, *Civil War Citizens*, 127; Partridge, *History of the Ninety-Sixth*, 664, 764, 826; Veterans Associations, BBDM.

28. Partridge, *History of the Ninety-Sixth*, 491–92; Jordan, *Marching*, 17, 25; Dunkelman, *Brothers*, 251.

29. Partridge, *History of the Ninety-Sixth*, 491–93.

30. Ibid.

31. Ibid.; "Reception of the 96th Regiment: Speeches, Incidents, Etc. Welcome to the Heroes," *Waukegan Gazette*, July 1, 1865; Currey, "Mr. Lincoln's Visit," 181.

32. "Reception of the 96th Regiment: Speeches, Incidents, Etc. Welcome to the Heroes," *Waukegan Gazette*, July 1, 1865; Jordan, *Marching*, 18; Faust, *This Republic*, 135.

33. Henshaw, *Our Branch*, 899; Partridge, *History of the Ninety-Sixth*, 493–94.

34. Jordan, *Marching*, 6, 4, 41.

35. Ibid., 71, 79; Dunkelman, *Brothers*, 251; Hodes, *Mourning*, 246.

36. "Fourth of July at Druce's Lake," *Waukegan Gazette*, June 24, 1865; Smith Diary, July 4, 1865, BBDM.

37. Smith Diary, July 4, 1865, BBDM.

38. Schroeder-Lein "'H.G.': A Medical History," 38.

39. Smith Diary, July 4, 1865, BBDM; Jordan, *Marching*, 108.

40. Jordan, *Marching*, 109.

41. "Military Asylums," *Chicago Tribune*, May 9, 1865; Jordan, *Marching*, 44.

42. Jordan, *Marching*, 110–11; LOC, *Wm. Oland Bourne Papers*; Partridge, *History of the Ninety-Sixth*, 710.

43. LOC, *Wm. Oland Bourne Papers*; Jordan, *Marching*, 111, 122.

44. Faust, *This Republic*, 177; Philips, *Battling Stereotypes*; Mitchell, *Vacant Chair*, 138, 140, 142.

45. Faust, *This Republic*, 177, 265; Alexander Thain to Susie Smith, April 25, 1865, BBDM; Jordan, *Marching*, 6, 7, 44.

46. Smith Diary, July 4, 1865, BBDM.

47. Smith Diary, January 1, 1867, BBDM; "George E. Smith," HMCA, accessed February 17, 2020, http://www.historicmillburn.org/Families/1_gesmit.htm.

48. "Millburn Reveres the Memory of Its Beloved 'Father' Dodge," *Waukegan Post*, August 15, 1940; Isabella Low to James Taylor, June 21, 1864, ALPL; Smith Diary, August 2, 1865, BBDM.

49. U.S. Department of Veterans Affairs, "History and Development"; Faust, *This Republic*, 144, 236.
50. Faust, "Civil War Soldier"; TSLA.
51. Faust, *This Republic*, 229, 241.
52. "Civil War Era National Cemeteries: Honoring Those Who Served: Nashville National Cemetery Madison, Tennessee," NPS, last modified April 4, 2019, https://www.nps.gov/nr/travel/national_cemeteries/Tennessee/Nashville_National_Cemetery.html; TSLA; Mitchell, *Vacant Chair*, 145.
53. John Taylor to Isabella Low, May 23 1863, ALPL; Faust, *This Republic*, 248–49.
54. Faust, *This Republic*, 212–13, 215; Atwater and Barton, "List of the Union Soldiers."
55. Atwater and Barton, "List of the Union Soldiers."

10. Lest We Forget

1. Edward Murray, RG 15, NARA.
2. Ibid.
3. Jordan, *Marching*, 152–53; Partridge, *History of the Ninety-Sixth*, 517; Murray, *Soldier's Reminiscences*, 3; *Portrait and Biographical Album*, 379.
4. Costa, *Evolution of Retirement*, 198; United States Department of Labor, *History of Wages*, 225; Murray, *Soldier's Reminiscences*, 28; Haines, *Past and Present*, 419; *Portrait and Biographical Album*, 379; "Town Election, Held Tuesday April 4th 1865," *Waukegan Gazette*, June 17, 1865; Henshaw, *Our Branch and Its Tributaries*, 399.
5. Jordan, *Marching*, 103.
6. "Town of Newport," *Waukegan Weekly Gazette*, February 10, 1866.
7. Jordan, *Marching*, 124.
8. Edward Murray, "Application for Increase of Invalid Pension," 1867, copy, BBDM; Costa, *Evolution of Retirement*, 198–99.
9. Faust, *This Republic*, 267.
10. James Murrie, RG 94, NARA; William Lewin/James Murrie, RG 15, NARA;
11. James Murrie, RG 94, NARA; Halsey, *History of Lake County*, 710.
12. *Portrait and Biographical Album*, 395–96; *Map of Lake County*, 1861; David Minto Diary, October 1866, BBDM; Veterans Associations, BBDM.
13. Murrie, RG 15, NARA; Costa, *Evolution of Retirement*, 197–98.
14. U.S. Naturalization Record Indexes, Ancestry.com; 1870 U.S. Census; 1880 U.S. Census; Halsey, *History of Lake County*, 607; U.S. City Directories, Ancestry.com.

15. Jordan, *Marching*, 129–30.
16. "The Martyrs of Andersonville," *Chicago Tribune*, May 4, 1865; "Lake County Soldiers Starved at Andersonville," *Chicago Tribune*, June 3, 1865.
17. "Grand Union Demonstration," *Chicago Tribune*, August 11, 1866; David Minto Diary, 1866, BBDM; Jordan, *Marching*, 71, 73; Dunkelman, *Brothers*, 251; Joyner, "Dirty Work."
18. LCIRD; State of Illinois, "1908 Revised List of Veterinary Surgeons"; "Veterinarian Dies Very Suddenly," *Antioch News*, January 15, 1914.
19. Lewin, RG 15, NARA; 1880 U.S. Census; "Homestead Dr. Wm. Lewin Drawn from Memory 1878," by William Murray, 1912, Queen Family Files; Halsey, *History of Lake County*, 809.
20. Lewin, RG 15, NARA.
21. Lake County Soldiers' Monument Association, *Articles of Association*; *Portrait and Biographical Album*, 261.
22. "Lake County Soldiers and Sailors Monument," *Waukegan Daily Sun*, August 1899; Osling, *Historical Highlights*, 54–55; Jordan, *Marching*, 72, 100, 127.
23. "The Ninety-Sixth Re-union," *Waukegan Gazette*, September 4, 1875; "The Ninety-Sixth," *Chicago Daily Tribune*, October 3, 1875, 7.
24. "96th Ill. Vol. Informal Social Gathering," invitation, November 25, 1878, BBDM; Jordan, *Marching*, 74; "The Ninety-Sixth," *Chicago Tribune*, November 26, 1878, 2.
25. "96th Ill. Vol. Informal Social Gathering," invitation, November 25, 1878, BBDM; "The Ninety-Sixth and Gen. John C. Smith," *Chicago Tribune*, November 26, 1878.
26. Sheehan-Dean, *Long Civil War*, 142; Dunkelman, *Brothers*, 251, 256.
27. Veterans Associations, BBDM.
28. Ibid.; U.S. Civil War Soldier Records and Profiles, 1861–1865, "Henry S. Vail," Ancestry.com.
29. Sons of Union Veterans of the Civil War "Illinois"; Veterans Associations, BBDM; Jordan, *Marching*, 79; Northcott, *Grand Army*.
30. Partridge, *History of the Ninety-Sixth*, 559, 566.
31. Jordan, *Marching*, 86, 130, 140; Anna E. Heath Williamson and William B. Lewin, ca. 1905, Queen Family Files.
32. Dunkelman, *Brothers*, 251; Partridge, *History of the Ninety-Sixth*, iii–iv.
33. Partridge, *History of the Ninety-Sixth*, iv.
34. Jordan, *Marching*, 83; Smith, *Reception to the Members*.
35. Smith, *Reception to the Members*.
36. Jordan, *Marching*, 95–96; "In Death Edward Murray Passed Away Wednesday. Bullet Caused Death," *Waukegan Daily Sun*, November 30, 1900.

37. Smith, *Reception to the Members*; Gallagher, *Union War*, 6; Doyle, "Civil War Was Won."

38. Robertson et al., *Staff Ride*; Jordan, *Marching*, 98–99.

39. Powell, "Battles for Horseshoe Ridge."

40. Evangelist J. Gilmore to Wife, October 5, 1863, CWM; Orson Young to Parents, September 24, 1863, BBDM; Partridge, *History of the Ninety-Sixth*, 202.

41. Powell, "Battles for Horseshoe Ridge"; "General Boynton Explains," *The Inter Ocean*, December 12, 1894.

42. Jordan, *Marching*, 100.

43. "Lake County Soldiers and Sailors Monument," *Waukegan Daily Sun*, August 1899; Osling, *Historical Highlights*, 54–55; "Will Honor War Heroes," *Chicago Daily Tribune*, August 28, 1899.

44. "3000 There," *Lake County Independent*, September 9, 1898; "Plan a Big Reunion," *Lake County Independent*, July 7, 1899.

45. Gallagher, *Union Cause*, 121; "Lake County Soldiers and Sailors Monument," *Waukegan Daily Sun*, August 1899.

46. "Lake County Soldiers and Sailors Monument," *Waukegan Daily Sun*, August 1899; "Unveil Shaft to Heroes," *Chicago Daily Tribune*, August 30, 1899; Photo of Monument Dedication, BBDM.

47. "Unveil Shaft to Heroes," *Chicago Daily Tribune*, August 30, 1899.

48. Mitchell, *Vacant Chair*, 145; Gallagher, *Union War*, 120; Jordan, *Marching*, 103.

49. Jordan, *Marching*, 104.

50. Faust, *This Republic*, 249.

51. *Portrait and Biographical Album*, 378.

52. Edward Murray, RG 15, NARA.

53. Ibid.; Jordan, *Marching*, 127; "In Death Edward Murray Passed Away Wednesday. Bullet Caused Death," *Waukegan Daily Sun*, November 30, 1900.

54. "A Soldier's Funeral: Edward Murray Laid at Rest by Comrades," *Waukegan Daily Sun*, December 1, 1900.

55. Ibid.; "In Death Edward Murray Passed Away Wednesday. Bullet Caused Death," *Waukegan Daily Sun*, November 30, 1900; Headquarters GAR, Services.

56. Will and Probate, Edward Murray, LCIGS.

57. Murray, RG 15, NARA; Charles Partridge to H. Clay Evans, BBDM; *Portrait and Biographical Album*, 553; Whitney, *Waukegan City* (1902).

58. Hapke, "Lake County, IL Veterans," 34; "Pioneer Resident of Lake County Expired Sunday Eve," *Lake County Independent/Waukegan Weekly Sun*, February 4, 1916.

59. William B. Lewin, LCIRD; Lewin, RG 15, NARA.

60. Lewin, RG 15, NARA; *Antioch News*, February 28, 1907; "Russell," *Waukegan Daily Sun*, December 14, 1907.

61. Meier, *Nature's Civil War*, 25; "A Horse Doctor Who Knew How to Attend People," *Waukegan Daily Sun*, January 13, 1914, 2; "Dr. W. B. Lewin Dead," *Southport Telegraph*, January 15, 1914.

62. *Antioch News*, April 4, 1907; "The Farmers Institute," *Antioch News*, February 7, 1901.

63. *Antioch News*, March 30, 1911; Lewin, RG 15, NARA.

64. "A Horse Doctor Who Knew How to Attend People," *Waukegan Daily Sun*, January 13, 1914, 2; *Antioch News*, March 30, 1911; "Veterinarian Died Suddenly at Home in Russell," *Waukegan Daily Sun*, n.d., 1914, BBDM.

65. Anna E. Heath Williamson and William B. Lewin, "Honor the Flag," ca. 1906, Queen Family Files.

66. Dunkelman, *Brothers*, 238.

67. Whitney, *Bumstead's Waukegan*, 1902; Veterans Associations, BBDM; "Personal War Sketch of James B. Murrie," WHS; 1920 U.S. Census.

68. 1920 U.S. Census; "Jas. Murrie, Civil War Veteran Dies at Home," *Libertyville Independent*, November 24, 1921; Murrie, RG 15, NARA; Barnard, "Excerpts from Barnard-Walldan."

69. "Jas. Murrie, Civil War Veteran Dies at Home," *Libertyville Independent*, November 24, 1921.

70. Barnard, "Excerpts from Barnard-Walldan"; Prechtel-Kluskens, "For Love and Money"; "Mary Jane Murrie, Old Resident of Lake County Taken by Death," *Waukegan News-Sun*, June 1928.

71. Dunkelman, *Brothers*, 276; Athlyn Deshais, "Capt. Blodgett Honored by His Brave Soldiers," *Waukegan Daily Sun*, n.d., 1939, BBDM.

72. Anna E. Heath Williamson and William B. Lewin, ca. 1905, Queen Family Files.

73. Doyle, *Cause of All Nations*, 170.

74. Ibid., 167.

75. Ibid., 10; Doyle, *Civil War Was Won*; Ural, *Civil War Citizens*, 4; Jellison, "Campaign of the 96th," Orson V. Young Collection, BBDM.

76. Twain and Warner, *Gilded Age*.

77. James Y. Cory, "Lake County and the War," *Waukegan Gazette*, August 16, 1862.

Bibliography

Manuscripts and Unpublished Sources

ABRAHAM LINCOLN PRESIDENTIAL LIBRARY, MANUSCRIPTS DEPARTMENT, SPRINGFIELD, ILLINOIS

Taylor Family (James M.) Papers

BESS BOWER DUNN MUSEUM OF LAKE COUNTY, LAKE COUNTY FOREST PRESERVES, LIBERTYVILLE, ILLINOIS

Minto Family Papers
Orson V. Young Collection
96th Illinois Collection
Civil War Collection
Civil War Veterans Associations Collection
Records and Histories of Township Schools Collection
Millburn Union Casket Collection
Journal of a Pioneer: John Delany, Newport Township File

CHICAGO HISTORY MUSEUM

Wilson Family Papers, [Manuscript] 1847–1920

CIVIL WAR MUSEUM, KENOSHA, WISCONSIN

Captain Evangelist J. Gilmore Collection

GALENA–JO DAVIESS COUNTY HISTORICAL SOCIETY, GALENA, ILLINOIS

Brevet Brigadier General John C. Smith Collection

ILLINOIS STATE ARCHIVES, SPRINGFIELD, ILLINOIS

Illinois Civil War Detail Report
Abstract of Votes County Elections

LAKE COUNTY (IL) CLERK, WAUKEGAN, ILLINOIS

Election Records

LAKE COUNTY (IL) GENEALOGICAL SOCIETY, VERNON HILLS, ILLINOIS

Records of Circuit Court of Lake County, Illinois, Will and Probate Book

LAKE COUNTY (IL) RECORDER OF DEEDS, WAUKEGAN, ILLINOIS

Land Records, Deeds and Mortgages

LAKE FOREST COLLEGE ARCHIVES

E. B. Payne Civil War Letters

NATIONAL ARCHIVES AND RECORDS ADMINISTRATION, WASHINGTON, D.C.

Compiled Service Records of Volunteer Union Soldiers, 96th Illinois Infantry, Records of Adjutant General's Office (AGO), 1780s–1917, Record Group 94

96th Illinois Infantry, Records of Movements and Activities of Volunteer Union Organizations, Records of Adjutant General's Office (AGO), 1780s–1917, Record Group 94

Pension Files of Veterans Who Served Between 1861 and 1900, Record Group 15

PRIVATE COLLECTIONS

Lewin, William B. Family History, Margie Queen Personal Family Files

Murrie, James B. Family History, Jack Murrie Personal Family Files

UNIVERSITY OF WISCONSIN–PARKSIDE, ARCHIVES AND AREA RESEARCH CENTER, KENOSHA, WISCONSIN

Public School Ledger 1850–1860s, Vol. 1, 1849–1855

WARREN TOWNSHIP HISTORICAL SOCIETY, GURNEE, ILLINOIS

Ida Bennett Scrapbook

WAUKEGAN HISTORICAL SOCIETY

Grand Army of the Republic, Waukegan Post 374 Collection

Newspapers

Antioch (IL) News
Chicago Press and Tribune
Chicago Daily Tribune

Chicago Tribune
Herald and Mail (Columbia, Tennessee)
Inter Ocean (Chicago, Illinois)
Kenosha (WI) Times
Lake County Citizen (Waukegan, Illinois)
Lake County Independent (Libertyville, Illinois)
Libertyville (IL) Independent
Metropolitan News-Enterprise (Los Angeles, California)
Nashville (TN) Daily Union
Richmond (IN) Weekly Palladium
Rock River Times (Rockford, Illinois)
Southport Telegraph (Kenosha, Wisconsin)
Voice of the Fair (Chicago, Illinois)
Waukegan (IL) Daily Sun
Waukegan (IL) Gazette/Waukegan Weekly Gazette
Waukegan (IL) Post
Waukegan (IL) Weekly Sun

Books

Atwater, Dorence, and Clara Barton. *A List of the Union Soldiers Buried at Andersonville.* New York: Tribune Association, 1866. Accessed February 17, 2020. https://archive.org/details/listofunionsoldi00atwa.

Beach, John N. *History of the Fortieth Ohio Volunteer Infantry.* London, OH: Shepherd & Craig, 1884. Accessed February 16, 2020. https://archive.org/stream/historyoffortiet00beac/historyoffortiet00beac_djvu.txt.

Bennett, William. *Post Office and Bon-Accord Directory, 1846–1847, Aberdeen and Banff, Scotland.* Aberdeen: William Bennett, 1846 and 1847. National Library of Scotland. Accessed February 2020. http://digital.nls.uk/86824624.

Blockson, Charles L. *The Underground Railroad: First-Person Narrative of Escapes to Freedom in the North.* New York: Prentice Hall Press, 1987.

Blodgett, Henry W. *Autobiography of Henry W. Blodgett.* Waukegan: 1906.

Bowery, Charles R., Jr. "The Civil War in the Western Theater 1862." Washington, DC: Center of Military History United States Army, 2014.

Bradley, Mark L. *The Civil War Ends 1865.* Washington DC: Center of Military History United States Army, 2015.

Bradley, Michael R. *Tullahoma: The 1863 Campaign for the Control of Middle Tennessee.* Shippensburg, PA: Burd Street Press, 2000.

Bruce, Susannah Ural. *The Harp and the Eagle: Irish-American Volunteers and the Union Army, 1861–1865.* New York: New York University Press, 2006.

Buckley, James Monroe. *A History of Methodism in the United States*. New York: Harper and Brothers Publishers, 1898. Accessed February 17, 2020. https://archive.org/details/ahistorymethodi01buckgoog.

Burton, William L. *Melting Pot Soldiers: The Union's Ethnic Regiments*. New York: Fordham University Press, 1998.

Byrd, Marvin. *A Unionist in East Tennessee: Captain William K. Byrd and the Mysterious Raid of 1861*. Mount Pleasant, SC: Arcadia Publishing, 2011.

Campey, Lucille H. *Fast Sailing and Copper-Bottomed: Aberdeen Sailing Ships and the Emigrant Scots They Carried to Canada 1774–1855*. Toronto: Natural Heritage Books, 2002.

Clifton, James A. *The Prairie People: Continuity and Change in Potawatomi Indian Culture 1665—1965*. Lawrence, KS: Regent Press of Kansas, 1977.

Cole, Arthur Charles. Collections of the Illinois State Historical Library. Vol. 14, Constitutional Series. Vol. 2. *The Constitutional Debates of 1847*. Springfield, IL: Trustees of the Illinois State Historical Library, 1919. Accessed February 17, 2020. https://archive.org/details/constitutionalde00illi.

Corris, William and Mildred. *Russell Illinois 100 Years of Memories 1873–1973*. Russell, IL: Centennial Committee, 1973.

Costa, Dora L. *The Evolution of Retirement: An American Economic History, 1880–1990*. Chicago: University of Chicago Press, 1998. Accessed February 17, 2020. https://www.nber.org/chapters/c6116.

Devitt, Fr. Leo A. *Centenary Program: St. Patrick's Church Wadsworth, Illinois, 1849–1949*. Wadsworth, IL: Centennial Souvenir Program Committee, 1949.

Dobson, David. *Ships from Scotland to North America, 1830–1860*. Vol. 2. Genealogical Publishing Co., 2009.

Doyle, Don H. *The Cause of All Nations: An International History of the American Civil War*. New York: Basic Books, 2015.

Dunkelman, Mark H. *Brothers One and All: Esprit de Corps in a Civil War Regiment*. Baton Rouge: Louisiana State University Press, 2004.

Eddy, T. M. *The Patriotism of Illinois*. Vol. 1. Chicago: Clarke & Company, 1865. Accessed February 17, 2020. https://archive.org/details/patriotismofilli01eddy.

Evans, Paul Lavern. *96th Illinois Volunteer Infantry Jo Daviess and Lake Counties*. Mobile, AL: Paul Lavern Evans, 1999.

Faust, Drew Gilpin. *This Republic of Suffering: Death and the American Civil War*. New York: Vintage Books, 2008.

Fonvielle, Chris E., Jr. *The Wilmington Campaign: Last Rays of Departing Hope*. Mechanicsburg, PA: Stackpole Books, 2001.

Frisby, Derek W. *Campaigns in Mississippi and Tennessee February—December 1864*. Washington, DC: Center of Military History United States Army, 2014.

Gallagher, Gary W. *The Union War*. Cambridge, MA: Harvard University Press, 2011.

Gates, Henry Louis, Jr. *Lincoln on Race and Slavery*. Princeton, NJ: Princeton University Press, 2009.

Goodspeed Historical Association. *History of Cook County, Illinois*. Chicago: Goodspeed Historical Association, 1909.

Gordon, Lesley J. *A Broken Regiment: The 16th Connecticut's Civil War*. Baton Rouge: Louisiana State University Press, 2014.

Goudy, Calvin. *History of Christian County, Illinois*. Philadelphia: Brink, McDonough & Co., 1880. Accessed February 17, 2020. https://archive.org/stream /historyofchristi00goud/historyofchristi00goud_djvu.txt.

Griffith, Paddy. *Battle Tactics of the Civil War*. New Haven, CT: Yale University Press, 2001.

Guasco, Suzanne Cooper. *Confronting Slavery: Edward Coles and the Rise of Antislavery Politics in Nineteenth-Century America*. DeKalb: Northern Illinois University Press, 2013.

Hahn, Steven, Steven F. Miller, Susan E. O'Donovan, John C. Rodrigue, and Leslie S. Rowland, eds. *Freedom: A Documentary History of Emancipation, 1861–1867*. 3rd ser., Vol. 1: *Land and Labor, 1865*. Chapel Hill: University of North Carolina Press, 2008.

Haines, Elijah M. *Past and Present of Lake County, Illinois*. Chicago: Le Baron, 1877.

Halsey, John J. *A History of Lake County, Illinois*. Chicago: Roy S. Bates, 1912.

Hapke, Aileen Potterton. *Lake County, IL Veterans of the Armed Forces of the United States Buried Prior to June 1, 1955*. Extracted and transcribed from microfilm housed at Fremont Public Library, Mundelein, Illinois, n.d.

Haynes, Nathaniel S. *History of the Disciples of Christ in Illinois, 1819–1914*. Cincinnati: Standard Publishing Company, 1915. Accessed February 17, 2020. https://archive.org/stream/historyofdiscip100hayn/historyofdiscip100hayn _djvu.txt.

Headquarters Grand Army of the Republic. *Services for the Use of the Grand Army of the Republic*. Philadelphia: Burk & McFetridge Co., 1894.

Henshaw, Mrs. Sarah Edwards. *Our Branch and Its Tributaries: Being a History of the Work of the Northwestern Sanitary Commission and Its Auxiliaries during the War of the Rebellion*. Chicago: Alfred L. Sewell, 1868.

Herdegen, Lance J. *The Iron Brigade in Civil War and Memory*. El Dorado Hills, CA: Savas Beatie, 2012.

Hicks, George. *Personal Recollections of Chickamauga: By Geo. Hicks, Captain Company A, Ninety-Sixth Illinois Volunteers; Extracts from an Address Delivered in Kingston, Jamaica, West Indies.* Chicago: Brown, Pettibone & Co., Printers, 1886.

Hodes, Martha. *Mourning Lincoln.* New Haven, CT: Yale University Press, 2015.

House of Representatives. *Constitution of the State of Illinois, November 16, 1818: Read and Ordered to Lie upon the Table; Printed by the Order of the House of Representatives.* Washington City: E. DeKrafft, 1818. Accessed February 17, 2020. https://archive.org/stream/constitutionofst00inilli#page/n0 /mode/2up.

Humphreys, Margaret. *Marrow of Tragedy: The Health Crisis of the American Civil War.* Baltimore: Johns Hopkins University Press, 2013.

Hunter, Robert, and William Henry Chamberlin. *Sketches of War History, 1861–1865: Papers Read before the Ohio Commandery of the Military Order of the Loyal Legion of the United States, 1883–1903,* 5. Cincinnati: R. Clarke & Company, 1903. https://archive.org/details/sketcheswarhist00unkngoog.

Illinois Adjutant General. *Report of the Adjutant General of the State of Illinois.* Vol. 5. Springfield, IL: Phillips Bros., State Printers, 1901.

Johnson, Reinhard O. *The Liberty Party, 1840–1848: Antislavery Third-Party Politics in the United States.* Baton Rouge: Louisiana State University Press, 2009.

Johnson, Robert Underwood. *Battles and Leaders of the Civil War: Being for the Most Part Contributions by Union and Confederate Officers.* Vol. 3, pt. 2. New York: Century Company, 1884. Accessed February 2020. https://archive. org/details/battlesleadersof32john.

Jordan, Brian Matthew. *Marching Home: Union Veterans and Their Unending Civil War.* New York: Liveright, 2014.

Klement, Frank L. *Lincoln's Critics: The Copperheads of the North.* Shippensburg, PA: White Mane Books, 1999.

Kolakowski, Christopher L. *The Stones River and Tullahoma Campaigns.* Charleston, SC: History Press, 2011.

Lake City Publishing Company. *Portrait and Biographical Album of Lake County, Illinois.* Chicago: Lake City Publishing Company, 1891.

———. *Portrait and Biographical Record of Christian County, Illinois.* Chicago: Lake City Publishing Company, 1893.

Lake County (IL) Genealogical Society. *1838–1888 Report of the Semi-Centennial Anniversary of the Fremont Congregational Church, Ivanhoe, Illinois, Monday, February 20, 1888.* Libertyville, IL: Lake County (IL) Genealogical Society, 2004.

————. *Lake County, Illinois Marriages: 1839 to 1859.* Vol. 1. Libertyville, IL: Lake County (IL) Genealogical Society, 1993.

————. *Lake County, Illinois Marriages: 1860 to 1880.* Vol. 2. Libertyville, IL: Lake County (IL) Genealogical Society, 1993.

Lake County Soldiers' Monument Association. *Articles of Association, and By-Laws, Rules and Regulations of the Lake County Soldiers' Monument Association: Organized at Waukegan, Ill. Nov 9, 1865.* Waukegan: Gazette Power Press Print, 1866.

Lawson, Edward S. *A History of Warren Township.* Gurnee, IL: Warren-Newport Public Library, 1974.

Lyman, Frank H. *The City of Kenosha and Kenosha County Wisconsin: A Record of Settlement, Organization, Progress and Achievement.* Vol. 1. Chicago: S. J. Clarke, 1916.

Manning, Chandra. *What This Cruel War Was Over: Soldiers, Slavery, and the Civil War.* New York: Vintage Civil War Library, 2008.

McCarley, J. Britt. *The Atlanta and Savannah Campaigns 1864.* Washington, DC: Center of Military History United States Army, 2014.

McManus, Michael J. *Political Abolitionism in Wisconsin, 1840–1861.* Kent, OH: Kent State University Press, 1998.

McMurry, Richard M. *The Road Past Kennesaw: The Atlanta Campaign of 1864.* Washington, DC: Office of Publications, National Park Service, 1972.

McPherson, James M. *For Cause and Comrades: Why Men Fought in the Civil War.* New York: Oxford University Press, 1997.

Meier, Kathryn Shively. *Nature's Civil War: Common Soldiers and the Environment in 1862 Virginia.* Chapel Hill: University of North Carolina Press, 2013.

Methodist Churches Centennial Pageant Committee. *Historical Centennial Pageant: "A Century Passes" North Prairie, Yorkhouse, East Benton Methodist Churches, 1838–1938.* Benton Township, Lake County, IL: Centennial Pageant Committee, 1938.

Millburn Congregational Church. *The First Hundred Years Plus Forty: The Story of the Millburn Congregational Church, 1840–1980,* Millburn, IL: Millburn Congregational Church, 1980.

Miller, Kerby A. *Emigrants and Exiles: Ireland and the Irish Exodus to North America.* New York: Oxford University Press, 1985.

Mitchell, Reid. *The Vacant Chair: The Northern Soldier Leaves Home.* New York: Oxford University Press, 1993.

Murray, Edward. *A Soldier's Reminiscences.* Waukegan, n.d. (ca. 1900).

Neely, Mark E., Jr. *The Union Divided: Party Conflict in the Civil War North.* Cambridge, MA: Harvard University Press, 2002.

Northcott, Dennis, and Thomas Brooks. *Grand Army of the Republic Department of Illinois: Transcription of the Death Rolls, 1879–1947.* St. Louis, MO: Dennis Northcott, 2003.

Osling, Louise A., and Julia Osling. *Historical Highlights of the Waukegan Area.* Waukegan, IL: City of Waukegan, 1976.

Palmer, Friend. *Early Days in Detroit.* Detroit: Hunt & June, 1906.

Partridge, Charles A. *The Battle of Chickamauga.* Waukegan, IL: Gazette Publishing Establishment, 1881.

———. *History of Lake County, Illinois.* Chicago: Munsell, 1902.

———. *History of the Ninety-Sixth Regiment Illinois Volunteer Infantry.* Chicago: Historical Society of the Regiment, 1887.

———. "Lake County War History and Records." In Elijah M. Haines, *Past and Present of Lake County, Illinois.* Chicago: Le Baron, 1877.

Powell, David A. *The Chickamauga Campaign: The Barren Victory; The Retreat into Chattanooga, the Confederate Pursuit, and the Aftermath of the Battle, September 21 to October 20, 1863.* El Dorado Hills, CA: Savas Beatie, 2017.

———. *The Chickamauga Campaign: Glory or the Grave; The Breakthrough, the Union Collapse, and the Defense of Horseshoe Ridge, September 20, 1863.* El Dorado Hills, CA: Savas Beatie, 2017.

Reinhart, Joseph R. *Two Germans in the Civil War: The Diary of John Daeuble and the Letters of Gottfried Rentschler, 6th Kentucky Volunteer Infantry.* Knoxville: University of Tennessee Press, 2004.

Report of the Adjutant General of the State of Illinois. Vol. 5, *1861–1866.* Springfield, IL: Phillips Bros., 1901.

Robertson, William Glen, Edward P. Shanahan, John I. Boxberger, George E. Knapp. *Staff Ride Handbook for the Battle of Chickamauga 18–20 September 1863.* Fort Leavenworth, KS: U.S. Army Command and General Staff College, 1992.

Rutkow, Ira. *Bleeding Blue and Gray: Civil War Surgery and the Evolution of American Medicine.* Mechanicsburg, PA: Stackpole Books, 2005.

Samito, Christian G. *Becoming American under Fire: Irish Americans, African Americans, and the Politics of Citizenship during the Civil War Era.* Ithaca, NY: Cornell University Press, 2009.

Simpkin, Marshall, and Company. *The Nautical Magazine and Naval Chronicle: A Journal of Papers on Subjects Connected with Maritime Affairs.* London: Simpkin, Marshall, and Company, 1851.

Smith, General John C. *Reception to the Members of the Ninety-Sixth Regiment, Illinois Infantry Volunteers, at the Residence of Their Old Commander, General John C. Smith of the Twenty-Ninth Anniversary of the Battle of Peach Tree Creek,*

Georgia, July 20, 1893. Chicago: Knight, Leonard & Co., 1893. Accessed May 2015. https://archive.org/details/receptiontomembe00unit/page/n6 /mode/2up.

Smith, Du Moulin & Co. *The Kenosha City Directory, 1858.* Kenosha: Smith, Du Moulin & Co., 1858.

State of Illinois. "1908 Revised List of Veterinary Surgeons Licensed by the Board of Livestock Commissioners of Illinois to Practice Veterinary Medicine and Surgery, Under the Terms of an Act Entitled 'An Act to Regulate the Practice of Veterinary Medicine and Surgery in the State of Illinois.' With a Copy of the Law. July 1, 1908."

Steplyk, Jonathan M. "Killing at Franklin: Anatomy of Slaughter." In *The Tennessee Campaign of 1864,* edited by Steven E. Woodworth and Charles D. Grear, 81–104. Carbondale: Southern Illinois University Press, 2016.

Teters, Kristopher A. *Practical Liberators: Union Officers in the Western Theater during the Civil War.* Chapel Hill: University of North Carolina Press, 2018.

Turner, Glennette Tilley. *The Underground Railroad in Illinois.* Glen Ellyn, IL: Newman Educational Publishing, 2001.

Twain, Mark, and Charles Dudley Warner. *The Gilded Age: A Tale of Today.* Hartford, CT: American Publishing Company, 1873.

Unadilla Valley Historical Society. *Historical Sketches of Old New Berlin.* New Berlin: George H. Willard, 1907. Accessed February 2020. http://www. usgenweb.info/nychenango/books/hsoldnb.htm.

United States Congress. United States Senate. *Supplemental Report of the Joint Committee on the Conduct of War in Two Volumes.* Supplemental to Senate Report No. 142, 38th Congress 2nd Session. Vol. 1. Washington, DC: Government Printing Office, 1866.

United States Department of Labor. *History of Wages in the United States from Colonial Times to 1928: Revision of Bulletin No. 499 with supplement, 1929–1933.* Washington, DC: United States Government Printing Office, 1934. Accessed February 17, 2020. https://hdl.handle.net/2027/uc1.32106007458745.

United States War Department. *The War of the Rebellion: A Compilation of the Official Records of the Union and Confederate Armies.* 1st ser., vol. 23, pt. 2. Washington, DC: Government Printing Office, 1889.

———. *The War of the Rebellion: A Compilation of the Official Records of the Union and Confederate Armies.* 1st ser., vol. 45, pt. 2. Washington: Government Printing Office, 1894.

———. *The War of the Rebellion: A Compilation of the Official Records of the Union and Confederate Armies.* 1st ser., vol. 49, pt. 2. Washington, DC: Government Printing Office, 1897.

———. *The War of the Rebellion: A Compilation of the Official Records of the Union and Confederate Armies.* 2nd ser., vol. 1. Washington, DC: Government Printing Office, 1894.

University of Aberdeen. *Catalogue of the Taylor Collection of Psalm Variations.* Aberdeen: Aberdeen University Press, 1921. Accessed February 17, 2020. https://archive.org/stream/catalogueoftayl000aberrich/catalogueoftayl000 aberrich_djvu.txt.

Ural, Susannah J. *Civil War Citizens: Race, Ethnicity, and Identity in America's Bloodiest Conflict.* New York: New York University Press, 2010.

Weber, Jennifer L. *Copperheads: The Rise and Fall of Lincoln's Opponents in the North.* New York: Oxford University Press, 2006.

Westerman, Al. *A History of Waukegan Township, Lake County, Illinois 1835–1850.* Zion, IL: 2013.

Whitney. *Bumstead's Waukegan City and Lake County Directory, 1901–1902.* Chicago: Whitney Publishing Co., 1902.

———. *Bumstead's Waukegan City and Lake County Directory, 1903–1904.* Vol. 5. Chicago: Whitney Publishing Co., 1904.

———. *The Waukegan City Directory 1897–98.* Vol. 2. Chicago: Whitney Publishing Co., 1897.

Wilder, Jeremy H. *The Thirty Seventh Illinois: Civil War Stories from the Back of the Battle.* Teaneck, NJ: English Garden Press, 2016.

Woodward, Joseph Janvier. *The Medical and Surgical History of the War of the Rebellion: 1861–65.* Washington, DC: U.S. Government Printing Office, 1870. Accessed February 17, 2020. https://archive.org/details/medicalsurgica132barnrich.

Woodworth, Steven E. *Six Armies in Tennessee: The Chickamauga and Chattanooga Campaigns.* Lincoln: University of Nebraska Press, 1998.

Zion Genealogical Society. "Newport Mt. Rest Cemetery." Zion, IL, 1985.

Articles

Barnard, Gladys. "Excerpts from Barnard-Walldan and Allied Families: Life Story of James Murrie and Mary J. Dixon Murrie." Last modified December 19, 2009. http://person.ancestry.com/tree/1601777/person/-1383352214/gallery.

Berg, Gordon. "Battle of Chickamauga and Gordon Granger's Reserve Corps." *America's Civil War* (January 2007). http://www.historynet.com/battle-of-chickamauga-and-gordon-grangers-reserve-corps.htm.

Brown, Richard D. "Microhistory and the Post-Modern Challenge." *Journal of the Early Republic* 23, no. 1 (Spring 2003): 1–20. https://www.jstor.org/stable/3124983.

Burton, William L. "Illinois Ethnics in the Civil War." Illinois Periodicals Online, Northern Illinois University Libraries. Accessed February 2020. http://www.lib.niu.edu/1997/iht429702.html.

Cubbison, Douglas R. "Tactical Genius above the Clouds: 'Fighting Joe' Hooker and John White Geary at the Battle of Lookout Mountain, November 24, 1863." *Tennessee Historical Quarterly* 61, no. 4 (2002): 266–89. www.jstor .org/stable/42627728.

———. "'That Awful Storm of Iron and Smoke': Union Artillery at Moccasin Bend, Chattanooga, September–November, 1863." *Tennessee Historical Quarterly* 58, no. 4 (1999): 266–83. http://www.jstor.org/stable/42627497.

Currey, J. Seymour. "Mr. Lincoln's Visit to Waukegan in 1860." *Journal of the Illinois State Historical Society* 4, no. 2 (1911): 178–83. http://www.jstor.org /stable/40193848.

Dillon, Merton Lynn. "The Antislavery Movement in Illinois: 1824–1835." *Journal of the Illinois State Historical Society* 47, no. 2 (1954): 149–66. http:// www.jstor.org/stable/40189370.

Doyle, Don H. "The Civil War Was Won by Immigrant Soldiers." *Time*. Last modified December 23, 2019. http://time.com/3940428/civil-war-immigrant -soldiers/.

Duerkes, Wayne N. "I for One Am Ready to Do My Part: The Initial Motivations That Inspired Men from Northern Illinois to Enlist in the U.S. Army, 1861–1862." *Journal of the Illinois State Historical Society* 105, no. 4 (Winter 2012): 313–32. doi:10.5406/jillistathistsoc.105.4.0313.

Engle, Stephen D. "Yankee Dutchmen: Germans, the Union, and the Construction of Wartime Identity." In *Civil War Citizens: Race, Ethnicity, and Identity in America's Bloodiest Conflict*, edited by Susannah J. Ural, 11–55. New York: New York University Press, 2010.

Faust, Drew Gilpin. "The Civil War Soldier and the Art of Dying." *Journal of Southern History* 67, no. 1 (2001): 3–38. doi:10.2307/3070083.

Gallagher, Gary W. "A Civil War Watershed: The 1862 Richmond Campaign in Perspective." In *The Richmond Campaign of 1862: The Peninsula and the Seven Days*, edited by Gary W. Gallagher, 3–27. Chapel Hill: University of North Carolina Press, 2000.

Gannon, Barbara A. "She Is a Member of the 23rd: Lucy Nichols and the Community of the Civil War Regiment." In *This Distracted and Anarchical People: New Answers for Old Questions about the Civil War–Era North*, edited by Andrew L. Slap and Michael Thomas Smith, 184–99. New York: Fordham University Press, 2013.

Girardi, Robert I. "'I Am for the President's Proclamation Teeth and Toe Nails': Illinois Soldiers Respond to the Emancipation Proclamation." *Journal of the Illinois State Historical Society (1998–)* 106, nos. 3–4 (Fall–Winter 2013): 395–421. https://www.jstor.org/stable/10.5406/jillistathistsoc.106.3–4.0395.

———. "Illinois' First Response to the Civil War." *Journal of the Illinois State Historical Society (1998–)* 105, nos. 2–3 (2012): 167–72. doi:10.5406/jillistathistsoc.105.2–3.0167.

Grinspan, Jon. "'Young Men for War': The Wide Awakes and Lincoln's 1860 Presidential Campaign." *Journal of American History* 96, no. 2 (Sept. 2009). https://www.jstor.org/stable/25622297.

Harrison, Lowell H. "The Civil War in Kentucky: Some Persistent Questions." *Register of the Kentucky Historical Society* 76, no. 1 (January 1978). http://www.jstor.org/stable/23378644.

Hébert, Keith S. "The Bitter Trial of Defeat and Emancipation: Reconstruction in Bartow County, Georgia, 1865–1872." *Georgia Historical Quarterly* 92, no. 1 (2008): 65–92. http://www.jstor.org/stable/40585039.

Heinzel, Sally. "'To Protect the Rights of the White Race': Illinois Republican Racial Politics in the 1860 Campaign and the Twenty-Second General Assembly." *Journal of the Illinois State Historical Society (1998–)* 108, no. 3–4 (2015): 374–406. doi:10.5406/jillistathistsoc.108.3–4.0374.

"History of Grub School by Former Students: Early Pupils, Later Buildings." Accessed February 17, 2020. http://www.historicmillburn.org/History/hgrubbs3.htm.

Jeansonne, Glen. "Southern Baptist Attitudes toward Slavery, 1845–1861." *Georgia Historical Quarterly* 55, no. 4 (1971): 510–22. https://www.jstor.org/stable/40579712.

Joyner, Benjamin. "Dirty Work: The Political Life of John A. Logan." *Historia* 21 (2012). http://www.eiu.edu/historia/2012Joyner.pdf.

Keating, Ryan W. "Immigrants and the Union Army." *Essential Civil War Curriculum*, Virginia Center for Civil War Studies at Virginia Tech, June 2014. https://www.essentialcivilwarcurriculum.com/immigrants-in-the-union-army.html.

King, Janet. "Civil War Medicine: Part II. The Microscopic War: Diseases and Medical Treatments." *Vermont in the Civil War.* Accessed March 12, 2018. http://www.vermontcivilwar.org/medic/medicine2.php.

Kisantal, Tamás. Review of *What Is Microhistory? Theory and Practice* by István M. Szijártó, Sigurður Gylfi Magnússon. *Hungarian Historical Review* 4, no. 2 (2015): 512–17. www.jstor.org/stable/24575830.

Lepore, Jill. "Historians Who Love Too Much: Reflections on Microhistory and Biography." *Journal of American History* 88, no. 1 (2001): 129–44. doi:10.2307/2674921.

McNamara, Robert. "Why Were Flags Enormously Important in the Civil War? As Morale Builders, Rallying Points, and Prizes, Flags Served Vital Purposes." Last modified December 13, 2018. http://history1800s.about .com/od/civilwar/f/Civil-War-Battle-Flags.htm.

Meites, Jerome B. "The 1847 Illinois Constitutional Convention and Persons of Color." *Journal of the Illinois State Historical Society (1998–)* 108, no. 3–4 (2015): 266–95. doi:10.5406/jillistathistsoc.108.3–4.0266.

Murray, Jennifer M. "Preserving the Nashville Battlefield: The South's True Lost Cause." In *The Tennessee Campaign of 1864*, edited by Steven E. Woodworth and Charles D. Grear, 233–47. Carbondale: Southern Illinois University Press, 2016.

National Museums Liverpool. Maritime Archives and Library, Information Sheet 64. "Liverpool and Emigration in the 19th and 20th Centuries." Accessed June 4, 2014. http://www.liverpoolmuseums.org.uk/maritime/archive /sheet/64.

Ó Danachair, Caoimhín. "Cottier and Landlord in Pre-famine Ireland." *Béaloideas* 48/49 (1980): 154–65. doi:10.2307/20522162.

Orr, Timothy. "Shot in the Lung." *Tales from the Army of the Potomac* (blog), posted January 29, 2016. http://talesfromaop.blogspot.com/2016/01/shot-in -lung.html.

Painter, Kyle. "The Pro-Slavery Argument in the Development of the American Methodist Church." *Constructing the Past* 2, no. 1, art. 5 (2001). http:// digitalcommons.iwu.edu/constructing/vol2/iss1/5.

Phillips, Jason. "Battling Stereotypes: A Taxonomy of Common Soldiers in Civil War History." *History Compass* 6, no. 6 (2008): 1407–25.

Plaisance, Aloysius F., and Leo F. Schelver. "Federal Military Hospitals in Nashville, May and June, 1863." *Tennessee Historical Quarterly* 29, no. 2 (1970): 166–75. http://www.jstor.org/stable/42623149.

Powell, Dave A. "The Battle of Chickamauga." *Essential Civil War Curriculum*, Virginia Center for Civil War Studies at Virginia Tech, December 2013.

———. "The Battles for Horseshoe Ridge: The 96th Illinois, 1863 and 1895." *North and South Magazine* 8, no. 2 (March 2005).

Prechtel-Kluskens, Claire. "For Love and Money: Pension Laws Affecting Widows of Military Veterans," *National Geographic Society* 42, no. 1 (January–March 2016).

Rubenstein, Major David A. "A Study of the Medical Support to the Union and Confederate Armies during the Battle of Chickamauga: Lessons and Implications for Today's US Army Medical Department Leaders." U.S. Army Medical Department, Office of Medical History. Last modified May 12, 2009. http://history.amedd.army.mil/booksdocs/civil/ThesisRubenstein/rubenstein.html.

Schroeder-Lein, Glenna R. "'H.G.': A Medical History of James M. Taylor of the Ninety-Sixth Illinois Infantry." *Journal of Illinois History* 15 (Spring 2012): 38.

Sidlo, Sid. "Civil War Roads." Cleveland Civil War Roundtable. Last modified 2008. http://clevelandcivilwarroundtable.com/articles/means/civil_war_roads.htm.

Simpson, Brooks D. "A Failure to Communicate: Grant, Thomas, and the Nashville Campaign." In *The Tennessee Campaign of 1864*, edited by Steven E. Woodworth and Charles D. Grear, 105–22. Carbondale: Southern Illinois University Press, 2016.

Thompson, D. G. Brinton. "From Chancellorsville to Gettysburg, a Doctor's Diary." *Pennsylvania Magazine of History and Biography* 89, no. 3 (1965): 292–315. http://www.jstor.org/stable/20089816.

"Traveling the Erie Canal, 1836." EyeWitness to History. Last Modified 2004. http://eyewitnesstohistory.com/eriecanal.htm.

Turner, D. L. and Scott L. Stabler. "No More Auction Block for Me: The Fight for Freedom by the U.S. Colored Troops at the Battles of Nashville." In *The Tennessee Campaign of 1864*, edited by Steven E. Woodworth and Charles D. Grear, 144–61. Carbondale: Southern Illinois University Press, 2016.

Uzelac, Peter. "The G. P. Griffith: The Great Lakes Second Worst Passenger Steamer Disaster." Accessed February 17, 2020. https://tripsintohistory.com/2012/03/17/the-g-p-griffith-the-great-lakes-second-worst-passenger-steamer-disaster/.

Welch, Richard F. "America's Civil War: Why the Irish Fought for the Union." *Civil War Times* (October 2006).

Wolf, Wayne L., and Bruce S. Allardice. "General John Corson Smith and the Early Days of the Fighting Ninety-Sixth Illinois Infantry." *Journal of the Illinois State Historical Society* 107 (Fall/Winter 2014): 285–94.

Maps

Illustrated Atlas of Lake County, Illinois. Chicago: H. R. Page & Co., 1885.

Kenosha, Wisconsin City Map. New York: Snyder, Black and Sturn, 1857.

Map of Lake County, Illinois. Chicago: Frost & Mc. Lennan, 1873.

Map of Lake County, Illinois. St. Louis: L. Gast & Brothers, 1861.

Internet Sources

Ancestry. 1997–2019. Ancestry.com.

Bailey, Joe R. "The Other Side of the Monument: Memory, Preservation, and the Battles of Franklin and Nashville." PhD diss., Kansas State University, 2015. http://hdl.handle.net/2097/20573.

Bodie, Glen C. Bodie-Antle Family and Ancestors. 1999–2006. Accessed December 10, 2018. http://bodie.ca/FreePages/MyTree/bodie_antle .htm.

The Civil War in Art. Terra Foundation of American Art. "Funeral Procession outside Cook County Court House, May 1, 1865," photograph, Chicago History Museum (Gift of R. Hamlin Petty Sr. ICHi-52359). http://www. civilwarinart.org.

Civil War Richmond. "Crew & Pemberton's Warehouse." Last modified 2015. https://www.civilwarrichmond.com/prisons/crew-pemberton-s -warehouse.

Elliott, Geoff, ed. "Chicago's Huge Funeral for Lincoln." *Abraham Lincoln Blog.* May 1, 2010. http://abrahamlincolnblog.blogspot.com/.

FamilySearch.org. "Louisiana Civil War Service Records of Confederate Soldiers, 1861–1865." https://familysearch.org.

Grand Army of the Republic (GAR) Records Project. "Illinois." Sons of Union Veterans of the Civil War. Last modified February 3, 2019. http:// www.suvcw.org/garrecords/garposts/il.htm.

Groom, Winston. "Why Shiloh Matters." *Opinionator* (blog). *New York Times,* April 6, 2012. https://opinionator.blogs.nytimes.com/2012/04/06 /why-shiloh-matters/.

Historic Millburn Community Association, Inc. historicmillburn.org.

The Historical Marker Database. "Choosing a President." https://www.hmdb .org/marker.asp?marker=56911.

Illinois in the Civil War. "92nd Illinois Infantry." Last modified 2007. http:// www.illinoiscivilwar.org/cw92.html.

Illinois State Archives. Illinois Civil War Muster and Descriptive Rolls. https://www.cyberdriveillinois.com/departments/archives/home.html.

The Internet Archive. Archive.org.

Irish-Genealogy-Toolkit. Claire Santry. 2008–2019. Irish-Genealogy-Tool kit.com.

Library of Congress. Chronicling America. Historic American Newspapers. https://chroniclingamerica.loc.gov/

Library of Congress. Notated Music. https://www.loc.gov/notated-music/.

Library of Congress. *Wm. Oland Bourne Papers: Left-Hand Penmanship Contest; Soldier and Sailor Contributions; Series I; $1,000 in Prizes, Awarded in: Entries 91–100.* 1866. Manuscript/Mixed Material. https://www.loc.gov /item/mss13375015/.

Minnesota Historical Society. "History and Development of Great Lakes Water Craft: Passenger and Package Freight Steamers." http://www. mnhs.org/places/nationalregister/shipwrecks/mpdf/wrecks.php. Adapted from Patrick Labadie, Brina J. Agranat, and Scott Anfinson, "Minnesota's Lake Superior Shipwrecks A.D. 1650–1945," The National Register's Multiple Property Documentation (MPDF).

National Park Service. http://www.nps.gov.

National Records of Scotland. "ScotlandsPeople." ScotlandsPeople.gov.uk.

Newspapers.com by Ancestry.

Office of Illinois Secretary of State. "100 Most Valuable Documents at the Illinois State Archives, the Online Exhibit." Accessed February 2020. https://www.cyberdriveillinois.com/departments/archives/online _exhibits/100_documents/home.html.

Records of Adjutant General's Office (AGO), 1780s–1917, Record Group 94, 96th Illinois Volunteer Infantry, National Archives and Records Administration (NARA), Washington, D.C. Last modified July 7, 2010. https:// archive.org/details/compiledrecordss0028unit.

Sitemason.com. "The Battles for Chattanooga, 1863–1865: The Chickamauga-Chattanooga Civil War Sites, 1863–1950 Multiple Property Nomination(MPN)." Accessed February 2020. http://www.sitemason.com/files /gLTn7a/Chickamauga%20and%20Chattanooga%20Muliple%20Property %20Nomination.pdf.

Southfield in the War. Website to honor Civil War veterans from Southfield Township, Michigan created by Southfield Public Library. https:// southfieldinthewar.wordpress.com.

Tennessee State Library and Archives. Tennessee Department of State. "Federal Civil War Burial Sheets Project." Last modified 2011. http:// www.tnsos.net/TSLA/BurialSheetsProject/index.php.

U.S. Department of Veterans Affairs. "History and Development of the National Cemetery Administration." Last modified October 2015. https:// www.cem.va.gov/docs/factsheets/history.pdf.

Index

Page locators in italics indicate illustrations.

Diana L. Dretske is a curator and Lake County historian for the Bess Bower Dunn Museum of Lake County, Illinois. For more than thirty years she has explored the history of northeastern Illinois through her research, presentations, and blog—www.LakeCountyHistory.blogspot.com—and she has written three books, including *Views of America: Fort Sheridan* and *Lake County, Illinois: An Illustrated History*. The Illinois State Historical Society recognized her with a lifetime achievement award for outstanding contributions in promoting, preserving, and commemorating Illinois history.

ENGAGING
the
CIVIL WAR

Engaging the Civil War, a series founded by the historians at the blog Emerging Civil War (www.emergingcivilwar.com), adopts the sensibility and accessibility of public history while adhering to the standards of academic scholarship. To engage readers and bring them to a new understanding of America's great story, series authors draw on insights they gained while working with the public—walking the ground where history happened at battlefields and historic sites, talking with visitors in museums, and educating students in classrooms. With fresh perspectives, field-tested ideas, and in-depth research, volumes in the series connect readers with the story of the Civil War in ways that make history meaningful to them while underscoring the continued relevance of the war, its causes, and its effects. All Americans can claim the Civil War as part of their history. This series , which was cofounded by Chris Mackowski and Kristopher D. White, helps them engage with it.

Chris Mackowski and Brian Matthew Jordan, Series Editors

Queries and submissions
emergingcivilwar@gmail.com

Other books in Engaging the Civil War